'If there was a time for *Belonging*, the[...] underscores the need and importance of diversity but also makes the case that diversity is not just a "nice to have" endeavour but a true competitive edge that allows companies to unleash innovation, employee joy, corporate reputation and value creation.'

Rishad Tobaccowala, author of Restoring the Soul of Business: Staying Human in the Age of Data

'At a time when things need to change, and change fast, the authors of *Belonging* have written a new guidebook for running businesses today. Current leaders – and those who hope to become leaders – will gain critical and actionable insights on diversity and inclusion from this important book.'

Bob Pittman, Chairman and CEO, iHeartMedia, Inc.

'Creating a sense of belonging should be a priority for every leader. This book is essential reading for anyone interested in creating happier, more productive and more effective workplaces.'

Tanya Joseph, Managing Director at Hill+Knowlton Strategies

'*Belonging* is full of brilliantly practical advice for anyone who is seeking to improve the culture of their team or business. It should be required reading for first time managers to FTSE 100 CEOs.'

Josh Graff, UK Country Manager & Vice President, Marketing Solutions EMEA & LATAM, LinkedIn

'Written by a triumvirate of serious leadership thinkers who understand and practice the value – and values – of equality, diversity and inclusion; and can evidence the tangible business benefits of *Belonging* from their own direct experience.'

Stevie Spring CBE, Chairman, British Council

'*Belonging* never forgets that diversity is not a problem to be solved but an opportunity to be grasped. It's essential reading for anyone who wants to take diversity in their organization from fine words to reality.'

Mark Thompson, former President and Chief Executive, The New York Times

The Key to Transforming and Maintaining
Diversity, Inclusion and Equality at Work

belonging

Kathryn Jacob, Sue Unerman
and Mark Edwards

BLOOMSBURY BUSINESS
LONDON · OXFORD · NEW YORK · NEW DELHI · SYDNEY

BLOOMSBURY BUSINESS
Bloomsbury Publishing Plc
50 Bedford Square, London, WC1B 3DP, UK
29 Earlsfort Terrace, Dublin 2, Ireland

BLOOMSBURY, BLOOMSBURY BUSINESS and the Diana logo are trademarks of
Bloomsbury Publishing Plc

First published in Great Britain 2020
This edition published 2022

A catalogue record for this book is available from the British Library

Library of Congress Cataloguing-in-Publication data has been applied for

ISBN: 978-1-3994-0139-5; eBook: 978-1-4729-7960-5

2 4 6 8 10 9 7 5 3 1

Typeset in Minion Pro by Deanta Global Publishing Services, Chennai, India
Printed and bound in Great Britain by CPI Group (UK) Ltd, Croydon CR0 4YY

To find out more about our authors and books visit www.bloomsbury.com
and sign up for our newsletters

The authors would like to dedicate this book
to our wonderful families.

Contents

Contents

Foreword
by Karen Blackett OBE

Diversity is not a problem to fix. Diversity is the solution.

Diversity offers us the solution to unlocking greater creativity in our businesses, and to finding growth in today's competitive markets. I have been passionately advocating the benefits of diversity for many years now, and I like to use an unlikely – but I think very powerful – analogy.

I am a single mum to a 10-year-old boy, who is obsessed with The Avengers. As well as being a hugely successful movie franchise, The Avengers provide a brilliant analogy for a high-performing team and for the benefits of diversity. Are the Avengers all the same? No. They are very different people, with very different attitudes and beliefs. Do they always get on? No. But when it matters, they come together as a team. And their very different skills combine to form a whole that is much greater than the sum of its parts.

I genuinely believe it is our job as leaders to put together teams of individuals with very different talents, then champion and nourish them, so that we can create an 'Avengers Assemble!' of talent in our businesses who can creatively problem solve and deliver. Survey after survey underlines the benefits to organizations of diversity. And we are making progress towards greater diversity at work. But that progress is very slow. Why? The authors of *Belonging* have identified one of the key barriers to progress that is overlooked time and again, and also outline a clear and achievable solution.

Recruiting a more diverse team of people is only the start. Leaders then have to ensure that they create a culture where everyone in this diverse team feels that they belong. In the old paradigm we would expect new people to 'fit in' – to simply absorb and replicate the behaviours of everyone around them. But if we do that, we lose out on the benefits of diversity, because we remove the diverse thinking, behaviour and attitudes that will spark creativity. How often have we heard of people leaving a company because they 'just weren't the right fit?' And on how many of those occasions might that person have actually been trying to bring the diversity of thought that the company needed?

Today we need to do more than be open to this possibility. We need to create a work environment where new people feel free to bring their different ways of thinking and where those already in place welcome this. That means a workplace where everyone fundamentally feels that they belong – that they are accepted and will be supported. This won't always be easy for any of us. Diversity of thought naturally means that consensus will be harder to get to, and tensions can exist. But with open minds and mutual respect we can work through that. A certain amount of healthy conflict, tension and challenge can be a vital spark to creativity – and so will help us create better ideas.

It will take true leadership.

It will take rethinking not only our approach to attracting talent, but also to keeping and progressing them. Culture is set from the top, middle and at the roots of any organization.

It will take commitment.

But it will be worth it.

Karen Blackett OBE
CEO Group M, UK, WPP country manager

Foreword
by Duncan Edwards

The economic case for diversity in the workplace has been proven: study after study has shown that greater diversity, especially at the most senior level, leads to better results. So too, the case that making your organizational culture inclusive will lead, over time, to greater diversity. And yet, despite the overwhelming evidence, and the good intentions of most leaders, progress, measured by outcomes, has slowed. In this important new book, Kathryn, Sue and Mark make a powerful argument to add 'Belonging' to the business lexicon and address the challenge to increase the pace of change at people like me.

As a 'straight white male' I have been in some form of leadership role for more than 30 of my 35 years in business. And, I should add to my self-description, I am the product of a more than comfortable and supportive upbringing and a private education. The authors' challenge to people like me, people with either direct power or significant influence, is not to be just a silent supporter of change but an active participant. And the challenge to others, the campaigners for change inside the organization, is to see the 'straight white male' not as the enemy but as an ally.

In my own former career in media I was lucky enough to work in an environment where women have long held senior roles, often in the majority, and our sector was always a safe and welcoming place for the LBGTQ+ community. But I would be the first to recognize that our record on BAME and socio-economic diversity, especially at senior levels, was poor. Looking back, there is no question we could have done more to make the environment more inclusive, from recruitment to board level, and to give all of our colleagues the same sense that they truly belonged with us.

For the last two years at BritishAmerican Business, we have run a series of workshops and seminars for our member companies on workplace change, called 'The Stir'. This series has looked at multiple aspects of the D&I challenge with speakers from every sector, consultancies like McKinsey, and the authors of this book! All of these sessions have advanced the understanding of the challenge and helped spread good practice and benchmark results but, more often than not, we have been talking to the already committed. Our most powerful sessions have been workshop discussions with 'allies'; these are the (usually) straight white men in leadership positions who are trying hard to support change in their own organizations. Rather than seeing these men as the enemy, advocates for change need to embrace their willingness to help and support them in the process. With your help, more of us will step forward on this issue, overcome our fear of saying the wrong thing or having our motives questioned, and demonstrate to everyone what it means to belong in our organization.

Duncan Edwards
CEO, BritishAmerican Business

Introduction

Every business sector has been, is being or will be disrupted. Even the disrupters fear disruption nowadays. The times when a technical- or skills-based advantage gave you a longer-term competitive edge are long gone. Change and volatility are the new normal.

In such an environment any advantage is worth exploring. It has long been proven that having a more diverse senior team can offer such an advantage: many research studies have shown that increased profitability and better decision-making come from a more diverse workforce. One such study from Boston Consulting Group found that companies with more diverse management teams have 19 per cent higher revenues due to innovation. McKinsey reported in 2019 that companies in the top quartile for racial and ethnic diversity are 36 per cent more likely to have financial returns above their industry medians, and those in the top quartile for gender diversity are 25 per cent more likely to have such returns – yet delivering diversity seems elusive to many businesses and organizations at the top level.

This has to change. It must change because this lack of diversity is seriously problematic. Problematic not just in terms of profitability, and not just in terms of competitive advantage, but in terms of fairness too. Fairness and justice for everyone, where everyone can have a chance at the career they deserve. A workplace where everyone feels that they belong is better for the mental health of the people who work there and the financial health of the company. Beyond the moral imperative, there is every reason for a company to build and to maintain a more positive culture for everyone.

Proof of profit

There's plenty of evidence, too, about the impact of diverse boards on profit. In terms of gender, S&P Global's market intelligence team reported in early 2019 that companies with women as chief executives or as chief financial officers delivered more profit and drove share prices. In the 24 months post-appointment, women CEOs saw a 20 per cent increase in stock price momentum, while women CFOs saw a 6 per cent increase in profitability and 8 per cent larger stock returns. These results are economically and statistically significant.

And it isn't only gender that drives financial performance. Companies with more culturally and ethnically diverse executive teams were 33 per cent more likely to see better-than-average profits, according to a 2018 study from McKinsey. In the UK, the potential benefit to the economy from full representation of black and minority ethnic individuals across the labour market through improved participation and progression was estimated by the McGregor-Smith Review to be £24bn a year.

Under-represented and underpaid

McKinsey also report in their 2020 *Women in the Workplace* report that parity in the workplace remains out of reach for the foreseeable future, and has significantly worsened because of the COVID-19 pandemic. In the US, the top boards are dominated by white men, who take two-thirds of the available seats.

The UK's top companies remain dominated by men and the 2020 Hampton Alexander review of the FTSE, which covers more than 23,000 leadership roles, states that while there has been some progress, the pace of change is too slow. At the time of writing, there are only eight women CEOs of FTSE 100 boards. Indeed, there are only nine even if you include the FTSE 250 and only 11 women chairs on the FTSE 100.

There are only 10 Black, Asian and Minority Ethnic (BAME) people working in leadership roles across companies in the FTSE 100, according to the annual 2021 Green Park 2021 Leadership Index. BAME, of course, is not just about skin colour. Minority ethnic communities encompass white minority groups too. There are currently no black executives as CEOs, chairs or CFOs. Diversity expert Trevor Phillips commented: 'People of colour seem to be superglued to the floor.'

In the UK, large businesses report their median and mean gender pay gap. Of all the companies in the 2019 report, an overwhelming majority favour men. And in many businesses the discrepancy has increased year on year (the report was suspended for 2020).

In the companies that make up the US Fortune 500, 38 per cent of seats are held by women and minorities, according to 2020 statistics; there are only 41 women CEOs overall. The editor-in-chief of Fast Company, Stephanie Mehta, observed: 'Despite spending billions, companies can't buy diversity.'

The backlash

Even though the reins of power remain firmly in the hands of white men, there is a growing belief amongst some of them that they don't have a future in the workplace.

Some white men feel that women and ethnic groups get a better deal. Writer and presenter Jeremy Clarkson said in an interview in January 2019: 'Anyone who has a scrotum, forget it… they [the BBC] just aren't giving jobs to men at the moment.'

Professor Clara Wilkins from Wesleyan University in America says: 'There's this perception of a zero sum relationship – men and women are in competition. So if things are better for women, things get worse for men.'

Furthermore, the Lean In institute reported in 2019 that an increasing number of men are nervous about spending time with subordinate women. In the US, 60 per cent of male managers are uncomfortable participating in common workplace activities such as mentoring, working one-to-one and socializing. This drops to 40 per cent in the UK, but even there the figure has grown by a third, year on year. As founder Sheryl Sandberg asks: Who are those senior men likely to sponsor and promote? The women that they're afraid to be alone with or the men that they have got to know much better?

Getting real

Diversity and inclusion doesn't have to be a zero-sum game – it never did. On 1 November 1848, in Boston, Massachusetts, Samuel Gregory founded the first college in the world to train women for the medical profession. He said at the time: 'There are said to be 40,000 physicians in the United States. 20,000 of these ought to give place to this number of women.' Indeed, about 50 per cent of physicians in the US are now women, but it is 50 per cent of more than 1 million doctors – 20,000 men did not have to give up the role.

Diversity helps businesses outperform the competition and so they grow. Therefore, there are more opportunities for all of their people. One set getting a fair opportunity does not have to mean that another set of people lose their opportunities. Those businesses who have managed diversity and inclusion successfully, who have different points of view represented on their top boards, are the businesses that have grown, even in tough times. With more diversity at the top, decision-making is better, stronger and more effective, and everyone's career benefits from this.

VUCA times

This is particularly true now. From political upheavals to the spread of the coronavirus, we live in times of Volatility, Uncertainty, Complexity and Ambiguity (VUCA). This US military term used in modern warfare also represents the situation in nearly every sector of business.

At times like these you need fast, agile and creative leaders. You need boards that can disrupt themselves and by not being authoritarian and controlling can take lessons from every diverse perspective. A board where everyone looks, speaks and thinks the same is going to find it more difficult to do this than a board full of difference.

Traditional values are not enough

Many workplaces, even in newer sectors, are built on traditionally 'masculine' traits: the office norms are often authoritarian, status-driven and dominant. This patriarchal alpha environment is no good for all kinds of people, including many men. Traditional 'pale, stale, male' company cultures remain a remarkably tough nut to crack. If success means having to give unsustainable efforts to work at the expense of health and family, then the kind of people who succeed will be of one type only. Traditionally, that will be a workaholic with a full-time, stay-at-home partner who co-ordinates all aspects of their life away from work. And that type of person will continue to perpetuate the current system that's become so toxic to many people of talent.

Current initiatives are simply not enough

Many diversity initiatives have become echo chambers, where responsibility for change seems to be laid at the door of disadvantaged groups themselves. The converted are preaching to themselves; perhaps influencing to the extent of starting the discussion, but then failing to make real, practical progress and effect long-lasting organization-wide change.

In the drive towards greater diversity at work, phase one has been all about empowering these disadvantaged groups. This work has been crucial, removing more overt cultures of sexism, racism, homophobia and other forms of discrimination, but it has not, in itself, been sufficient to bring about more widespread or lasting change.

From diversity fatigue to Belonging

Even when the business concerned has the best of intentions, some employees are put off by new diversity and inclusion (D&I) initiatives. The CEO has made a speech, training and awaydays are scheduled, yet many simply roll their eyes because they know, deep down, nothing will really change.

'When a company pays lip service to diversity but the message doesn't sink into the culture, the day-to-day experiences of individual employees may not change,' says Dnika Travis, vice president of research at Catalyst, a change-driving agency.

It's often referred to as 'Bake Sale Syndrome', where because someone senior has voiced support for a cause there's suddenly a flurry of activity. If it's for a charity, someone will arrange a bake sale. Then once this has happened, everyone goes back to their old habits and behaviours, secure in the knowledge that they've 'done something'. Many feel the same thing is going on at work in terms of diversity. If there's a policy written, or you can tweet a picture of the panel you've just run, then there's that box ticked. It doesn't mean there's necessarily been a change. Hive Learning's 2019 report on Diversity Fatigue found that minority groups are often expected to be the champions of D&I initiatives. This involves not only showing up for themselves at work, but also showing up for everyone else. They're also likely to feel a burden proactively to champion D&I initiatives. This can be tiring in itself when you're already working hard to speak up for your own identity. In addition to this heavy mental load, underrepresented groups often don't have access to power, budget or, crucially, emotional budget, to drive organization-wide change, resulting in a feeling of fatigue and helplessness. One commentator,

Julie Thomas, global head of diversity at law firm Hogan Lovells, has said: 'I wouldn't call it fatigue, more disappointment.' And as Asif Sadiq, head of equity and inclusion at WarnerMedia, Int., says: 'Diversity is great; we need to realize difference. We're trying to make that diversity mix work. But where we really need to get to is Belonging. Creating a sense of Belonging for all people.'

What needs to happen?

Without the involvement of *everyone* in the workplace, diversity initiatives will not succeed. We need *everyone* to understand and implement strategies for *Belonging*. That is the mission of this book.

To do this, we need to understand why more men aren't more engaged with D&I initiatives in organizations. At the extreme, some may be actively hostile, angry that they're being treated as 'the problem' and threatened by the changing cultural landscape. Others will be unmotivated to change: they may see diversity as a good thing in abstract, but can't immediately see what's in it for them. Many will be motivated, open-minded and supportive, but feel unsure about what to do. In short, they need help. Current diversity initiatives in companies today often put straight white men on the back foot to begin with. Perhaps they've referred to 'the girls' and a woman takes offence, even if they'd refer to their men colleagues as 'the boys', too. There might be an invitation to unconscious bias training. This immediately signals '*You* need this, because *you* are the problem that needs fixing.' Diversity will happen more quickly if those white men can see a clear pathway to becoming part of the solution.

If the men currently in power are brought on board, diversity initiatives will have more chance of actually succeeding. White men who feel excluded need to understand how they will benefit from more diverse cultures and how they can become champions of a new way of working. Everyone in the workplace needs to understand where those men are right now and the best ways to bring them on board, with compassion, understanding and empathy to make sure diversity initiatives do not founder.

More empathy is needed in the workplace

It will be good for everyone in work when old-fashioned masculine values are not the only way. Just as women and minority groups suffer from having to 'code-switch' constantly – i.e. pretending to be other than they are in order to fit in – so do even those who look like and seem the epitome of the alpha man. Business leader Daniele Fiandaca wrote in *People Management* about his own experiences: 'As a one-time member of the "in" male leader fraternity, I've experienced first-hand the negative impact that "manning up" can have. It wasn't until my brother passed away in 2011 that I really understood the value of allowing yourself to be vulnerable... understanding that vulnerability is the root of courage... a starting point for effective change.'

He adds, 'so too is empathy', but points out that, for most people, empathy in the workplace is in short supply. As we will go on to show, feeling empathy doesn't come easily to most and must be worked at; the chances are that where you work isn't all that empathetic, at the moment, but your boss doesn't realize it. A 2018 study by Businessolver found that while 92 per cent of top bosses described their organizations as empathetic, only 50 per cent of employees agreed. With empathy, you're able to really put yourself in the shoes of others.

And this empathy goes both ways, in every direction. This might be controversial, but it cannot be okay for women or minority groups to mock men behind their backs for getting things wrong, or to humiliate them in the working environment, even though currently this frequently comes from frustration and the inability to speak truth to power without damage. We need to create a culture of safe expression.

Everyone must act with empathy and compassion and no one gets it all right all the time.

The first woman MP to take her seat in Parliament was Nancy Astor, who was elected in November 1919. For at least two years she was ignored by all her colleagues in what was effectively a men's club. At that point, she was at a dinner with Winston Churchill, who told her that he really admired the way she handled herself. She asked him why he hadn't spoken to her and he replied: 'I felt when you entered the House of Commons that a woman had entered my bathroom and I had nothing to protect myself with but the sponge.' There are men who are still feeling this way about women in their boardroom – feeling exposed, feeling dread, and out of their depth – and we need to acknowledge this while at the same time continuing to insist on the change the boardrooms need.

Zero tolerance

There must be **zero** tolerance of sexism, racism and exclusionary behaviour towards people who are different in terms of their sexuality, disability, neurodiversity, social class, background, health and indeed any and every marginalized group. This includes **zero** tolerance of inappropriate comments, even if they are disguised as so-called banter.

In professional environments there is no question of senior expert men being able to skip rules about procedure. No one thinks it is OK if the CEO doesn't pay attention to accounting rules. Or if a top pilot makes light of safety procedures. Yet this is still what happens in the workplace: 'Sure, he's a bit inappropriate sometimes, but he's so good at bringing in business or schmoozing customers, we'll let it go this time.' Or you might hear: 'We don't want to drive all the fun out of the business.'

Inappropriate behaviour of any kind is the equivalent of any other important rule in the workplace. There is no excuse, no exceptions and there must be zero tolerance at all times in order to create a safe space for everyone.

There are three essential ingredients of change:

1) Every organization must set a course with clear targets informed by real data (including gender and ethnicity pay gaps).
2) There must be a programme to support diverse groups.
3) Crucially, those in power (predominantly white men) in the organization must want change to happen and for it to be credible and lasting. This is where diversity efforts and initiatives are currently failing.

Ingredient 3 is rarely addressed. Those in power, and in the pipeline to power, must want change to happen and to be part of that change. One of the causes of the failure to change thus far is a function of the permafrost of middle management, which frequently prevents change through a behaviour of 'plausible deniability'. For example, a course will be set by the CEO or chair, and diversity and inclusion bias will be discussed. Yet no change takes place because that particular tier of management has absolutely no desire or appetite for it. No one has explained what the benefits are for them. Those men will often say: 'Well, there were no women/people of colour with the right experience available' or 'There was a possible candidate but s/he didn't really have the appetite for the role'. And just as with plausible deniability in law, it is impossible to prove that this isn't the case.

The benefits of Belonging are for everyone

One of the reasons why RMS *Titanic* was such a terrible disaster in the early years of the twentieth century was that there weren't enough lifeboats. There were slightly more in fact than the legal requirement, but this requirement was inadequate and only provided sufficient space for about a third of the people on board.

The idea was that men would be… well, manly… about sinking. 'Women and children first' was the plan. And then it was the women and children in first class who literally were rescued first. The scale of the disaster was tragic and very public. So too was the longstanding call from the suffragette movement for the law to be changed so that there would be enough room for everyone to be rescued, regardless of gender, race, age or class, with the famous rallying cry: 'Votes for women, boats for men!'

Outdated patriarchal practices and belief systems were disastrous for the passengers on the *Titanic*. But today, many businesses are sinking under similar outdated beliefs and practices.

Building a culture of Belonging

The job of building a culture of Belonging in the workplace is down to everyone, from top to bottom. The board must set the vision of inclusion, but it's up to everyone to make sure that it is lived every day. Just as old-fashioned traditional culture is kept alive by thousands of tiny acts of exclusion and alienation of those who are different from the supposed norm, then a new positive culture of Belonging will be created from everyday actions and positive affirmations of inclusivity.

We cannot hope that this book will speak for everyone, but we do hope to use these pages to channel the voices and experiences of others. Everything within these pages is true, as told to us. Our interviews have been diverse and extensive, and we thank everyone for being so generous with their time, and so open and honest with us, even in the context of some difficult conversations and situations. We cannot put ourselves in the positions of others; all we can do is report from the frontline of business and do our best to represent those who have shared their stories and experiences with us.

These strategies of Belonging are simple and open to everyone. In every chapter there will be easy-to-follow examples of these strategies.

And every chapter contains a set of exercises to follow to help you become a hero and a champion of Belonging at work.

WE BELIEVE THE FOLLOWING:

- Equality of opportunity is a basic condition of a civilized society.
- There is both a moral imperative and a strong business case for companies to develop a more diverse workforce at all levels.
- In a business world characterized by rapid change and constant disruption, diversity of thought is increasingly essential to success.

We have seen some progress made towards greater diversity and inclusion in business in recent years, but overall progress has been painfully slow. Up until now, the D&I agenda has often been an 'echo-chamber' of groups who are preaching to the converted (e.g., a company runs an event to discuss gender equality and 98 per cent of the attendees are women).

While each group that is currently under-represented in senior positions at work has its own unique grievances, issues and needs, the Venn diagram of their grievances, issues and needs also overlaps to a great extent. If we focus on these commonalities, we can make more progress more quickly. Unless a significant number of straight white men rally behind the diversity agenda, progress will continue to be slower than we would like.

Forty-five per cent of straight white men currently 'cover' at work (i.e. hide their true identity) according to Deloitte's 2013 report. These people are not happy with the status quo and we should encourage them to add their voices to the push for greater D&I.

Having a more diverse workforce is only the start. Diversity of people will not automatically translate into diversity of thought and improved business performance unless organizations create the right culture and individuals have high emotional intelligence. Remote working and working from home, which is a reality for many workplaces, doesn't help to promote a culture of Belonging. Even more effort is needed in these circumstances to ensure that the workplace works at inclusiveness for everyone. During 2020 many workplaces moved to remote working as a necessity because of the worldwide coronavirus pandemic. It is too soon to know how many of those companies will undergo a permanent transformation because of this, so that remote working becomes the norm rather than the exception. What is likely is that this will make inclusion and Belonging even more of a challenge, especially where some people choose to return to the office and some of their colleagues continue to work remotely. During the pandemic working from home where possible was not a choice; it was mandatory, and every effort was made to be inclusive of everyone and in fact to be as kind as possible. Under more normal conditions, the effort to be inclusive of those working remotely may fade away. One interviewee that we spoke to, in late 2019, often worked from home as she is in a wheelchair. She told us that she did not feel as though she belonged in the workplace, but that she was sure that this was because she was a remote worker, not because of her disability. If remote working becomes more commonplace, the active effort to make sure that everyone belongs is even more crucial. In late May 2020 the world was stunned by the brutal killing of George Floyd and the protests that followed. In the corporate world we saw the roots of a palpable change; a feeling that those in positions of power and privilege were finally ready to acknowledge that they must play an active role in ending racism and in promoting all kinds of diversity. This sense must translate into action. There must be a real shift and transformation.

Throughout the book we have used the stories told to us in many interviews. The names, jobs and even sectors of some of those interviewed have been changed to protect their anonymity and confidentiality. We thank those who gave us their time, and their insights into the workplace. We do not expect every reader to agree with every opinion expressed in this book. That would be impossible. We do believe, however, that the shared experiences in this book will help everyone at work on the journey to a better culture of Belonging.

A MANIFESTO FOR BELONGING

We are aiming to create a business world where...

- Everyone should feel safe to bring their real selves to work.
- Everyone should feel that they belong in their workplace.
- Everyone should believe that success at their organization is based on how they can contribute.

To make this a reality, the following has to happen...

- As far as is humanly possible, recruitment and promotion should be made free of bias.
- Decision-making within the organization should follow a clear process and should be transparent.
- Organizations must create a psychologically safe environment, where people can be themselves. Where they feel free to express opinions, challenge others (respectfully) and make mistakes (occasionally).
- Organizations should train their people to develop their emotional intelligence and empathy, their self-awareness and their awareness of others. Individuals must also take responsibility to behave in an emotionally intelligent way.

Change is never ceasing, disruption is everywhere. The workplaces that will thrive are those who can combine the best talent to solve problems and drive growth. The only way to achieve this is to ensure that everyone with a contribution to make feels like they belong there. And to do this, everyone must be a champion of Belonging. Progress may have stalled in terms of diversity, but it is in your hands, as a reader of this book, to make that change real.

Preface

Belonging: the state of the nations

More than £6bn ($7.5bn) is spent on diversity and inclusion initiatives every year. There is very little evidence, however, that this expenditure in fact leads to increased diversity, especially at the top of business.

Unique research conducted by Dynata for this book in January and February 2020 and August 2021, across the United Kingdom and United States, shows that the workplace is still full of inequality and unfairness, prejudice and discrimination. This book is about addressing those issues head-on in a new way, not just by throwing money at the problem, but creating change collectively throughout the organization that you work for.

What you will read within the following pages are the voices, ideas and the opinions of those who feel that current diversity initiatives just aren't working for them (not just the voices and opinions of the authors). Overall there is not enough change, nor is it fast enough. Here is a snapshot of the research findings:

Belonging

One in three people in the UK still *don't* feel as though they belong at their workplace. One in four feel this in the US.

Leadership

Only *half* the UK workforce think that the leader of their company takes personal responsibility for diversity. Sixty-five per cent believe this in the US. These figures show some improvement since 2020.

Forty-nine per cent believe that their organization goes out of its way to hire for diversity in the UK; 61 per cent in the US.

Feeling uncomfortable or disadvantaged at work

One in five people in the UK and US have felt excluded or marginalized at work because of their beliefs, personal circumstances or identity; 28 per cent in the US. However, in both countries, this rises to 49 per cent of 18–24-year-olds, 48 per cent of mums returning from maternity leave, over a third of BAME (black, Asian and minority ethnic), 62 per cent of people who are registered disabled, and 62 per cent who are neurodivergent ('neurodiversity' refers to how the brain can process and interpret information in different ways. It has become an umbrella term for diverse conditions such as autism, ADHD, dyspraxia and dyslexia). More than half of women expecting their first child have felt excluded in the UK and the US. Disappointingly many of these numbers have risen despite increased spending by corporations on inclusion.

A third of people in the workplace find office banter uncomfortable. This rises to half of 18–24-year-olds in the UK (46 per cent in the US); 37 per cent of LGBTQ+ (lesbian, gay, bisexual, transgender, questioning or queer, and plus – other sexual communities) in the UK, 43 per cent in the US; and 38 per cent BAME UK, 41 per cent in the US.

One in three people feel that they can't bring their whole self to work and that they cannot be truly open about themselves. And more women than men feel this is the case.

Over a third of the workforce across both the UK and US say that no one senior at work looks like they do, which rises to over half of 18–24-year-olds and 48 per cent of 25–34-year-olds. Fifty-seven per cent of women expecting their first child say this, as do 45 per cent of the BAME work community and 60 per cent of those registered disabled or neurodiverse.

Experience of harassment at work

Shockingly, one in three people have experienced bias, harassment or inappropriate behaviour at work. This rises to 50 per cent of 18–24-year-olds (where there's a sharp rise), 40 per cent BAME, 61 per cent disabled, 70 per cent neurodiverse, 53 per cent of people diagnosed with mental illness, 48 per cent of LGBTQ+ and 59 per cent of women expecting their first child.

One in three people have witnessed harassment, with similar levels across gender. It's higher levels here: 52 per cent under 24, 45 per cent BAME, 49 per cent LGBTQ+, 65 per cent disabled, 72 per cent neurodiverse, 58 per cent diagnosed with mental illness. Overall, 60 per cent of the workforce, that's your colleagues and ours, feel comfortable at the moment to challenge this behaviour. This is one of the most important aspects to change, and it is encouraging news that this has grown since the last round of research. We all sometimes play the role of bystanders. Instead, we need to speak up for each other and to take on the very important role of being champions of Belonging at work.

There are charts detailing this research in the Appendix (*see* pp. 246–52) for those interested in more data. For now, let's get on with stories and experiences that will help us understand what is really going on in the workplace and how to change it for the better for everyone.

CHAPTER ONE

What is going on, and is it working?

Let's look at the 'progress' that's been made

There has been a lot of talk – in companies, on platforms, in the media, online and in books – about how diversity and inclusion are big priorities in the workplace. Lots of claims that we are moving forward. How much is this borne out by the facts?

Let's start with gender as it's the area of diversity that companies have been working on the longest and, given that women make up roughly 50 per cent of the population, you'd expect real progress. And indeed, there has been some.

Headlines about progress – for instance, that 30 per cent of UK FTSE 100 board directors are women – are seen as positive signs and there is a perception that even if it isn't all equal right now, it soon will be. After all, we have had equal pay legislation for decades, women are achieving the same level of academic success as men and, overall, the momentum is strong. Many companies talk about how their graduate intake has been 50/50 for an extensive period and that they are guaranteeing the pipeline of talent to ensure there is more broad diversity and inclusion.

And then you look at the detail. Where there are more women directors, this improvement, while admirable, has been attained mostly by improving the number of women non-executive directors. The percentage of executive board directors in the FTSE 100 (those active within the business on a daily basis and who run the company) was at 2 per cent back in 2015, reached the giddy heights of 3 per cent briefly and, in the latest report (2019), was back at 2 per cent. So, it's not quite as rosy a picture as we might have hoped for. Only 6 per cent of CEOs of top companies are women, in the UK and in the US.

In the UK, the gender pay gap between full-time employees in the 2019 government statistics is 8.9 per cent, virtually unchanged since 2018. The figure has only narrowed by 0.6 per cent since 2012. Amongst all employees, the gap fell from 17.8 per cent in 2018 to 17.3 per cent. At the most senior levels the gender pay gap between chief executives and senior officials is 13.4 per cent – so even when they are in the highest levels (where you would hope that that businesses could address the situation to level up the mismatch), there's still a pay gap of significance.

The diversity agenda today is much broader, but the fact that gender equality – the area of diversity and inclusion that has received the most long-term focus or effort – is stalling or even moving backwards is a worrying sign for everyone who wants to create a more inclusive workforce.

Divided we fall

How can it be that all this time, effort, thought and intent has barely moved the statistics and sentiment? Looking at the evidence of our latest research, we can see that far too many people still feel marginalized or excluded at work.

If it appears that focusing so intently on diversity and inclusion hasn't delivered the outcomes required, then there is a danger of it being seen as an intractable issue. After all, businesses have put in so much effort. Diversity and Inclusion is a billion-dollar industry worldwide.

It could be that in creating all these initiatives – to address gender, ethnicity, disability, neurodiversity, social mobility, sexuality – we are dissipating the intent and instead creating silos that define the groups but fail to bring people together. Where budgets are finite, you run the risk of picking one or two areas where you will focus in a year and allowing the rest to feel that their concerns aren't being addressed. Is it a year of women and the neurodiverse? Or will that be next year, as we're focusing on disability and LGBTQ+ this year? Or does everyone just get a week or a month in which we 'raise awareness'?

You have to take everyone with you

There seems to be an assumption that the rising tide will lift all the boats, but in reality, if you're not bringing your *whole* workforce with you, you are running the risk of more divisiveness. One example of this has been the backlash from those people who feel that everyone else is getting attention and more opportunity while they are being left behind – i.e. older, white men. As one of our interviewees put it, the tag of 'male, pale and stale' is attached to lots of men who find themselves defined by it – and it isn't helping. When you feel at the back of the queue for promotion, however hard you work and however strong your contribution, it doesn't encourage you to extend support to others.

Everyone has a role

One reason why so many of the well-intentioned diversity initiatives aren't working is, ironically, because of the series of micro-focused efforts to ensure that no one gets left behind. What we aren't doing is getting everyone to feel that they have a role to play. It's crucial that there is the creation of a set of values for every business, which means all individuals understand that having a diverse and inclusive workplace means better ideas, a better response to the changing nature of clients and customers, and increased profitability for everyone. And most importantly, that everyone knows that they have a role to play in making the better environment happen and that it won't unless each of them plays their part.

A culture of Belonging

Current efforts to improve diversity in the workplace tend to focus on entry-level recruitment and the 'pipeline'. Time and again business chiefs will try with the best intentions to change the organization over time by tasking their head of HR and recruitment with leading the change. And perhaps the intake of new entry-level recruits does change over time. This does not mean, however, that senior management will change over time. If the culture of the organizations doesn't pivot, the improvement to the pipeline will not yield board-level diversity.

Currently, the picture is most clear in terms of gender balance. In many sectors, gender is not an issue at intake level. Young women are graduating with great qualifications and have been for some time, and are well equipped to compete for entry-level jobs. Yet despite this 'pipeline', corporate Britain has moved backwards on progress towards gender equality at the top of the country's largest listed businesses, according to the director-general of business lobby group, the CBI, Dame Carolyn Fairbairn, who acknowledged that many public companies had a 'mountain to climb', with fewer women chief executives today than four years ago, adding that 'every man as well as every woman would be required to make efforts to improve the situation'.

So now, as efforts are made to improve entry on the basis of ethnicity, neurodiversity, physical disability or disadvantage in terms of background, what are the chances that we will see any better results than we have over gender? Even when those intakes arrive, we are yet to see much evidence that workplace culture has changed to be more encouraging of people who are different from the existing workplace norm in senior roles.

Unless the culture is a culture of Belonging, unless everyone not only gets invited in but feels welcome and listened to, then change will be incredibly slow. And all the best efforts of the HR team will be in vain.

Every man and every woman must **belong**, must be actively involved in change, must be free to express their views and must see the benefit of change. Is this the case generally now? Let's look at how everyone is doing.

How are straight white men doing?
(Part 1: the good guys)

Dan is in his 50s and a very senior manager in a multi-country entertainment business. We had a few conversations about what had been going on in the diversity and inclusion front over the past few months. He is a very open character and told us that he suspected a number of senior managers didn't know how to address the issue or how to articulate what they thought – sometimes because they didn't want to offend people, due to the fact that they hadn't even been aware that women and minority groups weren't thriving in the workplace.

Dan is very clear and highly articulate about the fact that a lot of businesses and most men are not fully engaged in the issue to the detriment of their companies, and openly shares his views on what needs to be done and why it isn't happening. Now, going into a meeting room full only of men, whatever the age mix at present, doesn't just strike him as regressive, it's also boring; he doesn't feel that he will be getting the breadth and perspective that a more mixed group would bring. We get the sense that he would just like to abandon any meeting like that purely because it is a waste of his time. He feels a meeting of heterogeneous men will miss out on many relevant points of view. Dan is sure that you get the very best outcomes when you get the true breadth of opinion. He is very clear about this and says it isn't a matter of him being 'woke' (which is a term referring to awareness of social or racial injustice, but which is sometimes used as a reference to too much 'political correctness') or implementing some HR diversity initiative, it is just the way that he feels and how he wants to work.

His main issue is in trying to get women to join the organization, as women historically have not been attracted to his sector as a career. Elements of it are technical, bordering on geeky. Finding the right talent mix for senior roles that require significant experience can be difficult. As a consequence of the sector norms, Dan has actively worked at creating an environment that attracts women and enables their development. His business has done this by being very outward-looking, not only in terms of their expansion, which has taken them from one European base into a multi-territory operation, but also in the way that they recruit. He says that he just wants the best people who can contribute to their culture and values and that the big breakthrough was the recognition that although they operate in the entertainment business, they can both learn from and develop colleagues who never thought of entertainment as a career choice.

This struck us as particularly insightful. So many sectors simply fish in the same pool to recruit top talent. Dan's openness to experience gained in other sectors and a willingness to accept learning from different fields is both unusual and resourceful. It's reaping rewards for his business as they are attracting and retaining talent that would otherwise not have considered entering the sector.

Everything starts with values

Dan has come to believe that the foundation of a successful employer that attracts a broad range of people starts with the values of that company. He explains that it is easy for any boss to write a list of ambitious values and to articulate them – no company is going to claim that they have no value system in place, are they? However, the crunch comes when you have to live the values that you state that you have. You must adhere to them, even if the easier path is to cut corners or tweak them from time to time as it's more expedient to do that than to have to execute a trickier, messier project brought about by staying on course with your stated values.

While it can seem that any minor aberrations aren't substantive, Dan insists this creates a sense that those values aren't that important to the leadership. Who knows how many hours have been spent in honing the value statements and then in sharing them with the wider teams, only for a quick 'win' or deviation to start the process of undermining all that work? So many really innovative and valuable efforts in this respect have ultimately failed because of the sheer number of small cracks that have destroyed the foundations of the values that a company claims to have at its heart. Once you acquire a habit of not quite hitting the standards that you say that you have, or you allow certain teams to interpret those values in a manner that fits the way that they would prefer them to be but which is a deviation from the initial intent behind that standard, you're on a slippery slope. Once the wider company sees that it's okay not to be up to standard, that those who don't live up to your values are not pulled up or put back on the right path, the original intent is diluted and you either end up with a shadow of a value set or a parody of it.

Dan is clear: any manager who says that they want honest, robust feedback and then doesn't listen to it, or stops the flow of feedback and information unless it's what they want to hear, is just mouthing platitudes. Everyone who works for his company knows this in their very core. The question is whether the wider management team and those operating above them in the company are always willing to act in accordance with the values, even if it is painful to do so. For the value system to resonate and to be lived by everyone, there will be the occasional difficulty – because we are human and it's inevitable that sometimes we don't all quite make it to our ideal standards – but these difficulties must be acknowledged and dealt with or the value system becomes wallpaper. Indeed, as we all know, corporate values are often written up on the walls but these worthy proclamations are as easily ignored as even garishly patterned wallpaper is over time.

Look outward

Dan spoke at length about the importance of being outward-looking as a business in order to be the very best you can be, to ensure there's openness to new and different experiences, both inside and outside his sector. This has been of great value to him as his operation has grown across multiple territories; it's enabled the business to adjust and adapt as it expanded into those different countries.

He said: 'It would have been easy for my senior team to take a highly successful model and just plant that into another country. Instead, we looked for best practices across the whole of our footprint, so that there was never a sense amongst any of the branches that you were just part of an amorphous mass.' This had added a number of benefits, as it encouraged individuals to be self-starting and to take personal responsibility for the job they do and the role that they can play. The danger of an inward-looking focus is that you allow for a siege mentality, where everyone is defending their own cultural model. Or if you remove challenge, that everyone falls into a blind and unquestioning acceptance of the status quo. This willingness to challenge any status quo is one of the hallmarks of a Belonging company – because it positively welcomes diversity of ideas.

Dan is an advocate of one of the key tenets of Belonging: honest internal assessment about every policy change. This doesn't mean you encourage a free-for-all, but it does mean encouraging everyone, in semi-formal groups, to ask the right questions (how will it affect people, profit and reputation?) and examining the risks and possible outcomes of what they plan to do. People who do well in his company tend to be those who can take an issue or a situation and, using their intelligence and knowledge, take their teams with them and get the culture right without waiting for an instruction manual from head office. The key central element of the process is to get any examples of best practice and ensure they are spread across the whole of the business. This is the only way to reap the real business benefits of diversity: without this element of culture, everyone tends to be flattened into a cookie-cutter sameness.

Dan wants all of his team to be both outward-looking and inclusive. Sometimes in the fast-moving environment in which he works (and don't we all?) this means having tough conversations. Creating an atmosphere of Belonging for everyone doesn't mean that difficult business challenges go away. Sometimes, to move forward, radical change has to take place. Here, Dan points out, it is crucial to be clear, honest and direct about the decisions that are necessary.

Straight talking

The commitment to honesty underpins the diversity and inclusion work that the business does. Working in entertainment, they know that they need to reflect *all* their audiences, not just the ones that turn up at Head Office for meetings. Dan knows that the only way the business can sustainably do this is to bring those customers' voices into the way that they work. They incessantly reach outward into new trends and interests. The recruitment policy is orientated to getting people who are *adding* to the talent and outlook of the company, not replicating it. Face-to-face interviews are naturally supported by psychometric tests. However, one of the key things they look for are people who interview the company, who seek to find out about the values and vision of the company and how they can contribute. This, in their view, is a crucial time to find out whether this is a place that the candidate will really want to work, rather than somewhere that they happen to have a job. It also plays back to the notion that they want people who are self-starting in the way that they approach their work, who will interrogate any situation and seek to put it right or improve it. This is in stark contrast to some organizations that not only want the interview process to be one-way, but even leave candidates with a sense that if you ask about maternity leave or enquire about any situation that implies you aren't 150 per cent focused on work, you won't do 'whatever it takes' and you are marking yourself out as a troublemaker or a candidate who is not fully embracing the job for which you are applying.

Dan has been very puzzled by why more companies aren't working full pelt at broadening their talent base. He's conscious too that at first glance he appears to be one of the very men who would feel challenged by more diversity in the workplace or who would not see the value of the expansion of opportunities to a wider palette of candidates. In some of the circles in which he moves, the norm is for decisions to be made by a small set of alpha males. Dan's policies of seeking diverse opinions are viewed as not just unusual but often judged as weak. His view is that there is significant competitive and profitable advantage in quietly getting on with the job at hand: of ensuring their diverse workforce all belong. Simply put, he believes that by ensuring that his business is human in its approach to both its own teams and potential customers, he is building a company with a bright and sustainable future. From each of the case studies in the book we will suggest a practical strategy for Belonging. Here's the first:

Strategies for Belonging

HOW MEN ARE DOING: PART I

At the end of every week, look back and identify a moment when you lived the company's values and a moment when you didn't (it happens, you're only human). Feel good about the first incident; ask yourself if there was a simple way that you could have been more aligned with those values during the second.

How are the men doing?
(Part 2: the ambivalent)

*'Men are being blamed for everything nowadays, **and** there's much more hate towards everything that has a word "man" or "men" in it. Men haven't changed but everything else has changed towards them! Soon a man won't be able to do or say anything anymore without being branded as horrible or sexist.'*

(Hearst, *The 4 Paradoxes of Modern Man* research quotation)

Based solely on the spoken declarations and sentiment of men at the top of business and government, you would be optimistic about the prospects of real change in terms of diversity of people in charge. However, if it were possible to measure the unspoken attitudes and sentiment of all men in the workplace, there might be a very different picture. Media conglomerate Hearst have done just that. A picture emerges that marries up much more consistently with the lack of progress towards diversity in top management.

In recent research entitled *The 4 Paradoxes of Modern Man*, Hearst describe some of the ambivalence and indeed difficulties that many men feel, including the opening quotation above. Paradox one: despite the fact there is more freedom of expression and fewer taboos than ever, many men feel that the risks attached to saying what they really feel now are higher than before. There's no template for how to behave anymore and 'many men feel weighed down by expectations of how they should act within the "new" behavioural frameworks that differ vastly from what was deemed acceptable behaviour in the past'.

Hearst's second paradox is that men today have the opportunity and indeed the responsibility to take a broader role in parenting than their own fathers did and are expected to take care of their appearance in a way that wasn't the norm a quarter of a century ago. Yet at the same time they are still expected to conform to traditional masculine stereotypes. Their fathers weren't expected to do both, so many of today's dads are feeling left adrift, with no role models from their own childhood experiences.

The third paradox is around mental health. While the awareness of mental well-being is much greater than three decades ago, many people still struggle to discuss it. This is true of all genders, but within their research, Hearst have framed it as a particularly masculine issue. It is a fact that most people who go missing are men, most rough sleepers are men and the majority of the prison population is men. There are wider societal contributing factors to this, of course, and we should not assume that women are necessarily experiencing much better mental well-being (although their outcomes are often different when they go through difficult times).

Hearst kindly allowed us to take a look at some of the hundreds of verbatim quotes behind their findings. This has given us a window into what many men are feeling, but rarely say out loud. These include considerable anxiety about how to behave: 'With the Me Too scandal, I think that men's behaviour is far more scrutinised than ever. I think that they are afraid of saying anything in case they offend.' There's also fear of not measuring up: 'The pressure from media has made men become insignificant'. And some men feel picked on: 'It is now expected that men should say and accept that they are privileged based solely on their gender. Due to this, men are no longer valued as they were in terms of opinion or ability. White men are *constantly* under attack in the media.'

In the US, a 2019 report from Pew Research Center makes clear that some white men feel that they're being harmed by efforts for gender and racial parity. Verbatim quotations from this study include: 'As a white male nothing is a given now, you have to fight harder to overcome institutional and government reverse discrimination'; 'Today the white male is the enemy. I've seen too many qualified white males passed over for promotions or advancement in favour of a woman and/or minority. Qualifications don't matter these days, rather your gender and race matter.'

Under pressure

A picture emerges of a wide section of society feeling under pressure like never before. Given this cohort is still actually on top, in terms of both pay and status, if they feel attacked they will understandably take measures to defend themselves, at the expense of those by whom they feel judged. That could be women, or it might be anyone in every other cohort than straight white men. If you seek an explanation for why there is so little progress despite all the HR diversity policies and investment in training, then it seems very clear that one reason lies in such a large and powerful proportion of the workplace actually now feeling under threat. Unless we confront this issue there can be no significant change: the benefit of more diversity has to be felt by everybody.

Jo Abeyie MBE runs the talent business Blue Moon, which is dedicated to increasing diversity in the workplace. Abeyie is clear that the workplace has to be fair for everybody, paraphrasing Martin Luther King: 'Injustice for one is injustice for all'. She is very certain that there will be no real progress if the movements for diversity alienate the people that are needed to buy into it.

The stark reality of what's going on in the workplace is evident in what happened to Peter. A middle management sales leader, in a manufacturing business based in Cardiff, he had been smashing his targets for five years on the trot. He was passionate about his organization and had his eyes firmly set on reaching the board within the year. Then there was a change at the top: the company hired a woman as chief executive for the first time in the 50-year history of the business. One of the outcomes of her recruitment was an immediate improvement in the gender pay gap – so far, so good for everyone.

Eliminating the gender pay gap was one of her priorities, along with increased productivity and profitability. She also had an eye on a potentially forthcoming ethnicity pay gap review.

Peter was initially an enthusiastic supporter of the new regime. He had, after all, always wanted to work at this particular business, had enormous enthusiasm for its product and no itchy feet. Within weeks of the new CEO's appointment his immediate boss was made redundant. There had been a reshaping and rationalization of the board in the spirit of improving efficiency, and joint heads of department had become a single role. Peter's boss had applied, but had lost out to his opposite number, perhaps because he'd always represented the softer side of the partnership. Despite this setback, Peter had every hope of forging as strong a relationship with his new line manager as with the old.

Six months later, he found himself made redundant. Six months of continuing to deliver on his targets and fulfilling every aspect of his role brilliantly. There was no question of unfair dismissal, his severance package was more than generous. He was left feeling very flat, however. As a straight white man in his late 30s, he felt like a victim of diversity politics. With a young family at home and with his wife taking a career break to look after them, his first priority had to be to find a new job to fulfil his designated role as breadwinner. Unquestionably, he felt angry, let down. He also felt as though his treatment was very unfair.

Privately, he is very clear that he was not made redundant for any performance-related reason. Had he been promoted, he understood that the board numbers in terms of diversity wouldn't have improved. And a promotion would not have helped the progress of the gender pay gap, or the upcoming ethnicity survey on pay. He was left feeling powerless.

Several men around him are feeling the same. The very men, in fact, who are still running the company, who still make up the majority of the board, which remains stubbornly uniform, in fact.

We spoke to Hugh, a strong supporter of Peter, who still sits on the board of the company: 'Mistakes are being made in the running of this business,' he observes privately and bitterly. He feels that decisions are being made without integrity: 'We owed it to Peter to consider his contribution to this business, his loyalty and his service. In my view making him redundant was not about his performance in the slightest, it was with an eye to a good headline.'

This is a painful dilemma. There is a lack of change in diversity at the top of business because leaders believe that the board is functioning just fine as it is. Time and again, we hear from business leaders who feel that they can't move on diversity because they'd have to get rid of good individuals who they don't wish to lose to the competition. And what about Peter's straight white male colleagues in middle management? If they are ambitious should they give up the idea of staying loyal to the current business? Is that a good signal for the organization to give? We'd question strongly whether this has to be a zero-sum game where one cohort loses for anyone else to win. Where does it end? Will staff wonder whether a physical diversity or neurodiversity of some kind needs to be evidenced before they can feel safe in their job?

Everyone feels judged

If people working at an organization feel judged for who they are then they are not going to be able to do their best work. You get an organization that has translated one form of conformity – to a white straight masculine norm – to another form, where everyone has to work on exhibiting their minority credentials. This is the opposite of Belonging behaviour by management and creates more divisions than before.

One comment about appearance norms from Hearst's Paradox research highlights the pitfalls of equalizing unfairness instead of solving the issue at hand. One man comments: 'There's much more pressure from advertising to look good, smell good, etc.' Well, it's not great that there is pressure from advertising for anyone to look unrealistically perfect. We're involved in the campaign against body dysmorphia that has come about because of the too-thin images of young women in the media. For a long time, there was far more pressure on women than men to look young and beautiful. It just wasn't fair. The solution to this inequity is *not* for it to be inflicted on men as well.

There is a better way

Back to the Hearst research for some clue to the way forward. Some of the quotations in the Hearst research speak of some release of the pressure on men to be traditionally stoic: 'It now seems acceptable for men to show their feelings and ask for help,' says one respondent. Here's an instance where the breaking down of old-fashioned and unhealthy masculine attributes to more human-shaped values has shown that there's a better way forward for everyone.

While it's unfair that women and people of minority ethnicities struggle to be promoted into top jobs, it isn't the answer for men to feel that they are now being treated unfairly, too. By making the workplace equal for all, this must include straight white men or all the efforts will simply equate to treading water.

One global CEO of an accountancy business, who has made significant efforts to appoint diverse candidates to top roles across his business, reacted with alarm when asked how things were going. His immediate response to a question about the pace of change was, 'Is this yet another attack on me for not moving fast enough?' Without a trace of irony, he observed: 'It feels like a witch-hunt for middle-aged white men.'

We need to call time on this unhelpful theme. There are no witch-hunts that will help, there never were. Continuing with old traditional attitudes that lack an understanding for the need for change, and the flexibility to do so, will leave individuals and their businesses at a disadvantage. The way forward lies in creating a culture of Belonging, where everyone can thrive.

Strategies for Belonging

HOW MEN ARE DOING: PART 2

Don't get rid of one set of norms that exclude people only to replace them with a set of norms that exclude others.

So, if some men are working positively to create change, and yet many are feeling defensive, let's look now at where women are at.

How are women doing?

There is a sense that things are changing. It seems that every other day we read about initiatives, groups set up to improve inclusion, the celebration of a woman CEO making the grade, changing the dynamic... So, yes, women are doing well, *if* you were to measure progress in terms of intent and interest. *If* it was true that when people write or talk a lot about what change is needed, then action and delivery inevitably follow and then everything *is* looking good for women.

In reality, for a number of women there is a stark contrast between perception and the everyday experience of what work is like. We have ended up with a sense of confusion – is there really anything happening? And if there is, why aren't we part of it? Why aren't I feeling the sense that things are changing? Am I in the wrong job/company/sector?

Speaking to women in the City of London, in plush, high-tech surroundings, we encountered one of these inclusion groups. They were a small cohort who had started their own network within the organization as there was no support structure to allow them to hear from each other or from external speakers. A fascinating group, they were really engaged and very high-performing. The dynamic between them was very strong and they clearly knew each other very well, encouraged the reluctant speakers to voice their opinions and were familiar with the challenges others in the group faced. They were a pleasure to spend time with.

It was an all-women group and they joked about all the rumours that accompanied their meetings – their men colleagues were intrigued, bemused, curious and a little threatened. The men wondered exactly what it was that was discussed: was it just a support group or were they plotting? Who did they chat about? Should they be worried? Some of it was teasing but there were some remarks that had a slight edge. The group thought it was funny and didn't feel the need to justify, explain or discuss what they had focused on. Better to leave the men guessing than open up the conversation to others.

At the end of our talk there was the usual exchange around how things were at their organization, what their goals were and how they saw their progress. What we learnt was quite shocking.

Every one of the women there was clear that once you hit a certain level in the company, you had to go to another company, do well there and only then would their current employer see their value – and headhunt them back. There were no internal promotions for women between two levels of management.

All the women knew it. The men knew it, too. No one talked about it openly. There were so many questions that emerged after this revelation that it was hard to decide which one to ask first.

Two-fold problems

For the women that we had talked to, the problems were on two levels. One was organizational, the other was personal. At an organizational level, the questions were how was it that this subject was both known about and yet never openly acknowledged, which in a place that espoused openness and co-operation in its stated values seemed perverse, if not downright strange? Also, why spend so much time and effort to recruit and train this cohort and then just let them go when they hit this magical job title?

Making the decision over who to promote when you have a number of strong candidates is never easy. The elation of the candidate who gets the role is more than matched by those who don't get the position feeling angry, disappointed and disillusioned. In situations where your candidates are primarily internal ones, it's even tougher. It can feel comforting to make the easy choice, one that doesn't create any ongoing problems afterwards. In fact, we had one woman who told us that after she didn't get a promotion, her boss had justified it by saying that the successful candidate's wife was expecting a baby and so he needed the bigger role (and, though he didn't articulate it, the bigger remuneration) more. She said she was so stunned at this feedback, she didn't know how to respond and just sat in a stunned silence, which her boss took as the end of the chat and left the meeting.

Probably feeling that he had got away quite lightly.

This City firm demonstrates one tiny example of the kind of common issues that are going on across business still. Even in those companies who are winning awards for their diversity and inclusion policies there is a lack of fairness for all humans at work. One woman at a large award-winning business confided in us: 'There's still sexism at play here, despite all the best attitudes. Every day I see or hear evidence of it.'

Strategies for Belonging

HOW WOMEN ARE DOING

Make sure that you don't lose talent to other firms because of your reluctance to promote people who don't look like the current board. Ensure the opposite. Check the board: if they all look and sound the same, it's essential to make an effort to add some difference.

If everyone else is divided, the established order wins

Martin runs a small kitchen sales business in the north of England, which is where he's originally from. Gay and white, his husband is black. He campaigns for attitudes to change to be more accepting of diversity, including running a course for people to learn to be a straight ally, to learn how to spot prejudice and call it out. For years he worked in London in a role where he felt somewhat excluded by colleagues who were straight and had kids. When there were events where you could take your partner, he was afraid to take a man. How terrible not to be able to fully be yourself at work. But he also believes that he was actually of particular use to his former employers because they felt he wasn't constrained by conventional family ties and so they would send him on last-minute business trips abroad, which made him a go-to guy for any mission that needed urgent attention. This gave him opportunities over others and put him in the spotlight when successful. Also, he had more one-to-one time with the overall boss. However, this was outweighed by feeling that he couldn't properly gel with those around him.

He felt disadvantaged because he apparently had less in common with colleagues. As he had no children, a point came when he felt left out of conversations about Center Parcs holidays and how to get into the best school in the area. On the other hand, he felt as though he had a secret advantage because the top management valued the way that he had fewer ties to stop him jumping on a plane or even moving the dates of a holiday (where mums and dads were not free to move it from the school holiday period).

A spokesman now for the gay community, Martin feels as though his old working life is behind him. He does have concerns about progress though and believes that militant attitudes are emerging in the LGBTQ+ community. There's considerable anger and there's a risk that this will end up alienating those who might otherwise be sympathetic. He feels it's important that he campaigns to take everyone with him. He also observed that there are people who sound sympathetic but by failing to change their behaviour, they just disappoint: 'I see people who are simply in it for themselves, concerned to look and sound positive but unchanging in how they act when people aren't watching them.'

Martin is also worried about the divisions within the LGBTQ+ communities themselves. He's witnessed arguments, for example, when a community of radical lesbians refused space on a march to a transgender community. Once again, we return to the theme that an inability to see the point of view of others only repeats the status quo. It might feel very different for the exclusions to be about transgender people for instance, but Martin questions if this echoes the way in which patriarchal institutions have excluded everyone who isn't a straight white man. Surely it's a better idea to develop a workforce where everyone has empathy for each other?

No one can expect this to come naturally. As best-selling author Yuval Noah Harari writes in *21 Lessons for the 21st Century*: 'Even if you personally belong to a disadvantaged group, and therefore have a deep first-hand understanding of its viewpoint, that does not mean you understand the viewpoint of all other such groups. For each group and subgroup faces a different maze of glass ceilings, double standards, coded insults and institutional discrimination. A thirty-year-old African American man has thirty years' experience of what it means to be an African American man. But he has no experience of what it means to be an African American woman, a Bulgarian Roma, a blind Russian or a Chinese lesbian.'

It takes effort

Diversity brings all kinds of benefits. It also takes work. No one has the capacity to instinctively empathize with everyone else's experiences. Martin, who is from a northern working-class background, has to really work at seeing the disadvantages that might be experienced by a middle-class white woman who is in her 50s and undergoing menopause. There is no set of rules that says that he would have more in common with a gay woman or more shared experiences than a straight woman would. There's no rule book nor a detailed roadmap for any of this. However, what is clear is that it is everyone's responsibility to take some action and to work at creating a workplace where everyone belongs.

When middle management in a company is not diverse, and where there is no visibility of role models in the most senior board, then there's a real likelihood that anyone who is different will simply internalize the message that they are unlikely to progress in that company. While it cannot be entirely true that 'you have to see it to be it' or there would be no change or progress, clearly a lack of role models hinders change. Furthermore, initiatives are often created by very well-meaning people who are actually removed from the talent that they are trying to attract and retain. In a not uncommon worst-case scenario, you end up with initiative overload (which alienates anyone who it is not designed for) but no outcomes that benefit those for whom it is designed.

If senior roles are still largely dominated by straight middle-class white men, there can be a feeling that the business is designed for straight middle-class white men with good connections and a full-time, stay-at-home wife to take care of the children, who in time will only recruit successors in their own image.

Language, and what passes in some sectors for banter, contributes to this. Martin recalls a dinner when he was much more junior and working in a large commercial firm. The team had secured a large and brilliant contract, unexpectedly and against stiff competition. To celebrate, the team, led by the director on the new account, took the client out for dinner. Of course, there was plenty of alcohol to drink – after all, it was a huge and profitable celebration. It wasn't really acceptable not to drink. And it wasn't acceptable to leave before the director. Finally, after the client had gone, the director asked the team to stay for one last celebratory brandy. One of the most junior team members had had enough to drink and instead asked the waiter for a peppermint tea. At which point the director, certainly the worse for wear after several glasses of wine, said: 'Peppermint tea, what's wrong with you? Are you gay or something?'

Is it any surprise that Martin took his talents elsewhere? And sooner rather than later.

According to the Office of National Statistics, 2 per cent of the UK population identify as lesbian, gay or bisexual. However, many LGBTQ+ organizations dispute the official figures and a recent YouGov survey found that 23 per cent of people chose something other than 100 per cent heterosexual when asked to plot themselves on a scale, which does suggest that the ONS figures are lower than reality, especially for younger people. The YouGov figures rose to 49 per cent self-assigning as other than 100 per cent heterosexual amongst 18–24-year-olds. Is this simply an issue of people feeling too uncomfortable to self-identify at work, or for a government enquiry? A recent survey of the advertising industry conducted by ad giant WPP found that 11 per cent of men stated that they were gay or bisexual versus 3 per cent of women. Does this further suggest that lesbian women don't feel comfortable being themselves at work, even in one of the creative sectors where traditional attitudes are less prevalent than in many others?

In a workplace where everyone belongs, everyone can share their personal stories. Of course, it should never be a requirement of employment that you have to reveal your private life, but life is too short to spend your working day covering up who you really are. It also requires energy that could be better deployed productively for your employer.

Sally is a trans woman who has not told any of her colleagues, her team or those who contract her business that she is transgender. Only her immediate boss knows. On the one hand there is no reason at all why anyone should know her personal story. On the other, normality for Sally is for there to be a conversation or a reference that makes her feel awkward. For example, this might be someone interrogating why a woman of her age has chosen not to have children. Sally feels this is none of their business and neither wishes to go into any complex explanation, nor to have to refuse to explain. She is aware that if people did know her story then she would be the centre of unwelcome attention, yet there is so much rhetoric about bringing your authentic self with all of your experiences to work that she sometimes wants to explain everything to everyone. She is certain though that this would expose her to some prejudice to which she is currently immune.

Imagine having to think about this, as well as doing your job well. Imagine having to calculate how much information you give out about your history and experiences. Sally's path is brave and not easy. She is considering coming out as transgender, but knows this isn't a door that she can open and then close. Attitudes to transgender people are not always welcoming and although everyone she has confided in has so far been positive, of course she has no way of knowing whether that will be the case if she goes public with her private history. Can she rely on everyone seeing things from her point of view?

The techniques we will describe at the close of this chapter to enable you to see the perspective of others are not for the timid. They will change you, and enable you to create change around you. And they are for everyone. No one knows each other's experiences. Back to Harari: 'As he grew up, the African American man was repeatedly stopped and searched by the police for no apparent reason – something a Chinese lesbian never had to undergo. In contrast, being born into an African American family in an African American neighbourhood meant that he was surrounded by people like him who taught him what he needed to know in order to survive and flourish as an African American man. The Chinese lesbian was not born into a lesbian family in a lesbian neighbourhood, and maybe had nobody in the world to teach her key lessons. Hence growing up black in Baltimore hardly makes it easy to understand the struggle of growing up lesbian in Hangzhou.'

Some disadvantages are more obvious than others.

Struggles with mental illness don't exhibit themselves obviously most of the time. And the experiences that people might assign to each other are often merely assumptions rather than the truth. The perfectly groomed tall white alpha male might have a wife or husband at home who is struggling with a breakdown. That same individual could have a child who is unwell or disabled. The idea that the workplace has evolved from one of conformity to a supposed masculine patriarchal norm to one where you need to compete to show your (socially acceptable) disadvantages is unhelpful and above all shows a terrible lack of humanity and compassion for each other. It is complicated, it is messy. The reasons for diversity at senior levels taking too long to manifest are themselves diverse. Current measures are not enough. Unconscious bias training scratches the surface, but doesn't really land empathy with those that are other. Away days and training efforts usually only land with people who are already on board. They don't reach everyone and though many may nod to the logic of diversity, it is not in their hearts to change.

There is, of course, a better way: the way of Belonging.

Strategies for Belonging

IF EVERYONE ELSE IS DIVIDED THEN THE PATRIARCHY WINS

Having empathy for people who are different to us doesn't come naturally to everyone. You can learn it, but you have to work at it. Whoever you are, put yourself in the others' shoes. Don't just imagine how you'd feel if you were them – sympathy and empathy are not equivalent.

How it feels to feel different

There's no single template for difference, so let's look at a variety of experiences. Sonya remembers being promoted a few years ago into a superb job at her then employer. It involved switching departments and her old team threw a big leaving party for her. During the course of the evening, once a few drinks had been downed, she heard one of her colleagues say to another: 'Well, you know the only reason she got the job is because she's a woman and she's black.'

Sonya said: 'I rang my new boss very first thing the next morning and said to him: "Why did you hire me?" He replied: "I hired you because you're good. Does it help that you're a black woman? Well, to be honest, yes. It means that you have a different perspective from the rest of the [all white] team. But I can assure you that I wouldn't have given you the job if I didn't know that you'd be good at it. I can't afford to carry anyone."'

This undermining from her ex-colleague probably stemmed from envy. It can be nicer to think that you've been passed over for promotion because of your ethnicity or your gender rather than that someone else has performed better than you. Sonya fortunately had the bravery and the good sense to ask her boss immediately and not allow the comment to fester and diminish her. Her new boss had been perceptive: you get better decisions from a team that complements each other's strengths and weaknesses, that goes beyond the comfort circle of each of its members.

Sonya knows a lot of chief executives. In her view there are the good guys, one of whom we talked about earlier in this chapter. The ones that you don't have to persuade of the benefits of diversity, who are true champions of change. And then the not-so-good guys. The ones who say that they've tried to employ a more diverse senior team but the candidates just aren't out there. She notes that many now tend to change the debate to talk about neurodiversity rather than ethnicity, gender or sexuality and she's scathing about this, saying: 'I think it is because frequently they've already achieved it. Particularly those with big tech teams. I think it's yet another way to stall the issue.'

Maurice McLeod is a social commentator and journalist. He points out that the challenge is to create a really fair organization, not just a so-called level playing field. The level playing field can trip up those who are without instinctive privileged assumptions and confidence. McLeod believes that the problem is about power: 'There's a propensity to give credence to people who we've always believed in. There's real deference to the language of power. If you don't have fluency in it (and I was 28 before I learnt the difference between "th" and "f"), then you're disadvantaged.' His advice is to find the aspect of yourself that is other and to learn how to deploy the practice of code-switching to your own advantage so that you can take control of the situation. He adds: 'We need to teach confidence and how to exploit being different.'

Harjot Singh would agree with finding a way to exploit your point of difference. He's a top EMEA strategy chief at advertising agency McCann. Writing in the *Huffington Post*, he explained that as a gay Indian man, he has experienced both racism and homophobia. Over time, he has found a way to harness the power of difference: 'Let me explain. Stereotypes are systemic. Oppression is systemic. It's the default setting of our society to maintain the status quo – it's what makes normal "normal"… I've learned that you don't have to accept the limits that other people impose on you, but you can learn from them, then set your own limits. You have the power not to FEEL oppressed. In my experience, feeling oppressed is a learned behaviour. You can acknowledge that it exists but you don't have to feed it…. Celebrate the fact that you're not like everyone else and don't let it ever hold you back. Instead, use your difference to propel yourself forwards.'

Singh is at the top of a leading ad agency. Perhaps you might be excused for thinking that he's now achieved power, but he explains that the lessons he's advocating are ones learnt in early life. He urges: 'There is no point in acknowledging what doesn't serve your best self.' He even thanks the naysayers for preparing him early in life to be adaptive and intelligent: 'If you're stuck in clichéd normality, surrounded by people who look just like you and think just like you, you're never going to have to truly challenge yourself and develop adaptive intelligence skills.' And of course, adaptive intelligence skills are what every business needs in the twenty-first century, a time where the pace of change only gets more rapid every year.

Daryl is a young black man working in a junior role in a large advertising network. He too feels different: 'Advertising culture in London is white. It's a drinking culture. That's how you bond, that's how you form relationships. It's not me.' Recently, he was told by a boss that you need to drink to be successful. He finds it old-fashioned and frankly disappointing in an industry that is meant to be progressive. So, on the one hand he doesn't fit in with that white culture. On the other, it took a black woman in his team six months to speak to him because she thought he was trying too hard to code-switch and fit in with the predominant culture. Frankly, he was then facing rejection on all sides.

Is Daryl hardening up in the way that Harjot would recommend? Almost inevitably. But being in a minority in the workplace is never easy. He will always speak up for himself. And Daryl tries to speak up for others too. He's very good at his job, but he's going to need recognition to progress and for the bosses at his workplace to appreciate the difference he brings to their culture.

Jasmine, a young black woman, works in sales at a large organization. She thinks that diversity is simply a buzzword for most: 'People want to be seen to be talking about it, [but] they don't mean it. Straight white men still have all the privilege. They don't have to adapt. Society and the workplace have been built for them. Everyone else has to adapt. From a personal standpoint I want to see people around me who look like me.'

Jasmine frequently experiences people touching her hair without permission. She doesn't think this is done with malicious intent.

Very often the action is preceded by a compliment. (It seems almost impossible to us to imagine that anyone could think that it is acceptable to touch anyone else in the workplace in any way without express permission these days.) Jasmine says that this happens all the time. And here's then a perfect example of a micro-aggression in the workplace. It seems a small action, it seems forgivable. Yet intentionally or not, it adds to the sense of difference and other-ness that can contribute to being undermined. Other examples include questions like: 'Where are you from? No, I mean where are you *really* from?' When the answer is Essex. Just Essex. Born there, brought up there. When you work for someone for months, but they still can't pronounce your name properly. When a white man addresses four men in the room, three of whom are white and says: 'Hi mate, hi mate, hi mate, yo brother.' Such micro-aggressions might seem small, but they undermine inclusion.

Micro-aggressions

When Ishika was in the middle of presenting a business proposal at her telecoms company, one of her white colleagues arrived late. He joined the meeting and by way of greeting said: 'Hi Ishika, can I just say you really do look beautiful, so beautiful. Have you considered modelling?'

She was taken aback, she was embarrassed and she lost her flow (understandably). When tackled, her colleague blustered: 'Can't I even pay someone a compliment these days?' Was his 'compliment' intentionally to throw Ishika, who is both younger and on a faster career track than him, off her stride? Possibly not consciously intentional, let's assume good intentions. But the effect of it, frankly, came to the same thing in the moment. The long-term effect though was to rally the other senior women in the room on her side. Ishika reflected that she might have lost out in the moment to that micro-aggression, but in the long term it confirmed her power.

Identity is not easy to define. It's not possible to make assumptions about what comes first: race, gender, sexuality, country of birth, religion or original country of origin of someone's parents, grandparents, great-grandparents (and so on down the line). Lloyds Banking Group conducted some research delving into ethnicity in advertising in 2018 to find out how well it was reflecting modern Britain. They found that black, mixed race/multiple ethnic groups and those who identify as Asian were all more likely to rank ethnicity over gender as an identity descriptor, but there were marked differences between men and women. It's clear that identity means different things to different individuals and there are no rules. Kimberlé Williams Crenshaw, American lawyer and civil rights activist, coined the term 'intersectionality' because she believes that identity politics 'frequently conflates or ignores intra-group differences'.

Would a religiously unobservant Jewish woman who has experienced being asked where she 'really comes from' when her family has been in London for five generations identify as white, British or Jewish? Stick with what it says on her passport, despite feeling that some of her colleagues didn't agree? Anyway, how is it anyone's business apart from her own?

Ruth, who now runs her own business, mentions that this has happened to her more than once when she was working in the corporate sector. She remembers one boss who persisted in saying 'Shalom' to her when he said, 'Good morning' to everyone else, and who thought it was funny to assert that she and his own personal assistant, who was also Jewish and who Ruth barely knew, spoke to each other in Hebrew behind his back. (Ruth only knows about five words of that language.) She admits that she had no way of telling him that she didn't find his attitude and words at all funny: 'I felt unwanted and soon found another job. He was surprised when I left and did everything he could to persuade me to stay but my mind was made up every morning. He lost me at "Shalom".'

Jasmine makes the very valid point that it's best if you find a way to ask what is appropriate, to ask quietly and privately. She says: 'I sit next to a gay white man at work. He and I have a pact. I'll ask him about things so as not to offend and he'll do the same.' She adds: 'I know as a fact that just because I don't find something offensive from my point of view that it doesn't mean it isn't offensive.'

'You know it's not a niche if one in six people in the world have a disability of some form. This is a huge opportunity for society,' says Hector Minto, accessibility evangelist at Microsoft. Minto here was speaking to Liam O'Dell, 'Mildly deaf freelance journalist', for *Metro*, discussing the lack of captions on many political videos released in the campaign for the UK's 2019 election.

Minto coined #nocaptionsnovotes after calling on MPs to add them to their campaigns. He runs a team at Microsoft dedicated to improving accessibility for disabled people through tech in the workplace. His boss, Jenny Lay-Flurrie, who is worldwide chief accessibility officer, has said: 'Every day, we have an opportunity to stand up for each other and work together to empower people to achieve more. For many people, including the 1+ billion people in the world with disabilities, employment is critical to a productive and purposeful life.' But she adds: 'The unemployment rate for people with disabilities is nearly double that of those without disabilities.'

Attitudes to disability

This is perhaps unsurprising if we examine attitudes to disability amongst leaders in many workplaces. A UK poll in the summer of 2019 revealed only 11 per cent of business leaders stated they'd have no concerns about recruiting a disabled person to a senior role, with 41 per cent of respondents saying they felt that disabled people might take a lot of sick leave and 45 per cent saying their offices wouldn't be accessible to those with disabilities.

Respondents voiced concerns including that disabled people's 'capabilities might not be enough to carry the job properly' and that disabled people might not be able to cope with 'the high stress involved with executive life'.

In the US, a 2019 survey by the National Organization on Disability indicated only 13 per cent of companies in the US have reached the Department of Labor's target of having 7 per cent disability representation in their workforce.

By excluding disabled people from the workforce, businesses are once again excluding talent with difference. One of the points of view they run the risk of missing out on is the accessibility of both their physical and digital spaces. The number of lawsuits focused on inaccessible websites is growing. According to UsableNet, a company that designs accessible technology, there were 2,200 cases in the United States in 2018, an increase of 181 per cent over 2017— plaintiffs have sued art galleries, wineries, fast food outlets and even Beyoncé. As journalist Katharine Schwab wrote in *Fast Company* magazine in May 2019: 'At stake is whether everyone should be included in the digital economy.'

Listening and respect

More listening. More respect and accommodation for difference. More patience. None of this is rocket science, yet all too often this is not the experience of many people in the workplace. The dominant culture in too many businesses is very constrained. Frequently, businesses congratulate themselves on having a culture of acceptance and friendliness, but time and again this just means that you have to conform to the norm to get on. If you employ in order to continue to sustain the existing culture, that's not good enough. If cultural fit is one of the main criteria to get on in the business, the business will not benefit from the input of diverse brains and experiences.

Strategies for Belonging

HOW IT FEELS TO BE DIFFERENT

Find a way of asking what's acceptable, quietly and politely. Just because you think you know, it doesn't mean that you do. Much better to sound out a friendly colleague than make someone feel unsafe or to become a laughing stock or worse by making the assumption that what you say is okay, even if it's the kind of language you're used to in your own social network.

Introducing Belonging exercises and techniques

The exercises and techniques in this book are designed to help create a workplace where everyone feels they belong. As such, they might not be the typical 'diversity training' that you may already have encountered. The exercises here are based on these fundamental ideas:

If D&I is seen as a zero-sum game – one group of people makes gains and another loses – then progress will be agonizingly slow. We will create a culture which is divisive and antagonistic. This will be the opposite of the culture we are trying to create and the diversity of thought we are hoping to unleash will not appear. Instead, we have to see diversity as based around a cultural shift towards more *human* values – respect, kindness, equality, inclusion – Belonging. We will get there if we all behave in a more emotionally intelligent way;

Getting us to that place is the responsibility both of the organization's leadership (through leading in a more emotionally intelligent way, through training and coaching, through rewarding supportive, collaborative emotionally intelligent behaviour), but it is also the responsibility of each individual – through committing to develop and grow their own emotional intelligence.

There are exercises in this book both for the organization, for leaders and managers developing teams, and also for individuals who are developing themselves.

Exercises and techniques for Chapter 1

We will all work more effectively and more collaboratively in a diverse culture if we are more aware of others (their needs, their feelings, the way they think and communicate), and if we understand that everyone has their own truth, their own beliefs and their own idea of what is right (and that these views may not be the same as ours):

The starting point for behaving in such an emotionally intelligent way is self-awareness. About 2,500 years ago, Socrates summed up the most important idea in all philosophy as 'Know yourself'. In the modern world this adage lives on as 'check yourself before you wreck yourself'.

It was good advice then; it's good advice now. So, why do we need to 'check' ourselves? As we go through life, we work on the basis that we are sane, balanced, calm, reasonably right about everything and very easy to get on with, while other people are sometimes erratic, unreasonable, weird, wrong about a lot of things and often extremely difficult to get on with.

Oddly, they're all thinking the same thing. Clearly, we can't all be right. In fact, none of us is – not even you. So, we need to 'check' ourselves in any situation where we're assuming that we're right, that what we believe is true, or the solution we recommend is obvious. Because our 'right', 'true' and 'obvious' might be different to someone else's.

The first step to greater emotional intelligence is to understand that you should never assume that there is a shared consensus of what is 'right' or 'true' or 'obvious'. Because everybody's reality looks different than everybody else's.

In a workplace which is actively encouraging diversity of thought, understanding that other people's viewpoints are as valid as your own is a vital life skill. If we don't appreciate this, we will speak to others with an attitude of 'I'm right, you're wrong'. And this will almost certainly be counterproductive and quite possibly, positively harmful.

As Al Siebert, author of *The Resiliency Advantage* says, 'You will not be effective with anyone you invalidate as a human being.' It's all too easy to do this, because, assuming we're in the right, we can overreact extremely quickly to anyone who doesn't immediately see our viewpoint or agree with us. This isn't our fault, it's evolution – we're hardwired to react instantly (and literally unthinkingly) to any threat, and have been for thousands of years. Our survival depended on it: if we'd stopped to check ourselves before acting, we would have been eaten by a predator.

Unfortunately, evolution hasn't quite caught up with our corporate progress. Every day in the workplace people are constantly being triggered into fight or flight mode, simply because someone has slightly disagreed with them. This is perceived as a 'threat' because even a slight disagreement might slow down the speed of the current project, which might mean a decision is delayed, which might mean a client fires your company, which might mean you lose your job, and so on. As a result, we spend a lot of our time in fight or flight mode, anxious, worried and expecting something to go wrong. While in this state, we don't think clearly and we don't communicate clearly; we're likely to not treat others with respect and kindness, not because we're bad people but because we're fighting lots of fires. So, one of the most important skills you can have in the modern workplace, especially one that actively encourages diversity of thought, is the ability to check yourself, to calm down and to bring yourself back out of fight or flight mode.

There are, however, several techniques that you can successfully employ to do this. If everyone in the workplace knew these techniques to check themselves, both individuals and companies would be much better-placed to reap the real benefits of diversity of thought.

Everyone is different (that's the point of this book), so not every technique works perfectly for everyone. Therefore, try out all the techniques and find out which one (or which combination) works best for you.

Check yourself: Technique 1 – The 4:7:8 Breath

The simplest way to stop yourself from being triggered or to pull yourself back after you've been triggered is via the breath. It sounds too simple to be true, but it does work.

We've all either told someone or been told ourselves to take a deep breath. It's great advice, but you have to know how to take a deep breath *effectively*. If you simply gasp a deep lungful of air, you're making things worse for yourself. A rapid in-breath maintains or exacerbates your fight or flight mode. What you need to do is focus on your out-breath. A slow prolonged out-breath is a powerful biological signal to your body that the threat is over and that it's okay to relax.

The American basketball legend Michael Jordan used a specific breath technique when he was about to face a high-pressure game. It's the 4:7:8 breath. You breathe in for a count of four, hold your breath for a count of seven and then breathe out for a count of eight.

As you can see, we're doing two things here. We're slowing our breath down by holding our breath in between the in- and out-breaths and we're putting increased focus on the out-breath. You want to make it roughly four seconds, seven seconds, eight seconds, but if you do it a little faster, that's okay. Just keep the ratio of 4:7:8. Do between three to five of these and you will have recovered your composure and be ready to function in a more emotionally intelligent way.

Check yourself: Technique 2 – Where Is My Mind?

One of the most powerful techniques to function more skilfully and purposefully at work – and in life in general – is cognitive diffusion.

That means creating a slight separation between yourself and your thoughts. This may sound odd, but essentially it comes down to simply remembering that the stream of thoughts rushing through your mind are thoughts and *only* thoughts; they may be helpful to you, they may not be helpful to you, and you can choose what you do with them. They are not the truth and they are not necessarily to be obeyed.

A simple cognitive diffusion technique drawn from the Buddhist practice 'The Four Right Efforts' is *Where is my Mind?* It's a four-stage process.

Let's imagine you're in a meeting with a group of people who are trying to choose between two possible strategies. The meeting isn't going well. You can tell you're not at your best: you're becoming wound up. So, you start the process...

Stage 1: Where Is My Mind?

Ask yourself, 'Where is my mind right now? What is it focusing on?'

You might immediately answer 'on the strategies, of course', and if this is true, great – you can carry on. But be honest with yourself. Is it possible that you're thinking more about the people in the room and their behaviour and how you feel about that behaviour than you are about the problem at hand?

What has your mind actually been focusing on? Is it the fact that someone in the meeting seems to wilfully be promoting a third strategy that the group decided not to consider at a previous meeting? Is it that someone in the meeting seems disengaged and you're annoyed at their attitude? Is it that you have another meeting in 10 minutes and if you don't get a decision by then, you're going to have to have another meeting about this sometime next week and then probably have to reschedule your whole week as a result? Is it that you originally made a recommendation about this matter two years ago and you can't believe you're still going round and round in the same conversation?

Stage 2: Is This Helpful?

All of these are thoughts that can occur to us and they may be perfectly legitimate ones, but they will probably derail us from being able to focus on the meeting and make a positive contribution to actually choosing the right strategy. The more frustrated we become at the fact that a decision hasn't been made, the less likely we are to contribute to a decision actually being made in the remainder of the meeting.

So, having worked out where your mind is focusing, ask yourself, 'Is this helpful? Is the fact that my mind is focusing on X actually going to help this meeting come to a productive and successful conclusion?' Hint: our minds – all of our minds, not just yours – are extremely proficient at wandering off to focus on things that aren't helpful!

Stage 3: Where Would I Like My Mind to Be?

Now, clarify for yourself exactly what you should be focusing on. For example, 'I would like my mind to be focusing on finding an area of agreement that will allow us to move forward.'

Stage 4: Place Your Mind Where You Want It

Now, actively choose to focus your thoughts on the area you named in Stage 3. If asking yourself these questions – or telling your mind where you would like it to focus – seems extremely strange (perhaps even a little ridiculous), then that means the technique is working, because its primary function is to disrupt your normal way of thinking. It's supposed to feel odd.

The *Where Is My Mind?* technique deliberately takes you out of your normal stream of thoughts to look at your thoughts and actively control them. We don't normally do this, so it will feel strange, but it is effective.

Introducing 'One Voice'

Throughout *Belonging*, you will read some extended extracts from our interviews with people with a strong point of view on the subject. The extracts are unedited and presented anonymously; as with all of the anonymous stories in the book, names and sectors have been changed. First, we hear from Anthony, a straight white man in his early 40s, who is head of sales in a start-up he joined, in part, to try and change the diversity agenda in a sector that still has the reputation of being a 'boys' club'.

One Voice: Anthony

'I've been at a start-up for nearly four years. I had been in corporate life, since graduation, without any breaks. I was working somewhere that I felt like I was just another number, struggling with getting the right rewards for very hardworking people. The shareholders were masters and how much money can you make them was the only real question, yet you couldn't get a hardworking graduate a bump in their starter salary.

'I started to become disillusioned. My voice wasn't being heard, and I didn't see enough positive change. There was generally a rise in talk about empathy in leadership, but I didn't see any of that where I worked. So, remarkably, I got an opportunity to leave and retrain and completely change careers, as I turned 40. I rang a friend of mine, a fishmonger – I love fish and I was a big customer. For 10 years, my holidays included finding the best fish and cooking it. Where I lived, there are fantastic butchers but no fishmongers, so I genuinely thought it was a great business opportunity. I suggested going into partnership, because I had an exit opportunity from the corporate. I went to work for £9.50 an hour and as much fish as I could eat. I only did three and a half months but I loved it, especially the interaction with the customers.

'Then I got a phone call, from my current CEO, asking if I would come back into the industry and help him put together the business plan for the start-up. Eventually, I went there full-time as MD at his start-up. I had told him all the reasons why I had been frustrated in my previous job and was clear that I wouldn't work somewhere like that again. Let's value our people's opinions, let's not have the loudest voice carry the most weight, let's have a gender-balanced workforce (which at the time was quite revolutionary in my sector). Let's build something really different.

'I even insisted that the CSR [corporate social responsibility] programme wouldn't be decided by top management, but by everyone who worked there. The owner said, "Go ahead, you make the company what you want it to be, I don't want to be involved." And so I went into the business.

'My first hire was a highly experienced woman; she is one of the reasons we have been a success and the growth has been strong. She brought passion, dedication, a wonderful work ethic and we built the team together. Even when we disagreed, which we did often, it never turned into a cock fight. Neither of us felt the need to be the dominant partner, that classic "alpha male" that I had experienced often in the past. We shared a common goal to grow quickly and successfully and surround ourselves with the best talent we could find.

'We have a new recruit, another woman at a very senior level, and I'm excited to see what she will bring to the business. I've been doing some thinking about where in my career I have experienced the differences between leadership of men and women. Do you know the bit in the movie As Good As It Gets? There's a funny line in it, where the protagonist is asked: "How do you write women so well?" And he replies: "I think of a man and I take away reason and accountability." This got me thinking; in my experience of working with some fantastic women, if I was to write what would define a great woman leader, I would say, "I'd start with a man and I would add empathy, loyalty and inclusivity." With almost all of the men leaders I have had, there's always been that element of their ego. Their willingness to share success is never the same as women, in my experience.

'I worked for some very capable men, very powerful in their roles, but only a few have been empathetic, inclusive or loyal. I would describe them mostly as in it for themselves. Some might be upset to hear that, but if they are honest, it is true and a fair comment. I have had two women bosses in my career and they have both stood out. They were as tough as the men, as capable, but crucially, they listened and understood me so much better. Both genuinely cared about the people in the teams' lives, which is rare in male bosses in my experience.

'I've had several excellent bosses in a 20-year career. Plenty of average bosses, including one male boss who when I asked for a written appraisal wrote on a Post-it note: "Make me look good". It took all my willpower not to say, "I can't do that, it's impossible!" My best bosses – men and women – we were in it together and that is something I try hard to bring to the teams I lead. The problem is with the egomaniacs – it's the people who have some doubts that should be in leadership, but actually the egomaniacs have no doubts.

'I am very proud to work in the sector I do, but there is a legacy issue. Critics point to not enough women leaders and I agree. It actually has been described as a safe sector for men with questioned reputations to go into – it has a reputation for being a bit of a boys' club. In some parts the whiff is worse than at the fishmonger's. It's really awful and something I'm keen to see changed, despite being a middle-aged white man myself. I think it is a slight on our sector and something we need to change. There are many people trying to get us away from that reputation. And I think things will change. The bigger picture in society as a whole means we are being better at understanding, better educated.

'My brother works in the City and you can see the changes there. The commentary as a whole is much better there for senior women. And that senior women are better for the company and better for society as a whole. Businesses should do the right thing and that has to mean a balanced workforce of men and women. We aren't all the same, and in my opinion women bring something different to the party at all levels. That leads to growth. The change is coming. I would say don't wait for it to happen to you, be a champion of the change, irrespective of your sex or position. Make the change happen yourself. If the first objective of the business is to grow profit, one of the answers is to have a more balanced workforce. The more balanced workforce the better. More interesting debate, conversations and a better place to work.'

CHAPTER TWO

The secret of Belonging

Belonging is an ancient human instinct. From the beginning of recorded humanity, people have clustered in tribes, and for most of history, to belong meant a significant improvement in a person's chances of survival. To be cast out was one of the most dangerous things that could happen to you.

The greatest punishment (apart from execution) the Roman Senate could impose was to cast someone into exile and therefore cut them off from the privileges of Empire. 'Beyond the pale' is an expression from the mid-seventeenth century, used to indicate when someone's behaviour has cast them outside of civilization, outside of the circles of Belonging.

The sense of Belonging is innate

We belong to teams, to friends, to groups of fans, to family. It's such a basic human drive and undeniably one of the differences that sets people apart from teams of robots. Yet it is rarely considered in strategies for the workplace and this is a mistake. The matrix management system is essential for most twenty-first-century businesses. Most businesses rightly regard traditional silos as an inhibitor to efficient growth. Projects can and do fall between the cracks of teams. Clients will be frustrated when one part of the business doesn't talk to another. Customers expect organizations to have a single customer view and their expectations are as high as the best experience that they have ever had. They are impatient with businesses or shops who don't join the dots. But a matrix reporting system creates a challenge for Belonging. If you report into one boss but have a dotted line of reporting into another, which one do you feel most loyal to? Managers can and do talk about smashing the silos, but this becomes a perennial thorny issue for the business plan as human nature demands that we pick a tribe.

Belonging is not something that a CEO or head of HR can impose

You can't put everyone through a training scheme for inclusion and leave it at that. Belonging has to be something that everyone who works in an organization truly believes in, truly feels. And it has to be a conscious consideration of all the management. In addition, everyone in the workplace must look out for each other. Is someone feeling left out? Then it is *each* staffer's job to do something about it.

It is *everyone's* job to make sure that everyone Belongs

This is the most important aspect of the culture of any organization that seeks to grow and thrive. It must rise to the top of the agenda of the whole team that runs the business and cannot be pushed into the valiant, yet necessarily limited, arms of the HR and Talent team to own.

In 1999, a mid-sized media agency called The Media Business was acquired by global advertising group Grey and merged into Grey's similar-sized UK media arm, MediaCom. Mergers in advertising tend not to go well. There are plenty of egos to rip each other apart and it is not unusual for the combined businesses to shrink rather than grow. This particular acquisition has been one of the most successful in Adland's history.

As someone who was there at the time, Sue puts it down to the attitudes of everyone involved. In the run-up to a moving day into one office, everyone was nervous. Sue had been through an acquisition before and when she'd arrived at her new office that time there had been no phone, and no computer, for weeks. The inefficiency was horrendous, but so too was the sense that she and her colleagues weren't welcome at that business. But this time that was not going to be allowed to happen. Teams were charged with ensuring the tools of the workplace were provided and working properly. The conversations in each company were the same, before the move and in the weeks and months following it. *Everyone* was concerned that *everyone* belonged. Any time a team meeting happened, someone would ask the question – do we have enough of the other lot here? Do they feel welcome? Are we mixing well enough?

One small incident on the day of the move characterized the tone of the merger. It indicated that everyone was involved in the initiative for Belonging for the newly formed company, from the very top of the business. The management had decided that it would be a nice idea to have a mug made with each person's name on it – that was about 300 mugs. Difficult logistically, but not impossible. The idea was to put them on everyone's desk before they arrived, for two reasons: (a) obviously, this way they'd know where to sit, and (b) it would encourage everyone to greet each other by name and accelerate getting to know each other.

It went extremely smoothly – apart from one mug. Sheila's was missing. Mid-management, Sheila was much-loved by her colleagues, but not on the board of the company. No matter, the CEO and chairman of the merged agency, Allan Rich, was distraught about the missing mug. It would never have occurred to him to delegate the issue. He spent hours hunting it down, made a huge amount of fuss of Sheila and eventually procured her mug from somewhere before the end of the first day.

Most CEOs wouldn't even have known that the mug was missing, being too busy with spreadsheets and profit. Or they might have just brushed over the incident, or blamed an assistant or the marketing department. But Rich's instinct was the correct one: making a fuss about the missing mug showed how important it was that everyone, *everyone*, was included. The businesses thrived together and now lead the industry in the UK. 'People First, Better Results' is the company slogan and in a sector renowned for short job tenures there are dozens of loyalists who remember that first day and are now running the company worldwide in the same spirit.

Let's be very clear. As we said in the introduction to this book, Belonging isn't the same as joining in. The joiners-in are the easy ones to give a sense of Belonging to. Great Belonging culture includes the outsiders, the geeks, the introverts, the alphas and the betas, the extroverts and the confident, the nervous and the timid, the optimistic and the anxious. And it gives each person who can contribute what they need and a reason to belong.

This then is the secret of Belonging: it must belong to everyone

Saying this is one thing, making it happen is another. Now we will examine some traps that come up in the Belonging journey. First, it's important that you don't just include the people who are easy to include.

Running a team ain't what it used to be

So much has changed in business this century so far. Means of distribution, customer service expectations and speed and agility of decisions. It should not really be a huge surprise that running a team isn't what it used to be and has changed dramatically too. But for too many businesses, the old ways of running teams still dominate.

Around 15 years ago, Angie, who is now chief technology officer at a manufacturing business, was taken on a team-bonding exercise out of the office. She spent the day paintballing. Her boss had assured her that she would love it, but Angie hated it and tried to hide out of the way for the majority of the time. At no point was she able to say how she felt. As far as her boss was concerned, a fun time was had by all.

She contrasts this with a subsequent, more recent team awayday at her next job. Here, there were a variety of exercises to choose from, including mindfulness and meditation and arts and crafts, as well as more alpha games. Her team leader had earned her affection by taking her aside at the beginning of the team events and privately saying to her that he only wanted her to participate in activities that she felt like doing. At the first awayday she felt like she was the odd one out, although she says now that she's sure there were other people there who must have hated it, too. At the more recent event, she felt like she belonged.

In his book *Alpha Girls*, Julian Guthrie chronicles the stories of women who succeeded in venture capital in Silicon Valley. The accounts are full of gender or class hurdles. Theresia Gouw, who helped to build Facebook, recounts being on a panel to discuss the growth of the internet. Her co-panellist was asked, what is your favourite tech website? Theresia was asked about her favourite cookery site. Sonja Hoel, the first woman investing partner at Menlo Ventures, was ordered to participate in a timed skiing race at a bonding weekend, despite barely ever having skied.

Guthrie writes: 'Being liked in Silicon Valley was a currency. It was a tacit requirement. For the few women in the game, being liked meant learning to be assertive without being aggressive, to be heard without being loud, and to like money without being seen as greedy.' In other words, it meant walking a thread-like line and mostly faking Belonging to a gang where you didn't fit in.

Imposing one set of values on a whole culture looks increasingly outdated. Every team needs diversity of thought, not just appearance, gender or background. It is essential for good decision-making to assemble a team of people with different perspectives and allow them to contribute and to have their voices heard. In the modern world, with its complexity, speed and contradictions, teams that are built to collaborate are more necessary than they used to be.

Challenge the norm

Currently, the norm in most businesses, both traditional and newer, is *not* particularly normal. It requires conformism to a dominant pattern of behaviour set by the alpha in the organization. When stripped down to the simplest version, it looks a lot like the kind of system that got the Emperor naked in Hans Christian Andersen's fable. You might remember that story from your childhood. The ruler is fooled into buying a new and expensive fabric that only the worthy can see. No one dares say that the Emperor is naked and it is left to a child to state the truth.

Matthew Syed argues, in his book *Rebel Ideas: The Power of Diverse Thinking*, that increasing the number and range of ideas on offer is the secret of resilience for business. The need to diversify revenue streams has intensified, since the challenge to existing revenues from start-ups or tech giants is so frequent.

Willingness to diversify is essential and statistics suggest that outsiders can spot profitable opportunities that insiders may miss. Immigrants account for 13 per cent of the US population but around 27.5 per cent of people who start a new business. To get the most out of a diverse team is a very different issue to recruiting them in the first place. To begin with, it's crucial to avoid stereotyping and we would recommend that you avoid this kind of commonplace gender stereotyping at all costs.

Bob is running an organization that was born in the last century and needs updating. The systems and operating models are outdated.

Unlike the majority of businesses, however, it is heavily staffed by senior women. After a frustrating six months, Bob confides that he's going to have to have a real clear-out of the old guard and replace them with some new people: 'There's too many women and the thing is that they're too *nice* to deal with the brutality of the changes that will have to take place,' he comments.

Dave has recently taken over an organization that was born in the last century and needs updating. The systems and operating models are outdated. Like many businesses, it is heavily staffed by senior men. After a frustrating few months Dave explains that he's going to have a real clear-out of the old guard and replace them with some new people. Do you imagine that Dave thinks for a moment that the fundamental problem is that because they are men they need to go? And that men are too *nice* to deal with brutal change? Does he stereotype all men? Of course not. Dave assumes that he needs more diversity, in fact. To allow new ideas to take root.

Bob has made an assumption about gender that is true to his personal upbringing – his mother and his wife both stayed at home rather than pursue careers and were predominantly caregivers. He's also working with the information that his own team have self-ascribed. The women who work for him have insisted on their own niceness. Quite what this means when it's broken down is unclear. A sustainable business is a nicer outcome for the employees than one that is going to be heavily disrupted and run out of options.

Bob's senior team of women are conforming to a way of representing themselves that is old-fashioned, clichéd and has little to do with facts. His own experiences make him happy to go along with it.

Research published in the *Harvard Business Review* in 2018 shows that men whose wives have careers are less likely to discriminate against women at work and more likely to facilitate their career development. Someone who experiences 'the other's' situation first-hand is much more likely to 'get them' and understand.

There's a common belief that men and women are fundamentally different in business, (other than biologically) and those differences in turn explain lagging achievements. In truth, objective evidence shows that the sexes are extraordinarily similar in respect to key attributes for the workplace, including confidence, appetite for risk and negotiating skills.

Bob doesn't have a team of women that need fixing; he has a *team* that needs fixing, exactly as Dave does with his team of mostly men.

Jennifer Petriglieri, associate professor at INSEAD, author of a study on how dual career couples make their careers work, explains that this gender difference myth persists partly because it is more comfortable. Many beliefs are repeated so often that mere familiarity makes it easier for us to accept rather than challenge them. Rigorous thinking is after all harder work and once you believe something is true, you tend to look for evidence that it is true rather than the opposite – this is confirmation bias. If you believe that gender stereotypes are accurate, you are more likely to notice and remember times when this view is reflected and to overlook times when it is challenged. Furthermore, those who don't fit the stereotypes easily at work may find that workplace a struggle. They don't belong and they are left with one of two options. To conform, which is tiring, and therefore not to deliver their full energy into positive work, or to struggle daily. Is it any great surprise that the first-rate amongst them will leave and go and work somewhere they do belong? If you're running a team, or a business, the opportunity to attract talent with the right kind of culture *will* give you a competitive advantage.

A closed culture in terms of conformity can take all kinds of shapes. When Angie left the business where she was made to join in with activities that made her uncomfortable, joining her current company was a revelation: 'I'd actually thought that the reason I got a decent salary in the former job was not just because I was good at my job but because it was a fairly miserable place to work.'

Paintballing was just one of the workplace issues she had to face. Locker-room banter and a culture of heavy drinking were also the norm: 'When I joined the company where I work now, it was so different. People went out of their way to include me and were immediately interested in my point of view even if it ran contrary to their existing beliefs. I had to substantiate any challenges, but nothing was off the table because it challenged existing ways of working. I think that this is why I have thrived here.' It is also true that the business she works for now has thrived and is sector-leading.

Traditional team-building tactics for every kind of team have changed in the last couple of decades. Running a sports team used to consist of bonding exercises, heavy socializing and team banter. Now it consists of precise and careful monitoring of how to get the best out of every team member and how to deploy them to best effect in competition. Any business that is still running a team according to the norms of the twentieth century is probably about to run out of future.

Strategies for Belonging

RUNNING A TEAM AIN'T WHAT IT USED TO BE

Don't work with traditional norms, challenge those assumptions about how office workers behave. Remember, you're not in an episode of the UK and US hit comedy, *The Office*. Clichés aren't going to help you create a true culture of Belonging.

Of course, whatever you do, you must do thoroughly. Another trap in landing a culture of Belonging is to throw everything at the launch of initiatives and then fail to follow through. Billions are spent worldwide on diversity and inclusion and much of it doesn't stick. In fact, now people are talking about diversity fatigue. This is both from those who are meant to benefit from those efforts, but who are fed up of joining in with initiatives that don't make a real difference to the numbers or the atmosphere, and from those straight white men who often don't participate as they don't believe it's for them.

Should you pioneer or should you play catch-up?

One question to decide in creating a culture of Belonging is whether you should be pioneering and leading the way for your sector in this respect, or be content to follow the more progressive firms when there's eventually evidence of the benefits of change. We'd advise leading, not waiting, but it will depend on your existing culture.

Organizations are dynamic. Not necessarily as in the slightly tired term that dominates management speak, but in the way every organization has its own momentum, behaviours and conventions. Every business has its own vibe and this vibe explains why you get a gut feeling about a company that this is the right place for you when you go for an interview or why you might feel that spending any longer than 30 minutes there could reduce you to boredom, tears or worse. This dynamic is the reason why cultural change and new initiatives can be so hard to land. You can't just make a new policy and expect instant change. Aside from the inertia that can hold any new idea back, you must be cognizant of the dynamics within your company. No amount of free yoga classes, massage therapy and Pizza Fridays will compensate for a management that regularly fails to recognize and reward the contribution of its employees.

Taking a long hard look at an organization that you lead or manage can be really tough. You must be willing to face uncomfortable truths and to have some of your most treasured ideas questioned, ridiculed or even trashed. And it's so hard not to be defensive when you feel that you have put your heart, soul, blood, sweat and tears into your ideas. However, until you really know where you are and what you need to do, you can never make long-term and lasting progress. The pattern of much-heralded initiatives, working groups and reports often becomes a black hole of effort, intention and stasis. The more of these you have, with no discernible change, the more people ignore them.

An interesting example we came across was a major bank that asked colleagues what change they would like in their working lives. The overwhelming response was for flexible working to be brought in. A number of the colleagues commuted every day and they felt that they could achieve more without the lengthy journeys to work and the tiring trek home.

This felt like a pioneering move for this organization. A decision was made to accommodate this and the bank's HR team worked hard to put it in place. After six months, the take-up had been minimal and the management were confused as to why the sentiment had apparently changed.

It emerged that no one of any seniority had been working flexibly, so the collective conclusion had been established that flexible working was a trap and anyone taking advantage of it was effectively signalling that they weren't serious about their job. No one knew where this idea had originated, or why it had taken such a hold and become a central tenet of the perception of flexible working, it was just what people believed. So, the management took the step of requiring every senior manager to visibly work flexibly for an extended period of time. They were asked to all speak openly and frequently about what they were doing and why they weren't in the office at those times. And this was hard to deliver; trying to encourage senior managers to do this proved tricky, as they were indeed wedded to the notion that they *had* to be present in the office, that they were too busy to do the flexible thing for more than a token amount of time. If the response had been token, it would have confirmed the erroneous perception of the majority of the company – it was a trick, a fad, a trap.

It took months to ingrain the belief that flexible working was what the company was happy to offer and that taking advantage of this wasn't the equivalent of throwing in the towel on your career. When the management initially consulted with staff and then gave them what they'd asked for with the flexible working policy, they could not have imagined that it would be so hard to deliver it. That's the strange things about companies and their people: they don't always do what you expect them to do and sentiment and perception can derail many well-thought-out theoretical plans.

Ruthless self-examination

This is where ruthless analysis and self-examination must come into play in any change of policy. If you don't know how your organization or all of your teams are reacting, you cannot create credible change. So, take time and be rigorous. This is not the time to be delusional, hopeful or unrealistic. Think about what possible bumps there may be on your journey and allow for them and be resilient about facing them. Change is a bit like the sea in that a number of small waves can alter geography over time and the occasional big storm will move you on a lot. (But big storms can create damage and they are uncontrollable.)

So, when should you pioneer? There are a number of options here. If you have a culture that is incredibly forward-facing and restless, this could be the right role for your organization. If you know that you are willing to take the risk, to break with existing patterns and commit to a pioneering move, then you could be in a position to pioneer. It can be incredibly invigorating to feel this rush of momentum, but we would add a few considerations that you might like to ponder.

Is this answering a genuine need or concern that is prevalent amongst your teams? I have never met anyone who felt that Pizza Fridays or a softball league would address some of their daily concerns if they were facing long-standing infrastructure issues or an expectation of regular, unpaid overtime. If there's an issue, don't always pioneer the first idea that comes to mind; you need to make it understandable, credible and above all deliverable. Get 360-degree feedback and be willing to adapt and refresh. Be your own worst critic, probing for those elements that might cause an issue.

This may sound harsh, but regular exposure to company cultures of all types can cause you to become quite cynical. We have often heard teams talk about a much-trumpeted and celebrated pioneering initiative as something that is meant to be happening, but no one has any proof that it is actually happening (in the UK, shared parental leave is the most frequent example). So, if you are in pioneering mode, be prepared for a beginning, middle and end phase.

Beginning

The beginning is the recognition of the issue and the development of a solution. This solution should be easily articulated and brutally simple – any reference to lots of detail on pages xx to yy of the employee handbook is to be avoided at all costs. It may sound obvious but stating that you have been listening to your teams is highly inclusive. Explain why your solution is the one that suits the way that you all work and the company culture. Give people a credible and deliverable timetable and explain why you will be doing regular checks to ensure that it is working for your colleagues. Try not to mention cost benefit analysis – it makes it sound like cost-cutting to those who don't quite get the management speak.

Middle

The middle is when the wrinkles can arise. You have congratulated yourselves on your sector-leading policy behaviour launch, initial feedback has been positive, it's so easy to feel the warm glow of a job well done and the anticipation of a congratulatory message from the board. But a launch is not a change of dynamic. Look for evidence of what is going right and what is going wrong. This might be a slow trickle of questions, lack of adaptation across the company, or even downright rejection from a cadre of management. Depending on the feedback and the strength of response, this is the time to reflect, review and respond. It could be that despite your clear articulation, some of the granularity may have been lost in translation to action and you are missing a key element or even a necessary detail. It could be that teams don't see how it could work for them and so haven't embraced the initiative. Be prepared to spend time with them and explain, revisit and explain again.

In the case of outright rejection, you and the wider company may have a bigger problem. Quite often companies can feel that there is a widespread acceptance of change and new development. In reality, some changes are only superficially rooted into the organization and unlikely to survive in the long term. Some of the companies that we have visited have been open that diversity and inclusion plans and programmes haven't actually shifted anything. In the middle of the organization is a stratum reluctant to change because they feel that the change won't work to their own benefit. They have worked their way up the hard way, in the existing system. Below them are people who want to change the dynamic and the reward and recognition system so they get an easier route to the top. Above this recalcitrant level is a board who have already 'made it' and aren't concerned about a reduction of opportunities open to them. The perception of a narrowing path to potential promotion and pay rises makes this mid-management level subtly undermine or fail to implement what they regard as threats to their own future. Outright rejection is rare; instead a series of what seem like hairline cracks in compliance with the new policies occurs and can be just as damaging in the long term.

End

To get to a successful end phase you need to address these issues and keep saying why it is a good thing for everyone. Provide tangible proof of why it has been a benefit and be prepared to keep on saying that for longer than you might think. The pace of change in some organizations makes geological changes look swift, but that doesn't mean that change is impossible – you must be prepared to keep on keeping on.

Sometimes the right policy is to simply follow the lead of the rest of your marketplace – to play catch-up. If playing catch-up rather than pioneering, you need to know where you want to get to and not just snatch at what seems to be working elsewhere. How far behind are you? No, *really* how far behind *are* you? This is no time to be glossing over the truth. Then be realistic about what you can achieve in a certain period of time. How much resource will you need? Add a bit more just in case.

Lateral

In either case, pioneering or catching-up, be prepared to think of all possible routes to change. Think laterally. One company we came across worked solidly for two years and reduced their gender pay gap by a few per cent. It was market leading in their sector and testament to the strong steps they had taken but the CEO realized that to make the gender pay gap negligible, the business would need to keep doing this for the next 28 years or more. Being data and tech people, their fully engaged CEO looked at another way of taking a big step.

They analyzed their management and worked out that if they promoted 90 women (they have 22,000 employees) into the top four management levels they could reduce the gender pay gap by double figures. Yes, some of those promoted might need a little more support initially but what a strong and credible statement by the company.

It also reduced the deliverable time on the gender pay gap at a stroke. This move didn't feel seismic internally, as so few individuals were actually affected by the change, but it was a massive step in terms of a statement, both internally and to its external clients. Other companies in this sector are now looking to emulate them.

It is a strength for a company to acknowledge and work with their own, sometimes uncomfortable, truths. To be self-critical is a necessary exercise as hubris is often the downfall of organizations. Falling in love with your projected image, fooling yourselves that you don't need to change or just paying lip service to the way that your teams want to work… that attitude and behaviour just won't work in the long term.

Strategies for Belonging

PIONEER OR PLAY CATCH-UP

Change in a business can take a long time. Don't expect your people to believe a new radical policy overnight, simply because you've made a statement. Whether you are a sector pioneer or playing catch-up, the same truth applies. Any new policy must be stuck to consistently, and shown in action at the most senior levels of the business, in the most public way possible. You must be ruthlessly honest about the outcomes, not deluded by your desired image.

Breaking closed thinking

'In business, the big prizes are found when you can ask a question that challenges corporate orthodoxy. In every business I've worked in, there's been a lot of cost and value locked up in things that are deemed to be "the way we do things round here". So, talk to people, ask them: "Why did you do that?'" says Andrew Cosslett, chair, Rugby Football Union; former CEO, Intercontinental Hotels.

One reason why change is hard is when there is a prevalence of what we would call closed thinking in the organization. There's one way we do things round here and the only alternative is not doing them properly. This kind of closed thinking stops the progress to Belonging and to reaping the rewards of diversity. Yet in our day-to-day lives it's so easy to get into routines and habits – the Monday morning meeting where you catch up on your projects and issues with colleagues, the quarterly KPI (key performance indicator) meetings where you analyze progress on your yearly plan. It's a rhythm and a path that is comfortable and adds a certain element of security to your working life.

The only problem with this routine is that it doesn't encourage you to think widely and broadly, so it is incredibly easy to just make assumptions about your workplace and your colleagues and to simply carry on the way you always have done. To ask for widespread reappraisal is rare. Those who question the whys and wherefores of a culture can be dismissed as 'not understanding how things work around here' or being ignorant of the particular issues and circumstances that have created the prevalent methods.

The temptation and tendency are that we carry on and just do what we do, even when there is disruption all around. So, it's just like binary counting where it's 1 or 0, plus or minus, and that's just how it is. No breadth or scope to try more extensive possibilities. Often it is only when there is change at the top that everyone is encouraged to look around and question the prevalent thinking, patterns and behaviours. Changing your senior management just to mix things up is a tad drastic.

It's not unusual for workplaces to struggle with change. Sometimes it can feel easier to get another organization like a management consultancy to come in to help you ask the tricky questions and to make you confront some uncomfortable truths. This can be a rather extreme decision if you don't need a full reappraisal of every element of your system and processes. On the other hand, it can feel very awkward being the person who is questioning your binary systems. After all, you have to face these people tomorrow and for the following weeks and months. Do you really want to be the tricky person questioning their way of working and how they operate?

Of course, there are people who relish that role and quite enjoy being the awkward voice in the room. You could give someone the excuse of playing that role for a few weeks, with the knowledge that it is just a temporary role and that everyone understands that the questioning comes from a desire to change things, to think beyond the current closed scope, rather than it being a personal attack.

Breaking closed thinking can't be done on a whim or just for a day or two. If the requirement is for the process to change, you need to commit to an extensive programme that will generate the long-term change that you need.

Breaking down barriers

There are some quick and inexpensive ways to break down barriers. Some companies advocate reverse mentoring, where a junior member of staff is paired with a senior person in order to create a dialogue that allows the younger person to offer their views in a way that is managed, respected and valid. This can sometimes be uncomfortable in a very hierarchical set-up where senior management are seen as the fount of all wisdom, but it is very good for the culture. By empowering the younger person to ask questions, offer their views and to work closely with the more senior person, you offer the opportunity to open up to new ideas and opportunities. There is mutuality there, too, in that the more junior person gets a more holistic view of the company rather than the team or operational group that may be their specialization. There needs to be a commitment to openness, a clear view on what the mentoring is focusing on and regular appraisal of what's being achieved.

When we spoke to a senior participant in reverse mentoring, he was surprised at how much he felt he had learnt and how he had implemented it in his work practices. He had felt that he would be asked about HR policies and his day-to-day role, with his learning coming from getting a feel for what was happening at grass roots. Instead, he was discussing how to recruit and retain talent in a competitive market, what the process was around product development and whether well-being should be a focus for the future. He came away thinking about his consumers rather than the technical developments that were possible ('just because we can create it doesn't mean there is a market for it'). His focus was too internal, he realized, and he needed to talk to his customers more.

Dialogue

In encouraging new entrants to the company to take part in a dialogue with the management, you also create a sense that everyone is part of the mission to grow and improve. It breaks that closed thinking routine. This can be so powerful in contrast to an archaic system of command and control, where people below senior management feel that they are just cogs in a machine, all interchangeable, and that someone – anyone – could slot into that role, rather than feeling that it is *their* particular attributes and personality which form part of the rich mix of talent, experience and attitude which characterizes a company with a route to growth. Reverse mentoring can help create a sense of Belonging.

Another method that is easily accessible and inexpensive is to question new team members about their previous roles and companies. No organization has everything completely right, and fresh insight and learning about the good (and the less than optimal) practices of another place can be helpful. The key is to encourage open and direct feedback. You won't learn much if every answer is a narrative of how amazing every element of the new company is and what a disaster their previous employer was.

Consideration should also be given to how internal meetings are run. Are they open and dynamic or just a succession of the various departments feeding back? Could you set aside time to change certain elements? Are you sure that people are really listening or are they just waiting their turn to report back? Can anyone ask questions of the participants or is it just the person whose meeting it is? Sometimes, just changing the questions we ask can alter perceptions and as a result, the feedback you get. Asking: 'What would you like more of and what would you like less of?' in a review meeting is a more relaxed and open way of discovering what works and what doesn't work rather than a direct question ('What is going wrong?'), which seems to apportion blame.

Diversity of training and development

Another way to break out of the trap of too much closed thinking is to look at the kind of training and development the business offers everyone. We often think that adding to the technical or practical skills we have in our teams is the only purpose of the development plan. Some organizations have found that a course or programme that focuses on personal development or developing communication skills can be as valuable, even if it isn't a practical skill that is used every day.

One company put their senior accounting team on a public speaking course. At first glance, you might think this is a waste of time and money but actually, members of the finance team are often asked to discuss budgets and planning and to provide feedback to other teams. How much more powerful and understandable would they be if they knew how to deliver those reports back in a way that was interesting, focused on their audience and paced appropriately? To know that you can communicate your knowledge effectively is a boost to confidence and to the knowledge of all the people that the accountancy team come into contact with.

To break closed thinking, you need to take away fear. The fear that you might be wrong, or you might lose face or damage your promotion prospects. We have all heard the supposed joke about 'Let me open up the session by saying there are no bad ideas here, except perhaps the ones that Sally and Simon seem to offer up'. It's meant to be funny, but it just shuts down two team members and discourages everyone else from doing anything other than propose ideas that they know the person who opened up the meeting will approve of. Creativity of thought is a key element of changing your thinking, but it can't exist, or hope to survive, in an atmosphere with fear at the heart of it.

Creativity is messy

The opposite of closed thinking, creativity is messy and an abstract concept. Most people think that they aren't creative – after all, you're not writing novels or painting all day, are you? In truth, most people are more than capable of thinking laterally and finding new ways to deal with issues and problems. Those solutions may not be perfect, but they are ways of getting to where you need to be. Even one spark of creative thought can set in motion thoughts in others that can build and become the solution you are looking for. In trying to break a pattern of closed thinking, you just need to start the process of reappraisal that you are aiming for. Be playful in your approach and start from a different place. If you were approaching the issue with a blank sheet of paper, would you operate the way that you do things now? What tiny shifts can you make? What big ones? Would you change the way that you work? Should you change it? You might be in a good place now, so try the idea that it could be EBI – 'Even Better If...'. What does Even Better look like?

Try to change things up by holding your meetings in a different environment. Not necessarily a cookie-cutter hotel with a good line in conference-friendly biscuits and grey carpets, but a meeting room in one of your partners' offices, a cinema, maybe even a picnic in the park as a team breakfast.

If you always have your meetings in the same place, at the same time, with the same agenda, how are you going to change? Why would anyone change? You are encouraging people to stay on autopilot and so you can't expect to generate creative thinking. Perhaps choose the topics you want to cover, get people to write down three ideas they and a partner come up with and collate them. Then get the group to vote for their favourite ideas so that they all feel involved in the creation of the solution. You can then pull that together and review as a whole. This puts an end to the endless sitting around in meetings with an increasingly urgent call of 'Anybody got ideas? Anything? Anyone?' Those much-heralded brainstorming sessions can fall into brain-fail sessions as the time passes by and nothing comes along to break the silence.

Consider asking outside speakers to come and talk about their experiences, good and bad, to provide another view. Think broadly about who could contribute to diverse thinking – if you work in logistics, the experience of a busy kitchen can be a useful insight into how you manage deadlines, customer demands and a highly competitive market to create a cohesive team. Also, of course consider the makeup of your team: are you recruiting to create a broad range of thinking and attitude? Do you encourage those individuals to bring their experiences and approach in a way that creates fresh and open dialogue? Or are you in a comfort zone of similar background, similar outlook and no-risk operations that isn't changing the way that you think and behave? Open it up and everyone can benefit. Everyone can feel they contribute and everyone can thrive.

Strategies for Belonging

BREAKING CLOSED THINKING

Closed, or either/or thinking is one of the big problems for rigid cultures. To create a culture of Belonging requires nuance. Rather than either/or, try 'and and and and...' One simple way to encourage openness is to organize reverse mentoring sessions at scale, where junior staff interact with your senior team and bring new ideas and a whole ream of benefits that you might otherwise miss.

CEOs need to belong too

Can the top management set the culture without being active participants? This is another trap that stops Belonging working in a company. If the CEO doesn't belong too, then the initiative won't work.

Apart from the recognition of your success, the rewards that go with it, it is easy to assume that once you have reached the top, you're in for plain sailing and an easy life. So yes, it can be hard for the rest of us to have much sympathy for those people 'struggling' at the top of the organization, particularly when you read about the many multiples of the company's average salary they can earn and the perks they get for holding down a job title.

Our perception of the role of the CEO is often that they have all the answers and that they are some kind of omniscient figure who knows *exactly* what's going on at a particular division (so why the heck aren't they sorting it out?). This skewed view was forged in a much more stratified and top-down management era.

What we want to do in this chapter is to look at this perception from the other side and how the CEO (plus all the senior team) needs to belong too. These individuals who are presumed to have all the answers, who must appear calm and in control no matter what, and who are often quite isolated. After all, no one is going to invite the CEO out for a quick drink and an analysis (or rather a major griping session) of exactly what is wrong with the new IT system, are they?

Meet Phil

When you meet Phil, you are immediately drawn to him because he has a really open and warm way of dealing with people – he is curious, he asks lots of questions and he has incredible focus. You genuinely feel that he is trying to establish a bond with you and to find a way of making you enjoy your time with him. He works at a very interesting company that has experienced substantial growth and which is celebrated for being at the leading edge of their sector. So how does he manage his teams? What lessons can we learn from him?

He tells the story of his career and how he has been successful for a while but that he felt something was missing, even as he was feted for his achievements. Through a long period of reflection and analysis, he realized that he had been shutting down his emotions in order to meet the image of a true leader, a totemic figure and a celebrated pioneer. He was a shell of a human being. He just wasn't getting any enjoyment or satisfaction from what was happening even as his company notched up success after success after success. Milestones of achievements were hit and surpassed while the architect of the plan felt detached from those who were helping him achieve it.

Phil realized that what was missing was a real connection with the people in his teams. He thought long and hard about how that would be possible and what he needed to do. He was conflicted and confused by all the voices and paths that were espoused as the very best way to manage your team and to ensure growth. It felt a bit like a trap. He also felt that in admitting that he was struggling, he would be letting down the people who relied on him to be the leader, to be the one who had created and sustained this company and who hadn't ever faltered. It was hard to do but he changed the way that he worked. He decided to open up more and be trusting of the people around him and to let them see his vulnerability.

Phil says: 'I realized I was tired from my commute and that I needed that energy to be better at my work. So I started leaving at 5 p.m. – gosh, that was so hard! I really thought that people would judge me for not being "always on" the way I had been. I worried they might think I was being lazy.' He waited nervously for the feedback and it was overwhelmingly positive: his team felt that he had taken a leadership stance in being flexible in his working policy. They trusted him to get his work done whenever he was working.

Trust and autonomy

Phil now thinks that trust and autonomy are essential to continuing his company on their growth path. He realized that he couldn't do it on his own and that he needed to change the language that was used in the business and give his team the chance to grow. He has become really passionate in ensuring that his colleagues have autonomy.

Your teams have the knowledge of the issues and requirements they face, so if they feel that an email doesn't need answering at the weekend, whatever the official or unofficial policy, then fine. If businesses realized that they had tens, hundreds, maybe thousands of smart, dedicated people all working for the same goal, namely a company that was good at what they did, just imagine how that collective could drive the business rather than relying on one overburdened person at the top. By getting your teams to commit to supporting each other, you create a network that is more powerful than anything one person can achieve and that support network is there for you as a leader and as a person too.

Phil now mentors three people in his organization on a regular basis – not the next level down from the C-suite, but across all levels of the company, so he can hear their pinch points, know the barriers or issues they face and fix them. Rather than look top down, he wants insight from the bottom up.

So many of the initial challenges around inclusion come from our assumptions of what we think people are doing and the reasons we attribute for that behaviour. The instinctive drive to classify someone as a type or as only having one side to them is part of our day-to-day shorthand and yet it can be incredibly limiting for both the classifier and the classified. You see someone as being distant and aloof; well, they may just be an introvert and need their space. Or they may feel that the way to appear businesslike is to become distant.

This journey for a CEO doesn't have to be part of a process of recovery and re-examination like Phil's. It can be the start of a new journey towards a different and better outcome for both you and your teams. It is continually emphasized that there is a struggle to find the right talent for companies and to create the workplaces that people stay in and thrive within. By being part of a bigger, more welcoming and human-shaped structure, you may well be creating the type of environment that delivers on both those criteria and which benefits the senior team too.

A final note on Phil: he takes encouragement from the fact that his own team are sharing their whole selves much more openly with him and not just saying what they think he wants to hear. An example that occurred recently was when he asked his mentee what they wanted to achieve now that they had spent time together. Of course, he expected a review of work plans and priorities. However, as well as those elements, the person he had mentored talked about her family background and how fractures in her personal relationships were hurting her and stopping her being the person she wanted to be. It emerged that amongst her top three plans was to fix that, to address that long-running situation and give herself the space and time to deal with it.

Phil was delighted at this revelation: she felt so comfortable with him that she opened up and included him in her thought process. She felt a connection with him that allowed that open dialogue and he knew that he had helped her. That was quite a big reward for a man who had struggled to reach out to other people and he is delighted.

Strategies for Belonging

CEOs MUST BELONG TOO

Belonging is not a policy that the top person in the business can mandate and then stay aloof from themselves. They have to open up, show vulnerability and humanity. Employees might like to think that the CEO is superhuman, that they are an omnipotent Dad or Mum replacement. And the CEO might quite enjoy this adulation. But this isn't healthy for the business: it's a fantasy and a trap. Get real, be human and show that you're all in this together!

Lead from every seat

Everyone in the organization must take responsibility for the culture. It is crucial for Belonging that in this sense therefore everyone leads from every single seat – including the seats at the top of the table, of course.

Emma runs the HR department at one of the UK's largest city firms. She also sits, pro bono, on the board of a large charity. Her role on that board for the last few years has been to raise the issue of their culture. Together with one of the other non-executive directors, she has insistently brought up the question of culture despite it not usually being on the official agenda. This is Emma's first non-executive role and her first work outside of the private sector. She has been astonished at the difference in the culture of her firm, which is focused on profits and which has faults but is consistently making efforts to improve, versus the culture of this company that is working to improve society.

'I've been surprised at how old-fashioned it seems. The digital transformation that every business has to undertake is slow. And the discomfort of the changes has played out in a very toxic way. During all of this, the executive board have consistently held the HR team responsible for the problem. Time and again, I and a fellow NED [non-executive director] have petitioned for this to be seen as the responsibility of everyone on the board. And, it is no surprise that the culture has not improved. Even as a head of HR, I can clearly see that this issue cannot be the responsibility of one person, however much the head of the organization believes he has empowered her.'

After the intervention of Emma and her colleague the organization spent a significant amount on a cultural consultancy project. The consultancy interviewed and observed. Generated a report with some guidelines and then bowed out. The report had delivered good recommendations, but no one owned making them happen and the issue once again faded back into the background.

What Emma has observed here is one of the many problems that can beset an unhealthy business. External issues (the economic trends essentially) had changed long-standing income expectations. The turmoil that resulted led to a blame game, where survival depended on dodging responsibility. This in turn led to a worsening of the culture of blame in the organization and no one was willing to stand up and take responsibility for anything that had gone wrong or for owning uncomfortable change.

Vulnerability

Vulnerability is important for everyone. Brené Brown writes in her book, *Dare to Lead*, that without vulnerability, leaders are simply not able to connect with their teams: 'It's about having the courage to show up, when you can't be sure of the outcome.' EMEA CEO Josh Krichefski believes that modelling what is often seen as traditionally feminine behaviour is crucial: 'My biggest learning from working with senior women is learning about empathy. Men simply need to role model softer, warmer, vulnerable selves. Be true to your whole self without worrying about being judged.'

Krichefski once had to explain to all of his staff that he couldn't go ahead with a promise he had made publicly to them all. He didn't hide from this circumstance. Instead, he owned it, he apologized and the general feeling for him was sympathy for being overcome by circumstances beyond his control. If anything, it made his position stronger. He adds: 'When you're secure in yourself, you can say what you feel, even when what you say is not necessarily what people want to hear.'

Krichefski introduced mental health allies in his organization – individuals trained to offer a sympathetic ear to those who needed it. It meant that no one needed to feel overwhelmed by their mental state and has set standards for the industry.

Former Secretary of State Mo Mowlam used her own vulnerability to further the peace agreement in Northern Ireland. She oversaw the negotiations which led to the historic 1998 Good Friday Agreement after decades of the Troubles. Her very unique style arguably allowed some of the rigidity to be drained from the negotiations and in 2005, the then First Minister of Northern Ireland Lord Peter Hain said, 'Mo Mowlam was the catalyst that allowed politics to move forward… She cut through conventions and made difficult decisions that gave momentum to political process.'

One of Mowlam's ways of cutting through convention was to remove her wig (which she was wearing because of treatment for cancer) and throw it on the table during heated discussions, in a show of vulnerability that showed her strength. Indeed, she was undeniably polarizing.

University academic Maria Dalton comments: 'Mowlam's visibility and her demonstrative interest in class and gender-based issues extended a sense of ownership and inclusion to constituencies who would become vital... The way in which she physically and metaphorically hugged these communities was uniquely Mo. Her outstanding legacy was her inclusiveness.'

Mowlam's behaviour, which was unconventional and included many unconventionally timed expletives and replacing handshakes with hugs, signalled breaking with previous British governmental norms – which was crucial at the time.

Actor Justin Baldoni is a prominent voice in Hollywood on the dangers of traditional masculinity norms. He says that what he most wishes women co-workers understood is that he constantly messes up: 'It is never my intention to say or do something hurtful, offensive or ignorant. Yet at the same time, I am human and it happens more often than I'd like it to. My advice to men is simple. Open yourself up to the possibility that you have more to learn – that you don't know the answers, may not be right, and in fact could be very wrong.'

This couldn't be more different from traditional masculine patriarchal leadership, could it? A crucial element to ensuring a good culture is for the leaders to take full responsibility for it and not to charge a team member or department with fixing a whole organization.

Extreme ownership

Another approach is to ensure whatever seat people occupy in the organization, from top to bottom, that they have a sense of ownership of the culture too. To create a great culture of Belonging, everyone must own responsibility for it. As the elite fighting team Navy SEALs call it: 'Extreme ownership'.

Justin Baldoni says that what he has understood from the Me Too movement is how crucial a role bystanders can play in stopping and preventing harassment: 'We must be part of the movement and call for respect and equality for women, act upon that call to action and continue to perpetuate positive behaviours.' Here, Baldoni is talking of course about overt harassment in Hollywood, but the same solution applies to every kind of micro-aggression that occurs in any workplace.

The term 'micro-aggression' was coined by psychiatrist and Harvard University professor Chester M. Pierce in 1970 to describe insults and dismissals which he regularly witnessed non-black Americans inflicting on African Americans. It's used to describe brief and commonplace daily verbal, behavioural or environmental indignities, whether intentional or unintentional, that communicate hostile, derogatory or negative prejudicial slights and insults towards any group, particularly culturally marginalized groups.

By the early twenty-first century, use of the term was applied to the casual degradation of any socially marginalized group, including LGBTQ+, people living in poverty and disabled people. Psychologist Derald Wing Sue defines micro-aggressions as 'brief, everyday exchanges that send denigrating messages to certain individuals because of their group membership'. The persons making the comments may be otherwise well intentioned and unaware of the potential impact of their words.

Micro-affirmations

One way to counter act micro-aggressions is to encourage their antidote in the workplace, the micro-affirmation. This phrase is rarely used and the much less well-known complete opposite to the micro-aggression. An article from Everfi Educational Network succinctly explains, however, just how powerful the micro-affirmation can be in the workplace. It cites MIT Sloan School of Management adjunct professor Mary Rowe: 'Micro-affirmations are tiny acts of opening doors to opportunity, gestures of inclusion and caring, and graceful acts of listening.' By affirming and practising good behaviours, Rowe suggests, we may be able to block unwanted ones. After all, she points out, 'Attitudes may follow behaviour just as behaviour may follow attitudes'. As a result, micro-affirmations are a way to counteract unconscious bias.

Some general examples of micro-affirmations are:

- Asking others for their opinions
- Recognizing the achievements of others
- Using friendly facial expressions and gestures
- Taking a genuine interest in someone's personal life

Micro-affirmations are a series of small acts of inclusion that add up to an overall feeling of inclusion and Belonging for everyone and this is part of leading from every seat. Each staffer must raise objections to micro-aggressions – even and especially when they are not the victim of them. No bystanding. And each staffer must make acts of micro-affirmation.

B.J. Fogg, a researcher of behaviour design at Stanford, suggests a similar approach to Rowe's. Fogg considers trying to stop old behaviours instead of creating new ones as a common mistake in behavioural change. He coaches individuals trying to change their behaviours to 'focus on action, not avoidance'.

Back to Emma and her own experience of running an HR team: 'I've seen senior leaders being told about the experience of micro-aggressions in their organization. The trouble is that they don't know what to do about it often because the behaviour is unconscious most of the time. Or at least those who are behaving in that way say that it is not intended. The benefit of talking about an antidote, about inclusive and Belonging behaviour, and of senior leaders mirroring this, is that it gives *everyone* a role in fixing the culture.'

Don't be a bystander

Refusing to be a bystander doesn't just prevent problem behaviours but also affirms and supports positive behaviours. If any member of staff sees someone else speak up, they can praise them. If any individual makes a positive change, colleagues can support that change. As Professor Mary Rowe explains, 'The hypothesis is that "on the spot" help and affirmation from bystanders may be especially effective because it is an immediate, positive, often unexpected reinforcement.'

You need bright sparks in the organization for change to happen. If the narrative is based on how poor the culture is, then what hope is there for change? If everyone works at highlighting positivity as well as critiquing poor behaviour then the likelihood of positive change is much better. This also gives everyone the power and capacity to make improvements.

Every organization needs the right leadership, but if everyone is always waiting for those leaders before they act then the culture is in turn too dependent on a pyramid peak. These days, leaders must promote a self-fixing culture. The old paradigm of one man setting the tone for the whole organization makes an organization less agile and flexible. Of course, the executive team must set the business plan and of course a company is not a democracy, but one leader must not pretend that they can create a positive culture alone. In good cultures there is cultural leadership from everyone. If everyone pledged never to be a bystander to any behaviour that made people feel other, whether conscious or unconscious, then of course everyone would believe that they belonged.

Strategies for Belonging

LEADING FROM EVERY SEAT

Everyone in the organization must take responsibility for the culture. It's not okay to complain without trying to do anything about it. A positive step is to encourage 'micro-affirmations' of Belonging.

Exercises and techniques for Chapter 2

Alongside self-awareness, another key element of emotional intelligence is awareness of others. So, here are some exercises that will help to develop those empathy skills further. If you want to bring your best self to work, and to encourage those around you to do the same, it really helps to develop your understanding of what other people are thinking and feeling. To really benefit from diversity of thought and a more inclusive workplace, it's important that we actively open ourselves to the fact that other people think differently and also that the way we feel about the situation may be very different from the way others feel about it.

You might think that some people just have these empathy skills and others don't. In fact, we can all develop our ability to step into someone else's shoes.

The 'No Personal Agenda' meeting

Have you ever been invited to a meeting that you really didn't need to attend? Stupid question, of course you have! The meeting you don't really need to be in but have to go to is one of the banes of the modern workplace. As you enter the meeting room, knowing there is nothing you can usefully contribute, knowing there are a dozen things on your to-do list that you should really be dealing with instead of sitting in this room, you think to yourself, *Well, here's an hour of my life that I'm never going to get back.*

Except now you are.

This technique turns a time-wasting meeting into an excellent training opportunity for you to develop your empathy skills. As you have nothing to contribute to the meeting, instead of bemoaning this fact, embrace and celebrate it. Acknowledge that this is a meeting in which you have no personal agenda.

Normally, when people come to a meeting with a personal agenda, they will listen in the meeting in a way that is hardly listening at all: simply waiting for a gap in the conversation so that they can say the next smart thing or make a comment that they believe will move the meeting towards their desired ending. When you have a personal agenda, it's so easy to listen in this superficial way. With no agenda, you can practise your active listening skills.

As the meeting begins, actively commit to listening to what everyone else is saying in order to really hear what they're telling you. If you find yourself thinking of clever things to say, let them go and return to active listening (if you find this hard, scribble things down if you like and send an email with any questions later). Actively notice how different this feels from a normal meeting. Try and capture what it feels like and take this feeling into other meetings where you do have an agenda, so that you can call on your active listening skills in every other meeting too.

If you feel awkward not contributing to the meeting at all, then write two headings on your notepad: 'What do they want?' and 'How can I help?' If – as you're actively listening – you identify someone with a clear need, issue or problem that you can help them with, note it down and offer your help.

How powerful is this exercise? Well, imagine you had a colleague who came to your meetings, listened intently to what you were saying, appeared to really understand your needs and regularly offered help. How valued would a colleague like that be?

If you use your 'waste of my time' meetings to practice in this way, you will naturally start to also bring these valuable active listening skills to the rest of your work.

'No Personal Agenda' meeting (version two)

Alternatively, when you find yourself in one of these meetings where you have no personal agenda, commit to practising your empathy skills. This time, as the meeting begins, commit to understanding what everyone else in the meeting is feeling.

Again, spend your time actively listening, really hearing what people are saying. And now go one stage further: as well as noting what they're saying, think about what they're feeling too. What are the feelings that lie behind the comments they're making? What are the feelings you can read on the faces and in the body language of those who are not saying anything?

Are they angry? Are they scared? Worried? Threatened? Are they excited? Are they enthusiastic, or are they bored? Actively examining how the other people in the meeting are feeling will hone your empathy skills and, once again, you will take these skills into other meetings where you are not doing this exercise.

Again, imagine a colleague who comes to your meetings and really seems to understand how you feel. Once more, how valued would a colleague like that be?

Three questions for every one statement

But what about the regular meetings – the ones where you do have a personal agenda, the ones where you will be expected to contribute? What about the meetings that you are running? How can you use these meetings to strengthen your empathy skills and to make sure that others in your team feel heard?

An effective technique is to commit to asking three questions in a meeting for every statement that you make. It's surprisingly hard to do (which rather indicates how much we all like expressing our own point of view more than we like listening to others). You don't need to keep an exact score, you'll know when you're not doing it.

Depending on your personality, you may choose to come to the meeting having already prepared some questions, but mainly allow yourself to react to what others are saying and to ask clarifying questions based on what they have said, so they can notice that you are listening and that you want to dig deeper into their views.

One Voice: Shereen

Shereen is 36, she's of French Arabic origin, living in London, a new mum and the CCO of a flourishing start-up:

'There is one particular experience at work that made me really realize I'm a woman. I'd moved from a very traditional business to a tech company. Basically, this was the very beginning of the company – I was employee number 10. Where I had worked before was very much a boys' club – you needed to play golf, you needed to be middle-aged, to have a beer belly to get promoted. I didn't fit in for a load of reasons. I wasn't aware of being different as a woman, but in the new job, I was the only girl in the sales team. I was working with lovely, lovely guys. But then I remember there was like a lot of rapid changes – like honestly, so it was every two months, there would be something new. And it was great to be in that environment because I've never been in such a fast-paced environment, and it was great for me because I'm a person that gets bored really quickly and I need things to be changing so I can be learning. But then one of those changes was that one of the worst performers in the team has been promoted to be our manager.

'I was so pissed off because until then I thought if you perform well, then you will be rewarded for it. I decided to work on a plan. Okay, I'm going to ask for promotion. I'm going to ask for a new role, I'm going to take a look at what I'm doing. And I'm going to see how is it that I can evolve from here to there and develop clients and tap into stuff that we're not doing at the moment and demonstrate my value from a business perspective, I thought. And I asked for that promotion. And then, I remember my boss got back to me with a new package. Which was exactly the job that I was doing at the time. The same package, but in charge of clients in Europe. But I was already in charge of clients across Asia. So, I thought, oh, there's

something I'm missing here. Maybe he's not explaining everything properly. It was really undermining. And I think it was because I am a woman. So, I refused it, and I left and I handed in my resignation.

'I've been managed by men my entire life. It was kind of like a repeat of everything, unfortunately, until I came into this company that I'm currently working for. Here, all of our team is 50:50 men and women. That's amazing!

'Some people leave this to their head of HR and they see it as a staffing issue. I don't see it as a staffing issue – it's a talent issue for sure. If I create an environment for my commercial team or my design team or my data team, that is representative of all of our common values and the culture of the company, then people will be more inclined to perform better. If you work in an environment where you don't fit then it's three steps forward, two steps back, because things get tough and people think, well, what's the point? Yeah, I don't like this company anyway. When things get tough, that's when you lose the best talent and the people that are the most open-minded and creative. And those are the people who challenge you. Yes, men and women are not the ones that are moving the needle in the company. The good ones can go get jobs elsewhere.

'I've noticed in the past five years now every single company I worked at was in a very tough sales environment. I was always one of the rare, if not the only, woman in the company, in the team. There were harsh targets, but I always reach my targets, always, always, always. And before I was in this company I would never have been promoted on my merits, I was never promoted on my performance. It would be tough on the back.

'In terms of diversity, everyone is saying the right thing. It's just like greenwashing, everyone wants to be sustainable, everyone wants to take care of the planet and everyone, but really about 2 per cent of businesses are truly, truly making an effort and actually implementing it concretely. I think it's the same thing happening

with diversity – I think there is a massive massive diversity washing. It's the right thing to say, so every business is perceived as good as the others. Everyone is using this as a marketing ploy and for instance saying: "Okay, let's do a rainbow flag on the week of Pride." I find it outrageous and it's undermining.

'I can be completely honest with you: I see it more subtly in the UK than, for example, in France. I go actually quite a lot to Paris to do big meetings with agencies and people will tell me to my face: "For an ethnic woman you're doing very well and you're quite smart." I'm outraged when I hear that. What do they mean? If I call this out and tell them, "What you just said is extremely racist and sexist," then they reply, "But what I just did was give you a compliment."

'In Paris, all the top level are men. Zero women. Everyone who's doing the work is a woman when in the UK, I think it's much better. And that's one of the reasons why I moved here 12 years ago. It's because of that, but at the same time, you know, I think there's a lot of work to be done here. And I really feel it now as a new mother.

'It's really tough. People make a lot of assumptions about your parenting. I think we should now put a massive focus on men as parents, then I think we'll see less discrimination towards women going back to work. My husband wanted to take more time off for parental leave, but he's in property, and it just isn't done. Also, dads, they have this ability to distance themselves emotionally more, I think. I'm not saying that fathers distanced themselves emotionally from their kids. That's not what I'm saying, what I'm saying is that they have this ability that when they're at work, they're at work. Yes, that's it. But when I'm at work, I'm like, let me check on my kid. Just check everything is alright, whereas he will just forget all day.

'I was at this workshop two days ago and we were talking about the whole imposter syndrome. We were talking about, you know, our biggest fears at work. And what is the worst-case scenario *associated with that. And I would say probably 70 per cent of the room (of 25 women) said: biggest fear at work is fear of making a mistake. And hence being labelled as not good enough at my job and being found out. And I've observed this, like, very carefully in the past two years – my team, young men and young women. I see how they behave towards others when they make a mistake and guys are very, very good at just snapping back, you know, they think, okay, it's fine. It was my screw-up but no problem, what do we do from here? And I'm going to be very honest with you, young women, they have to flagellate themselves for three days. They feel like it's going to be associated with them for ever, that it's going to be brought up at their performance review quarterly. You know, it's like a vicious circle – that ability to snap back and move on and get on to the next task and get on to the next project is an actual skill, because it shows that nothing – good or bad – affects you and that you're keeping going on and you learn from your mistakes.*

'I grew up with two brothers, older brothers, so I was always following them – you know, when they were playing. I would just do the same thing as them. I have a much more prominent masculine energy.

'Three years ago, I actively stopped doing something at work. Instead of saying sorry, now I say thank you. I used to say sorry all the time. Or sorry about this, this and that, you know, so sorry I'm a bit late when I was just on a client call. So now I'd be like, thank you for your patience, I was on another call. And now it's automatic. And I just feel because I'm less apologetic about being there, I feel it gives me a new sense of ownership about work that I wasn't owning before.

'I think you know nothing's impossible. And correct me if I'm wrong, there's not a lot of people, women, that say, I'm going to sit down and think how do I have a harmony with my intellectual life

which is work, and the books I'm reading and stuff like that, my parenting life, my life with my partner as a couple, and with my friends, how do I bring harmony into that, not go insane because I can't do everything? And I feel that a lot of people either go on autopilot and they burn out, or they have five years of a very shitty life, which I don't think is a nice thing, until the kids go to school and then they start breathing again. And even then, it's been tough. But you know, people don't stop and think that they do have a choice. You almost want to take someone out of the fog and say, "You do have a choice, you can work out a plan that makes you happy and there's absolutely nothing wrong with that." And yes, so I know it's very simple and very complicated, but my goal is to have harmony and balance.'

CHAPTER THREE

Belonging for everyone

Most boards now have diversity on their agenda. They spend time and money on diversity initiatives and yet, despite this, many businesses are not delivering change. More and more people are talking privately about the barriers between different groups at work increasing in number and intensity.

Why are the barriers getting worse?

One of the reasons (or excuses) given for this is the complications of intersectionality, which have left some people feeling as though it's just too complicated to do or say anything. Another is that it gets left to HR, the assumption being that the HR department are sorting out the pipeline and that things will take care of themselves, given time.

The problem with leaving it to HR

The pipeline improvements in terms of background, race, disability or sexuality are not at all guaranteed to turn into changes at the senior levels of a company. The 2019 FTSE board review concluded that despite some progress there is 'little sign of change' in women being under-represented in top jobs in business.

In the FTSE 350, only 25 women are in chair roles, with fewer chief executives, the Hampton-Alexander Review said. So, it's still the case that most businesses lack women at senior levels. The numbers of executive directors who are women on the FTSE 350 is less than 5 per cent. In most companies the gender pay gap figures favour men. Simple calculations show that 'sorting out the pipeline' won't have much impact in terms of more diversity on the board given that at entry level the pipeline in many businesses was not an issue in the first place as far as gender was concerned.

The backlash

Some indeed feel that there is a backlash which has come about as straight white men feel under threat. In extensive interviews there are essentially two predominant reactions from them to diversity and inclusion efforts in corporations. Either a feeling that the stakes are too high to try and help in case they get it wrong; in case they say or do the wrong thing, however well-intentioned. Or there is a feeling that they're under attack and whatever they do will be ridiculed or rejected.

The situation that we end up with is therefore that the men who still hold the reins of power are feeling threatened, feeling 'as though it is a witch-hunt'. Even that to be a straight white man in a senior position is to be part of 'an endangered species' (verbatim quotes from top executives running corporations). Another problem is that many of the men in question feel as though the current system has been very successful as far as business is concerned, so why should it need to change?

The current system suits many men and here's one reason why. Many senior men have stay-at-home partners (McKinsey 2019 research measured the proportion of men and women who are in dual career relationships, and far more women have partners who also work: 72 per cent of senior level women versus 37 per cent of men). It's not uncommon for senior men to have wives who pack their suitcases and certainly who take care of all of the childcare issues that come up during business trips, whereas often women who work will have most of the responsibility for this and will also find that an extra day might be tagged on to a business trip, with little warning given by those senior men who have everything taken care of at home.

An analogue culture of business in the modern world

It's as if the predominant culture of business has remained analogue in a digital world. As if people were still reliant on old-fashioned landline phones instead of carrying the internet in their pockets.

There is still often a culture that everything will get done urgently and immediately at once and that everyone will be always available at short notice. Of course, this takes its toll on everyone and you end up with people at senior levels who have been willing to make sacrifices. Because this is the way that things have always been in most organizations, there is a sense of inevitability about it. The world has changed, however. The behaviours that developed in business in the last century don't need to hold true in a world where everyone can be connected remotely and where so much else has changed. Where many younger people entering the workplace want more than to devote their whole lives to profit and to the old ways of capitalist economies.

Diversity and Inclusion talks: what we have learnt

We've given more than 150 talks at businesses over the last four years. Time and again, we hear similar issues come up. As we will continue to illustrate there are myriad micro-aggressions, which can vary from subtle to outrageous. Too many recipients of this end up feeling that the game simply isn't worth the candle and business loses out in terms of diverse talent. Here now are more case studies of changing the old narratives and delivering Belonging. Belonging, for everyone, means making sure that everyone feels that they belong.

Be the hero

You can truly be a hero to your organization and of your career by staging an intervention and being the champion of Belonging. Often these talks will be attended mostly by women. At one point, one of those women will raise her hand for a question that is actually directed at the rest of the attendees. She will say: 'Can I just ask, where are all the men? Why are there mainly women here and how can we expect to change anything if there are only women involved in the issue?' Sometimes one of the men present will attempt to respond on behalf of the men who are not there. He might say: 'We weren't sure that this was for us and if we take seats that are meant for women, isn't that bad again?'

Another common incident is the question of daughters. This is when one of the straight men in the room raises his hand and says: 'I have a daughter. Now that I have a daughter, I am realizing just how unequal the workplace is. It hasn't really occurred to me before now. How can I help to change the workplace so that my daughter is never at a disadvantage?'

Our answer is always that this is an opportunity for him to become a champion of Belonging for everyone in the workplace.

All my daughters

There is an Arthur Miller play called *All My Sons*. Written just after the Second World War, the plot revolves around the true story of a man who conspired with army inspection officers to approve defective aircraft engines destined for military use. This was covered up and the man's business flourished, but during the course of the play, the hidden cost of the conspiracy comes out. Many planes crashed as a result of the defects and eventually the protagonist's son is revealed to have crashed his own plane because he learnt of his father's involvement in the crime. At this point the grieving father says: 'Sure, he was my son. But I think to him they were all my sons. And I guess they were, I guess they were.'

So, what we would like to answer to every man who asks how to make the workplace a better place for his daughter is that he might choose to think of all the women in the workplace as his daughters (or sisters or loved friends). And only by doing so will the workplace change. Only if everyone at a senior level is invested in the idea of work being a place where everyone can thrive will there be sufficient collective energy to create a culture of Belonging. And only then will change really take hold.

You mean they're not all just treading water?

At one talk for the women in the fast stream at a large accountancy firm (which had only a tiny proportion of women as partners across the world), we asked the men in the audience what – if anything – they had learned. One of them stood and said: 'You talked about the fact that women seem less likely to show off than men. This resonated with me. I have worked for this business for nearly 20 years. I show off about my achievements all the time. That is how I got the job in the first place and how I have been promoted to a senior level. All around me there are men showing off too. And you're right: the women in the business show off much less.

'It has never occurred to me before that this might be for any reason other than that they have nothing to show off about. I have put this down to their "treading water". And I now see that this is a terrible shame. That it has meant that we haven't created a diverse senior team and that this is a loss to the business. A loss to the quality of work life. A loss to our ability to beat the competition. I truly hope that this will now change.'

Don't require employees to act like the dominant men

We hope that this will now change too, but we hope that it doesn't just change because the women we spoke to find a way to show off about their achievements more. We also hope that the senior men in the business look beyond the showing off to calibrate and then to champion the achievements of quieter, more internally focused workers, many of whom may be women but also many of whom will be men. Because at the moment what seems clear is that the people (largely, but not exclusively, men) who are great at showing off are the ones who are getting promoted. But being good at showing off and being good at getting promoted is not the same as being great at the job into which they are being promoted. This doesn't include introverts of any kind or simply anyone who focuses on the job rather than the career ladder. This is why where there is an inclusive approach, business benefits accrue: for the truly talented are added to the team, not just those who exhibit a talent for showing off and getting on with the boss.

Here's how to champion real Belonging to ensure your career and your business benefit.

'Over to the girls'

Bias is incredibly hard to eliminate entirely and extremely difficult to do just by asking people to behave differently or writing a new HR policy. It is though not as difficult to interrupt. Without interruption, bias tends to grow stronger. With an intervention, with a bit of what we might call 'an action of counter-bias', attitudes can shift and the 'norm' becomes healthier. One analogy is to think of an unhealthy norm as what happens if your leg breaks and you don't do any proper physio once the break has healed. Without an intervention (and sometimes a quite painful intervention, as those who have recuperated with the help of physiotherapy will attest), the norm for you will be unbalanced. And you will get used to it. You'll compensate, but you will certainly store up future back pain or vulnerability.

Many workplaces have an unbalanced norm. After decades of modelling patriarchal and alpha behaviour, they are a long way from a norm that works for everyone. They are storing up future trouble and are vulnerable to disruption and competition. However, it is never too late for a workplace to start to right itself and to come back to a more helpful balance, where everyone can be nourished and helped to be their best.

New companies, old bias

Once of the surprising things that has characterized the workplace this century so far is that bias seems to be built into very new companies, in some cases more strongly than in centuries-old institutions. Discussions with people in the Civil Service in the UK, obviously a well-established institution, seem to indicate that senior management have gone out of their way to be inclusive of diverse groups.

Liz, a very senior civil servant in her sixties, said that the Civil Service had been in the vanguard of flexibility: 'Having a family and continuing to work was pioneering when I joined. There were no role models who looked happy and had children and had success. But I was absolutely clear about what I wanted, and yes, I was on call during certain crucial periods, but mostly that just meant being at home with my children and being prepared to work if called on. It meant being organized. My husband completely believed in what I did and never questioned me, never made life difficult for me. I'd say start by being very good at what you do, make sure that you show that what you do is important and don't allow yourself to accept that things are different because you are not a straight white man.'

Another civil servant we spoke to agreed that it's crucial to have support, and of course from those in power, from those men who currently hold many top positions. Helene Reardon-Bond, OBE, who was the policy expert behind the UK Gender Pay Gap Reporting, points out that all too often male bosses will rule out promotions for women and that women all too often have less time to dedicate to managing their career paths because of caring duties. She says that women are as ambitious as men, but are responsible for 70 per cent of the caring that needs doing in the UK (kids, pets, parents and the vulnerable): 'At various stages, opportunities for women just get chipped away.'

Gender pay gap reporting is now statutory for large businesses. In the vast majority, the gender pay gap favours men and in its first two years of reporting the gender pay gap worsened in many companies. There are differences in behaviour in the workplace between men and women. Women can tend to be more retrospective during annual reviews, for example. Men tend to talk about what's next. Of course both are important, but this leads to a understanding gap if a man is reviewing a woman, expecting her to push for promotion and hearing instead a review of her previous performance only. Truly inspired leaders look for this and ask questions to bring out the best in those they manage. Helene concludes with the remarkable phrase: 'They used to say that behind every great man is a great woman. I say, behind every successful woman there is often a man without a chip on his shoulder.'

It's true that there are not usually battle lines drawn in the workplace. It's more a chaos of mostly good intentions and frequently undermining actions. Therefore, it's so important for everyone in the workplace to take action and not allow situations to pass by without comment.

'That's enough from me…'

Nicole tells us about a situation at a big conference for one of those newer industries – i.e. the tech sector – where she had been asked to talk about the subject of improving the diversity of boards with her colleague, Anne. They were introduced by the conference chairman, a distinguished white straight man in his forties, who ran his own business. He didn't spare their blushes, taking at least seven minutes to run through the highlights of their careers so far. Also emphasizing how important this issue was to him and his business, and indeed the future of profitable growth for the industry. At the end of this, he handed over to them with the comment: 'Anyway, that's enough from me, it's over to the girls.'

Nicole says she felt as though he had thrown a glass of cold water in her face at this point. Indeed, it was as though despite everything that had been said, he really didn't take her or her colleague seriously. However, saying something felt extremely ungracious, ungrateful and even aggressive. The decision was taken out of her hands, however, by Anne, who said light-heartedly as she took to the stage: 'Well, anyway, it's over to the *women* now!'

Standing shoulder-to-shoulder with Anne made a huge difference. Whether or not the conference chair had in some way intended to undermine them, even unconsciously, or whether he had simply misspoken, his use of language had thrown Nicole off her stride. She confesses: 'I probably would not have said anything, but I was immensely glad that Anne did.'

The talk went well. Undoubtedly, there will have been some in the audience who would have hated Anne's comment and regarded it as unnecessary. There will have been others who cheered.

Will there have been some in the audience who felt threatened by Anne's comment? Would it have been more reasonable to have taken the chair aside and said something privately? Undoubtedly, this is the case, but only tackling these issues in private de facto lends endorsement to the behaviour. There are pros and cons here, upsides and downsides. Nicole, however, felt that by standing up and saying something Anne ensured that the world changed a tiny bit to be fairer and friendlier for women. Did it become a little less friendly for some men though? Does it have to be that one group loses in order for the other group to win?

There will have been some who will have taken Belonging lessons from the incident. Some who will have noted the minor humiliation of the chair and taken note not to use such language themselves in future.

Others will have found the courage to stage such an intervention. Nicole observes: 'It might seem like a very small incident in the scheme of things, but I would never have referred to this man as a "boy" and if I had, he would have taken huge offence, so for him to describe us as "the girls" in this situation was ridiculous.

'One day, this won't matter perhaps, but in a year where the gender pay gap in the UK was revealed as being so skewed in favour of men it felt appropriate to pick up on the language. Plus, Anne did it in such a charming way. I was too upset – if I had said something, it would have sounded off, maybe petty or accusatory. But she was light-hearted. I know she knew what I was feeling, partly because I'm actually quite small and introvert and have suffered from feeling overlooked in my career in the past. I'm sure part of her motivation, at such a crucial moment, was to make sure that I had the courage of my convictions to speak up as we'd agreed, to not be diminished by the remark.'

A tough choice

Should we regret that the conference chair was slightly shown up in public? Ought we to be concerned that his status was undermined? We believe that this is, on balance, an example of restoring normality and hope that the chair would experience it not as an attack of any kind, but a reminder. The kind of reminder of more balanced behaviour that can jolt you out of a habit.

Anne staged an intervention and the business world norms in that conference hall changed as a result.

Here's one instance then of a slightly dismissive comment being dealt with by an antidote to bias. Some groups of people have to prove themselves over and over again when perhaps tall white straight men traditionally don't in the same way. Anne's remark back to the conference chair had interrupted the normal course of events and created a mini moment of truth, a moment where the norm was challenged and perhaps a new normal established. If everyone who believes in diversity and inclusion in the workplace were to interrupt the norms in this way, then there would be a greater sense of Belonging for everyone.

Language is vitally important in the workplace. As we will come on to discuss, one man's idea of banter is another's experience of being undermined. Rules of language, of what's generally regarded as acceptable, changes over time. Just as there are books that were popular for children half a century ago that are now banned from every bookshelf for their casual and unacceptable racism. There has been a conscious effort to change the norms in society to be more inclusive. Every leader in a business organization must take full responsibility for their language, for it to be inclusive. And once again, everyone should listen hard and stage an intervention on the behalf of others if they hear something that might undermine another's confidence or inclusion.

Strategies for Belonging

HERE'S THE GIRLS

If you overhear something that doesn't fit the culture, or diminishes someone in the workplace, find a way of staging an intervention. Make a conscious effort to do this yourself, not to wait for someone else to speak up – but be sure to do so with empathy and kindness.

We need to talk about banter

The business can have all the policies in the world for inclusion. The HR team can be working away on the diversity of the pipeline for senior management. The business can go out of its way to find senior hires from a diverse background. If the culture of banter is unchanged, there is really no point. The people the company employs from those backgrounds won't feel welcome, will not stay, or if they do stay then they will 'code-switch', i.e. change their behaviour to fit the predominant cultural norm to the extent that they are no longer free to focus on doing good work.

Ros works as a general counsel at one of the prestigious law firms in the City of London. She had been at a new company for a fortnight when she was asked to a meeting with her CEO. There were seven people at the meeting, she was the only woman. She was the only person of Asian origin. When she arrived at the meeting, her CEO greeted her like this: 'Hello there, Ros! Well, there don't seem to be enough chairs, want to come and sit on my lap?'

Now presumably this was intended as banter. There were indeed only six chairs. Not one of her colleagues offered to get her a chair. She was lost for words at this point. Her reply was to say that she was sure that she was too heavy to sit on his lap and that she would go and get another chair. She commented that when she told some other women later about her response they were a bit hostile, saying, 'that it was too soft a response, that I wasn't standing up for myself enough... This actually made me want to cry more than the original incident, which at the time just left me furious and numb.'

The firm had brought Ros in at a senior level and her boss had managed to publicly undermine her in a matter of weeks.

Amira works in marketing and talks about how her boss behaved towards her when she was unfortunately ill for a prolonged period a few years ago: 'In the end I was diagnosed with appendicitis, but unusually it was missed when I first went to the GP. I ended up having a series of tests over about two months and was in quite considerable pain. Clearly not at my best. The hospital where I was having the tests was near my home, not near work. As a consequence I had to work from home more than usual and wasn't always as available to be where my boss wanted me to be. He wasn't happy about this. To begin with, I tried to see this as a sign that he valued me, that he couldn't do without me. It was even flattering. But as the weeks went on his attitude became more hostile. I think perhaps he was bewildered by the whole episode, and frankly so was I, but the way he dealt with it was frankly very undermining, even embarrassing, certainly depressing at the time.'

Amira says that her boss called her into his office after lunch one day, clearly having worked himself up to some kind of confrontation. He asked her to explain exactly what was going on. She calmly and clearly recounted the tests that she had had, the tests that she was waiting for, the results so far and what the doctors had said to her. He listened and then said: 'Okay, Amira, do you want to know what I think is going on here?'

Amira says she literally had no idea what was coming next. She knew he had no medical training so couldn't imagine what he thought he was doing. He continued: 'I think it's "women's problems".' She was actually speechless. At a time when she needed sympathy, empathy and when she was rather frightened about her future health, he had delivered some kind of joke. Once again presumably this was banter, but highly ill-judged and unlikely to make her feel in any way supported.

Amira remarks that presumably she could have gone to the HR department, but that she chose to deal with this herself. She began by being very exact with him, very specific, and only talking to him about work tasks as her tests continued. Eventually, it turned out that she had appendicitis and would need surgery. When she told him this, he paused for a moment and then said: 'Well, I'd like to apologize to you then… I now understand why you haven't been yourself. It is a surprise though… the thing is, I'm normally very good with "women's issues".'

What was going on here? An attempt to diffuse an admittedly difficult situation with inappropriate banter? A clumsy version of sympathy? In any terms it was inexcusable as far as Amira was concerned and she didn't stay working for him for much longer.

Banter isn't funny

It is very important to establish here that banter is not the same as being funny. In fact, if the myriad attempts at banter in the workplace were actually funny, there probably wouldn't be an issue. Equally, let's state, as it still seems to be necessary, that women (and every other diverse group) have a sense of humour. The point here is that banter, which usually exhibits as more akin to mockery than to inclusive jokes, excels at driving home the point of otherness that is so undermining in the workplace.

This wasn't how banter was defined originally, of course. The Oxford English Dictionary defines it as 'the playful and friendly exchange of teasing remarks' but then gives this as the example: 'the men bantered with the waitresses'. One can't help but wonder exactly how 'playful and friendly' the 'waitresses' in question found the remarks. You can jump immediately to a black tie dinner, perhaps as exemplified by the now-redundant but infamous 'Presidents Club Dinner', where the so-called 'banter' aimed at the waitresses serving men-only guests was outed by an undercover *FT* journalist in 2018. This longstanding dinner, which was entirely well-meaning in its stated raison d'être to raise funds for good causes, was the subject of an exposé, where it was disclosed all of the waitresses were told to wear 'skimpy black outfits with matching underwear and high heels'. The story continued: 'At an after-party, many hostesses were groped, sexually harassed and propositioned.'

The dinner had been a mainstay of London's social business calendar for over 30 years – now it is no more.

The most salient point about banter is that it only works if it is genuinely 'banter with' and not 'banter at'. If it comes from a position of power then it is not actually banter. If, on the other hand, it's only funny from the point of view of the man on top, then it's better left outside the modern workplace. One company COO once remarked to us that he was sure that we were wrong about this: 'I've checked with the girls in my team and they said they find my comments very funny.' We replied: 'Shall we just check in on that comment: you've asked the women who are reliant on you for a job whether they think you, the boss, is funny. Exactly what did you expect them to say?'

Banter is not a habit that most women participate in – especially not in the workplace. We've previously quoted advertising creative director Dave Trott saying, 'Men insult each other all the time at work and they don't mean it. Women compliment each other all the time at work and they don't mean it either.' Whether the second part of this is true or not, what is certain is that a woman at work's first instinct is not to insult her co-workers whether she means it or not. And let's be clear, banter isn't funny if it comes from the boss and is directed at someone with less status, however it is intended. If you're not equal, if you're privileged and they aren't, then it isn't banter, and it may present as bullying.

Now it could be that a group of men who are habituated to banter as a way of showing affection for each other try and include someone new in that way. Again, let's be clear: it won't work and it won't make someone feel included if they're not from the same background. Therefore, it is not a strategy for Belonging. Some women or minorities will respond by joining in – one tactic for anyone who feels left out that can make you look like you're one of the group. As a short-term way of fitting in, it's often a pragmatic solution and may be the only way to respond. We would not necessarily argue against it. At one radio phone-in about diversity and inclusiveness, in fact, we were asked how to deal with this situation. A young woman called in and said that she worked in an office with a group of men who were also all older than she. They habitually 'bantered' that she should get in the kitchen and make them all a cup of tea. This was bringing her to the point of quitting, but she'd worked hard to get the job. She didn't want to leave and she didn't want to show that she was upset, although she was. Every effort to get them to pay more respect to her had just resulted in more so-called banter.

We suggested that she try bantering back. Perhaps making some kind of joke that all the best cooks were men these days and suggesting one of the 'Jamie Olivers' or 'Gordon Ramsays' present get in the kitchen instead. (Your banter back doesn't have to be funny either.) We hope this worked and wished her luck, but once again, the real issue was not one of the men really understood where she was coming from. It's possible that she made them nervous, she represented a change of the status quo and they didn't know how to respond to her. But by using the 'banter' technique to get her to become one of them, they massively miscalculated. You can't tease someone about their supposed status if they come from a place where their status is less than everyone else's. You can't tease an outsider about being an outsider and expect this to make them feel welcome. Once again, as told to us, not one of the men present tried to change the tone in the office. Again, the outsider was left to fight for themselves.

To create a really diverse office you need everyone to take responsibility for including everyone else.

Are women funny?

One final note… You might be wondering: are women funny? The fact that this remains as a question, even a question for academic scientists, is perhaps the biggest joke of all. In October 2019, an article was published on 'Sex differences in humor production ability: a meta-analysis'. This claims to be the first systematic quantitative meta-analysis on the differences in verbal humour production between the sexes. The results say that men's output is rated funnier than women's. An end to the question? Not exactly, as despite the headlines, the authors of the study immediately acknowledge that 'this difference is small-to-moderate and may reflect divergent preferences and experiences of humour for men and women, stemming from evolutionary and environmental influences'.

Commenting on the study at website funnywomen.com, Kate Stone says, 'Social stereotypes about sex differences in humour – particularly the stereotype that women are not funny – are culturally pervasive.' Stone goes on to say the survey itself suggests that the 'cis-het [cisgender; i.e. those whose gender matches that assigned at birth; and heterosexual] boy's brain is moulded and trained to make girls and then women laugh. Cis-het girls are moulded and trained to… I dunno, get the jokes they are told.' As banter humour, particularly in the workplace, is bound up with notions of power, who wields it and therefore who has to laugh at whose joke? Frankly, if you are telling a joke at the expense of someone who you have the power to fire or at least slow their career progression then take it from us: the joke isn't funny.

And for anyone unsure of the humour of funny women, we would refer you to the Lucille Ball Chocolate Factory sketch on YouTube: 'Lucy and Ethel wrap chocolates', of course, as well as a mountain of funny women in literature, on stage, on radio, podcasts and on screen.

The founder of funnywomen.com, Lynne Parker, set up her company in 2002 as a 'knee-jerk reaction to a misogynistic comedy promoter'. When asked why he hardly ever booked any female acts, he said there weren't any, and furthermore, 'women aren't funny'. Parker set up the business to help women find their voice through humour and recently observed, despite enormous pride in what she has achieved, that there is still much to be done.

In a nutshell, and just to be clear: women (and other diverse groups in the workplace) are funny and do have sense of humour. Banter isn't funny if you're more powerful than the recipient. In that case, banter is bullying and it needs to stop – now.

Strategies for Belonging

WE NEED TO TALK ABOUT BANTER

Cut out the banter! If you're telling a joke at the expense of someone else, it really isn't funny – even if they laugh along. They might be laughing at you, they might be laughing along because your status is higher than theirs. They're not laughing because they think you're funny, and they will feel excluded, not like they belong.

Crying

If you had asked us what we thought might be the most frequent subject that came up after the publication of our last book on gender equality in the workplace, we're not sure what we might have answered. We couldn't decide what we thought could be the most frequent issue that might affect our readers or potential talk participants. Money, as in salary equality or the issues around asking for a pay rise and managing your work/life balance, seemed to be the topic that dominated the contemporary chatter. In our talks, however, one subject is almost inevitable when we come to the Q&A.

It's crying. The why, the where, the who to and the whole gamut in between crying in the bathroom at work to full-on bawling in a meeting. Some of the stories made us stop and think. It particularly made us think when men asked what they should do in response to someone crying and how to handle the situation.

There are varying thoughts about whether crying at work is appropriate, ever. Some, including both men and women, firmly believe that you should never cry at work. It is either undignified (it signifies a lack of control – and lack of control is never a good thing at work) or it is a powerful tactic that women deploy because it's hard to handle a woman crying if you are the man being cried at.

Another thought is that if we're encouraging people to bring their whole selves to work, why is crying so taboo? Can you only bring your cheerful self in and must you leave the unacceptable bits at home? How does this suppression play out when one of the biggest killers of men under 35 is suicide? What if it's your only way of relieving or expressing stress? If you bottle up your emotions as your natural response, crying may be the ultimate signal that you need help.

I'll cry if I want to

For people who find themselves in the 'It's my work life and I'll cry if I want/need to' camp, your actions and reactions are varied and wide. From those who say that crying is the norm at their place of work and that it's normalized, to those who went through a stage where crying was just a regular occurrence (there is no general rule here, but we have observed that the combination of small, wakeful children and the associated sleep deprivation plus new routines, plus the return to a regular work pattern can be a trigger for some people, who stopped when the sleep and routine was established). All options and variations are playing out in companies across the world.

On both sides of the divide, either being cried at or if you are the one crying, there is a need to develop an awareness of what is happening in the moment and what is happening in the long term. If you are in the 'no crying at work' set, you may need to temper your view on what this crying incident is. You may see it as a lack of control and the person crying in front of you might see it as the only way to make you see exactly how they feel. Women, and many men too, generally are uncomfortable with anger. The main manifestations of anger in women are a rapid and staccato verbal release of the circumstances that have made them angry (and this can sometimes be hard to follow as it's generally not a measured narrative) or you might get an icy withdrawal from the situation creating the anger, or you get crying. Women are not encouraged to be comfortable with being angry or expressing it. 'Men get angry, women get hysterical' is a tired old cliché but one that has credence in certain circles.

Women are stereotypically seen as collaborative and as such it can be hard for them to raise concerns, even outwardly disagree. If you feel that you aren't being heard, you get angry and it can overwhelm you. You may cry. If this is the cause, the key thing for the other party is to ask questions. Make time to get some space into the situation – get them a glass of water/tissues/into a quiet and private space and just ask if they want to talk. If the answer is no, then accept that and ask for a follow-up session. In the interim, ensure there isn't an embarrassed or guilty silence. A quick communication saying that you want to hear their concerns, their issues and how you can help resolve the situation is far better than a long and regretful banishment and glossing over what happened.

You are human, they are human. Listen, be empathetic and try to find a solution or a resolution. Elsewhere in this book you will find exercises to help you develop that part of your working life. There is no doubt that in the modern workplace, where we look at screens for large parts of our day or we go to meetings with lots of colleagues, the crucial skill of sitting with one other person and having a big conversation is hard to do. There are a million distractions and if you are transaction oriented, it can be frustrating. Sometimes these situations and behaviours don't have a quick win.

If you suspect these cries are a tactic, you have other questions to ask. As frustrating as it may be, it can be worthwhile to examine the common behaviours of your team members. Do some of your colleagues drive their views by assertiveness, attention seeking or just sucking up? Is your crier doing it to get their moment with you? Could you encourage an open dialogue that might put a stop to some of these behaviours?

In a very time-starved, goal- or target-orientated organization, your diary can fill up quickly and you may find yourself communicating with your colleagues mainly by email. This has its uses in that it's quick and doesn't require you being face to face or even in the same location, but it can be impersonal, it clearly does not have personal impact and of course it is easy even to be misinterpreted. When composing the email, you might think you're being businesslike, yet it's read and interpreted as being cold and demanding. Try to put yourself in the position of someone who wants to raise an issue that they are sensitive or concerned about. Does your style of communication actually encourage communication or do you issue series of commands, instructions and factual information? We're not suggesting you write a full-blown description of your emotional state at every time of writing, but a little human touch is helpful. Have they just been on holiday? You had a great time in Boston/Barcelona/Bridgetown too – it is those people-orientated asides that make individuals feel that they belong and that you are interested in them too.

By expressing that interest in your people, you are encouraging an open dialogue. It's not simply based on shared interests (chat about sport can bring people together or drive them apart if their respective teams are sworn enemies), it's about you and them and your connection. When you feel that you can talk openly, the barriers to raising concerns are lowered. This works in two ways. First, the worriers who don't want to derail anything can position themselves as the ones who ask the awkward questions – having a professional Eeyore character is a must in any team. Sure, they don't get carried away with momentum and wild enthusiasm, but they do ask the awkward questions that need to be raised. Secondly, if you suspect crying is a tactic, the open dialogue addresses issues before they merit a dramatic outburst of sobbing.

It is, after all, far easier to respond to the crying tactic if, when a person comes to you and starts to sob, you can calmly and logically go through all the interactions you have had recently, and explain the number of opportunities the individual has had to raise this before being reduced to tears, and essentially respond with empathy but not emotion. In acting this way, you provide a framework for future interaction.

It may appear that this is an impersonal reaction to an extreme emotion. However, if you have been actively listening, responding and reacting to an open dialogue, this isn't cold or calculating. What you are doing is creating a level platform for everyone to engage with you, with no bias or reactions based on individuals seemingly playing with a human response.

If you work with someone who cries when they feel as if they don't know what to do, it could be that encouraging them to write down what is bothering them and why could help marshal their thoughts and frustrations. The piece shouldn't be more than one page. It may be that in writing down all of their concerns, they discover there is one cause for most of it. If you then take a look at what it is that's at the root of the emotion, you can either work out what support you need, what you need your manager/co-workers to do and what a successful resolution looks like. If you write a note, rehearse saying it out loud frequently and then raise your concerns. You may have a crack or some wobbles in your voice, but you probably won't end up crying. We also tell people that a very wise woman we know says you can't cry and whistle at the same time – which is true – as long as you only pretend you're whistling and you don't treat your manager to your very own rendition of a favourite David Bowie number.

Shouting instead

For a number of women managers, being shouted at has a similar response to that which crying elicits in men. It is uncomfortable, incredibly emotional and they don't want to respond in kind. As a woman manager faced with a serial shouter (they quite often like to send aggressive emails too), your best tactic is to keep your tone quiet and controlled and to let the shouter have their outburst – you can't be heard over them anyway – until they can't shout any more. Normally, they will now feel drained and flat. Now, respond by saying that while you appreciate that something extreme must have triggered this response, you couldn't get the full detail of the issue due to the shouting. Suggest both of you take some time away from the current situation so that you can revisit it in a calmer and more measured way. Make a note of any issues raised and address them quietly, calmly and without emotion the next time you meet. If the shouting starts again, wait and then calmly continue.

Should this behaviour begin to resemble a pattern, you need to dig deeper and find out why they feel it's appropriate. Make it clear that this isn't the way things work within your company (or if it is, then we think you might need to temper that as you may be excluding very talented individuals who don't like to work in a place seemingly dominated by confrontation).

Emotion of all types at work is a very nuanced concept. Some places feel like a family, with all the variants that this entails. Other organizations prefer to keep it cool and measured, with behaviours and expectations clearly defined, a logical and businesslike tone always in place and a level of detachment expected. This can be the most appropriate way for certain sectors to operate. What is important to remember though is that individuals need to know what the expectation is. The implications if it isn't your natural style can be very strong and may prevent individuals from giving their best contribution.

Strategies for Belonging

CRYING

Express a one-to-one interest in those you manage. If you have a real relationship, this will help you genuinely empathize with them. Be curious, be supportive. If they can bring their whole selves to work, you will get the best out of them. Don't assume that crying is an act of weakness, or even that the person crying is necessarily upset. They may just be furious and unable to express themselves clearly. Be patient. If you can be supportive, this might be the trigger to gaining real loyalty and support back.

Making sure everyone is heard

We have done a number of talks about diversity and inclusion in all types of organizations and in very varied business sectors.

As mentioned earlier, most of our audience are women and this can be because we're talking to the designated women fast streamers or a women's network, or sometimes just a group of women who like hanging out together and are happy to hear our views. At all these events, the representation from men is usually minimal. We always try to ask the men who are there what might have stopped more men from coming to hear the discussion. As discussed, in the majority of cases the reason given for men not attending is because they didn't feel that they would be welcome, or they didn't think that they could make any real contribution.

This perception is interesting for a number of reasons. After all, we are working side by side in the same organizations, yet some of our fellow workers don't think they have a role to play in creating a more equal and inclusive environment. Actually, they probably do know that they have a role to play, but how to step up, play your part and not mess up is a big unknown.

Another factor is the lack of exposure to any other mode of thinking. If you have only experienced work through your own perceptions, if you haven't attempted empathy with others unlike you, you might not think that there is a problem because you have never come across one. It's not part of your work every day so you are just unaware. This is a very different set of circumstances to those who know there is an issue but choose to ignore it, possibly in the hope that it will go away. This was brought home to us when we met a man who had experienced a 180-degree change in the way he thought...

Frank had always identified as a feminist and he is a vocal supporter of fairness and equality. A supporter of equal pay and female leadership, he was one of the good guys, wasn't he? So in tune was he that he attended a women's networking event, confident he was completely on side with everything that would be covered, and he was convinced that he was one of the believers, a true supporter and advocate of best practice, walking the walk, very in tune with the issues involved. However, as the day went on, he found himself blindsided.

As he says, he'd never grabbed a woman inappropriately, interviewed someone while in his dressing gown, behaved at all in a #metoo way. He was shocked by these stories, couldn't imagine how such behaviour was possible in the current workplace. What Frank had failed to recognize in the slightest was what was going on in his own workplace. That he worked in an industry with little flexibility in working practices, one where there was a 'boys' club' culture. He suddenly remembered all of the meetings where women were talked over, excluded or even downright ignored. And as a man in this sector, all those barriers didn't hamper his progress. He was in a situation where the behaviour of employers and the views and standards of the society around him worked for him but against the interests and opportunities of his female colleagues. He couldn't point to definitive examples of when they had been disadvantaged – it was more subtle than that – there was just the incremental build-up of barriers put in the way and he was suddenly confronted by it.

When he spoke to a woman delegate about her career ambitions, she said that she wanted to be managing director of her current company. She then said that she knew that she should have a more 'realistic' ambition than that. When Frank asked her the thought process behind having two ambitions, she said that she had two because as a woman, she was unlikely to achieve the more stretching one.

The fact that anyone would feel that their gender would limit the scope of their ambitions was an utter shock to Frank. Surely he didn't work in a sector where this could happen? This was an experience and a view that he had never encountered before. It was too close for comfort, unlike the terrible behaviour that he had read about in other workplaces. This wasn't some ego-driven monster using and abusing women and thinking that they could get away with it; this was right on his doorstep and he was staring the situation in the face.

Following this session, Frank decided to change his behaviour and to commit to being open in championing equality and calling out things when they were wrong. His opportunity came very quickly and required a measure of grit and a very deep breath.

A few weeks later, after a day when the new graduate intake had been introduced to the company, there was a welcome drink in the local bar. There was a bit of work chat and then the conversation turned to the new employees. Suddenly there was a new thread about which of the recruits was the best-looking and a comparative appraisal of their merits. Frank knew that he should say something, even though he knew these people and didn't think there was malice or bad intent. Mindful of his new perspective, he asked his colleagues if they thought that this type of chat was appropriate – after all, no one was rating the men in the same way, were they? There was a brief silence and then all of them said versions of 'Yeah, good point, that's not right, is it?' and they started talking about football. And that was that, no drama, no pushback, just the acceptance that it wasn't appropriate and that they shouldn't do it.

In the following days and weeks, nothing was said about the incident. Frank wasn't aware of any change in the way that the group involved dealt with him; it was merely accepted that they had made a mistake, they wouldn't do that again and that was that. Nothing to have a drama about, no one was ostracized as a result and he has never experienced another conversation like it at work. His action was that of a leader – he staged what he anticipated to be a dramatic intervention and it cost him nothing.

Don't catastrophize

That's how tame it was. Quite often, it's the anticipation of the reaction to a challenge that creates a perception that it will be damaging or intemperate, or will have far-reaching consequences. Our ability to catastrophize a situation knows no bounds (or is that just some of us?). So, if we find ourselves in a situation where there is a group that is being ignored, excluded or worse, how do we make sure they are heard?

It can be very difficult for an individual to feel comfortable or willing to address the void that they can find themselves in. Too many times, they think it's just them that is subject to that situation. After all, no one else is raising it as an issue, are they? Perhaps you aren't reading the situation properly – your boss is busy, so they can't help, or maybe you don't understand what's really going on.

A number of approaches can address this issue of exclusion. A robust and regular appraisal system allows colleagues to raise concerns, to seek support in structuring future progress and to articulate exactly how they feel. It needs to be a dialogue where both sides can be open. A tick-box exercise where you are just measuring performance against KPIs (key performance indicators) isn't the optimal way of allowing people to be heard. That's a process, not an appraisal. While process has a part to play in our daily lives, it doesn't generate a culture or a set of values. The issue with those transactional events is that they don't accommodate a pressure to change or look at things slightly differently. It can turn into a cookie-cutter way of operating, where people soon learn to play the system and the true value is lost.

Dialogue

So, creating a dialogue where there is an open approach to work and the challenges it brings is the foundation stone of creating a place where everyone is heard. Asking questions on a regular basis ensures issues aren't bottled up or lost in the process of time from where it was a concern but is now a (distant) painful or uncomfortable memory. How are people feeling/what would they like more of? What would they like less of? How can you support them more? Help them be effective, both as colleagues and as people. If they seem reluctant to talk, don't give in or assume this means you can move on to the next project/ person/thought. When your views are sought, be candid and as constructive as you can. This is about building the workplace where you are heard, not a general rant about the merits of the company policy on applying for annual leave or the position of your desk relative to the amount of vitamin D in your life or your pressing need for proximity to the coffee machine.

If you have introverts in your team, it may take time to get them to feel fully comfortable in the act of sharing or speaking openly. Make it clear that you are going to give them the space they need and recognize that this is how they operate: be flexible and appropriate.

With dominant extroverts, don't use their willingness to share as a substitute for the quieter groups – they cannot express the views of those more reluctant to voice their views. We all know that this can seem the easy path and a quick win, but it isn't a long-term solution or one that is really involving. Whatever you do, the ones who are quick to chat and happy to be heard *will* be heard and you need to ensure this dominance doesn't create a one-dimensional and distorted perspective.

In meetings, a quick check-in with those who seem distanced or quiet can encourage them to be open. It may be very hard to find the 'right' time to speak, and so observe the situation and act appropriately. Try to provide cues so that the unheard voices can contribute, preferably by avoiding questions such as, 'Lily, what do you think of Simon's plans for the engineering division?' as this can feel as if you are being asked to pass judgement publicly and you're likely to get mute assent. Perhaps ask a question such as 'I'm interested if anyone else can build on Simon's thoughts on engineering. Lily, you have extensive experience in this area, how have other plans you know worked, any learnings we could use?' Far less comparative and you've built up Lily as a wise sage. Or you could allocate time for each person to contribute in meetings. They get a turn to chat, it provides boundaries for those liable to expound their views at length *and* you get to have clarity of the issue the meeting is meant to be addressing. This is hugely useful as we have never met anyone who says their work life would be richer, more effective and deeply fulfilling personally if only they had more meetings in the diary. More often than not, they are seen as a waste of time and energy.

Outside of the more formal settings such as meetings, chatting one-on-one with the participants to encourage full feedback or asking what they need you to do so that they feel comfortable in participating is powerful. It shows you have noticed the situation, you recognize that they have something to say and you are going to help them get their voice heard. This is exactly what you need if you are going to encourage individuals to feel that they belong.

Strategies for Belonging

MAKING SURE EVERYONE IS HEARD

Commit to being open in championing equality and calling out things when they are wrong. Be open to diversity of personalities too. We have heard of one senior highly successful manager whose new boss leant over to her in a meeting, lightly placed his hand on her arm and said: 'It's okay, I really don't have a problem with introverts,' which immediately made her sure that he did. She didn't in fact work for him for much longer.

Some people in your workplace are joiners in – they're the easy ones to manage. Others are not. They might be extremely talented and contribute to the business, but they regard organized fun with dread – for them, it's 'Funishment'. To reap the rewards of diverse thinking, you need to create the conditions for all to thrive.

Exercises and techniques for Chapter 3

To create and lead a Belonging culture, everyone must be able to operate free from fear. They must feel that it is safe to be themselves and to express themselves. They need to feel confident, positive and motivated about the workplace and their own place in it. But a Belonging culture isn't a fairy-tale place where only nice things happen, everyone likes everyone else, all meetings are fun and all targets are always met.

Business can be tough. So the people in a Belonging culture also need to have resilience, willpower and the willingness to take personal responsibility (not blame, responsibility) when things don't go right. Those who exhibit these qualities can be said to have high levels of psychological capital and recent research indicates the single most important factor in determining the levels of psychological capital in a company's people is not their own personalities, but the behaviour of managers and leaders. As a manager, and especially as a leader, you must take ultimate responsibility for shaping a Belonging culture. In fact, whatever your notional title, as we have seen in Chapter 2, you can take a role in leading the culture. The way you talk, the way you behave in meetings, the way you write emails, your body language as you walk through the workplace all communicate powerfully what kind of company you want to work in and will determine the culture in which the people around you function.

If you act without awareness of this, it is easy to send out negative signals, signs that you do not value individuals or their contribution. And especially if you have any kind of manager role, this will eventually lead to a culture of fear. Conversely, if you bring self-awareness and some simple communication skills to your leadership role, it is also easy to send out powerful positive signals – signs that the people around you are accepted and valued.

This will eventually lead to a culture of Belonging

The Belonging Leader's Most Important Question: 'How can I help?'

Picture a typical company organogram – a diagram like a family tree that shows the CEO in a box at the top, the board in a row of boxes just below her, then the department heads in a row below them, and on down through managers, executives, assistants. Now, imagine it turned upside down. That's how a Belonging Organization works. The senior people aren't looking down on the junior people, watching their every move, picking up every mistake. They are supporting the juniors, using their valuable experience and expertise to help the rest of the company do their jobs as well as possible and to grow and develop.

If as a leader you can ask, 'How can I help?' more than, 'What went wrong?' or 'Whose fault was it?' then you will take a huge step towards creating a Belonging culture. If you can commit to never again saying 'Don't bring me problems, just bring me solutions', you've taken another major step in the right direction.

Four key skills of the Belonging leader

Asking for input from others

The way in which a leader (or the most senior person in a meeting) asks those attending for their input is a major indication of the emotional intelligence within an organization. Some, of course, don't ask at all, but simply move forward with their agenda. At this point, it's up to each individual who would like to comment to gauge whether it's okay to do so. Will their comment be welcomed as useful debate, or might it be treated as an unnecessary waste of time, even ridiculed?

In circumstances like this, anyone who feels slightly uncertain of their place in the company is likely to stay silent (and continue to feel uncertain about their place in the company). The only people who are likely to feel okay about talking are extroverts who are already firmly embedded in the culture. As a result, a potentially valuable contribution might be lost and the culture moves one small notch further along the spectrum away from diversity of thought and true Belonging, so the first thing a leader needs to do is actively solicit the opinions of others. And do so in a way that makes it clear that all contributions are genuinely welcome.

The leader who clearly states their own view before asking for any other thoughts isn't really soliciting opinions. Many people will choose not to speak under such circumstances. A leader who wants to genuinely encourage diversity of thought and to ensure everyone feels okay about speaking up needs to show that this is true and here's how...

Allow time for thought

In order to ensure real diversity of contributions you have to ask for them in an inclusive way. Go around everyone in the meeting, asking if they have any thoughts. But before you do this explain that it's okay for people to pause and think for a second before they answer. Let the quieter, more reflective, less confident people know that they can have their say without the louder attendees interrupting them.

Assigning a task

One of the most important indicators of a truly diverse and inclusive culture is that people feel that it's okay to fail. Sometimes leaders will naturally worry, 'Hang on, I don't want my people making lots of mistakes'. Getting the balance right is tricky but achievable. It's possible to make clear to people that they are allowed to fail, while at the same time minimizing the risks that they actually will – and indeed increasing the likelihood that they won't.

When assigning a new task to someone, consider asking the following questions. (The brackets contain the strong messages of Belonging that are implied by your words.)

Are you clear on what I'm asking you to do?
(If my brief isn't clear, it's okay to say so.)

How confident do you feel that we can achieve this?

(I've set you a target, but you're allowed to question it.)

Where do you foresee difficulties in this task?

(You're allowed to find this difficult. You don't have to pretend to be Superwoman/man.)

How might you respond if that happens?

(I trust you to deal with most difficulties.)

How can I help you?

(But you're not on your own)

How can the board/the rest of the team/other departments help you?

(Again, you're not on your own. We're all in this together.)

Would you like me to send them an email?

(If you feel unconfident approaching people you don't know in the company, I will help you by opening some doors.)

Leaders are busy people. The 'How can I help you?' question does not imply that you will roll up your sleeves and do the work yourself, but a quick phone call or email from you can soon overcome challenges a more junior person might take weeks to deal with.

Resetting a meeting, while respecting diverse agendas

When a group of people come to a meeting, you would think that they might be able to stick to the agenda. But anyone who's actually been in a meeting anywhere ever knows this rarely happens. The problem is that everyone brings their own agenda (actually, their many agendas) into the meeting with them and will raise those agendas, given the slightest excuse.

So, a meeting is called to make progress on Project X. After five minutes of productive work, Person A suggests they need to bring someone from HR on to the team.

'Good luck with that,' says Person B, who then tells an anecdote about how incredibly unhelpful HR have been over the past few weeks for them.

'That's nothing,' says Person C, who tells their own story of HR incompetence, launching into a story of how both HR and Finance have let their team down.

In a standard workplace, there are only two possible outcomes. Either the leader – frustrated – pulls everyone abruptly back onto the original agenda. Result: Project X might move forward, but Persons B and C are annoyed because their very real problems have been ignored – they've not been listened to or heard. Or the meeting zigzags from one issue to another, Project X makes no progress at all, but actually, it's also unlikely that Persons B or C will make any progress with their problems either. They've had a moan, but they've not really been listened to or heard because everyone else in the meeting was simply waiting for a gap in the conversation to raise their own personal issue.

An emotionally intelligent Belonging leader takes another approach, using what mediation experts referred to as a Process Move. That is, they step out of the conversation and comment on it, drawing everyone's attention to what is happening. They say something like this: 'Okay, we seem to be going nowhere. Instead of working on one agenda, we're now working on three separate agendas. [They then spell out the three agendas.] With all these separate agendas, we're not really going to make satisfactory progress on any one of them. We need to take them one at a time. Because we've got all the right people in the room now, I want to return to Project X first, but all the other issues have raised genuine needs to be addressed too. Before we leave the room, we will agree an action point to make progress on each of them.' Result: the meeting gets back on track and Project X moves forward. Persons B and C feel they have been listened to and heard and that their own agendas are important and will be addressed.

When things go wrong

One might not think of the military as a natural place to look for emotional intelligence, but a feedback model used widely in this area is an extremely fair and inclusive way of dealing with those times when things go badly wrong. The model has four questions:

- What did we expect to happen?
- What actually happened?
- Why was it different?
- What will we do differently next time?

Rather than begin a meeting with the usual question – either, 'What went wrong? or in some cultures, 'Who screwed up?', if a leader introduces the entire four-stage model and says that this is how they will manage the meeting, it instantly creates a Belonging environment where diverse perspectives, opinions and thoughts can be introduced rather than a fear environment where everyone is just trying to make sure they don't end up getting the blame.

Notice how the four stages open things up instead of closing them down. The questions allow people to question whether or not the original expectations were realistic. They allow them to put forward different interpretations of the results achieved (perhaps, by some measures, it isn't a failure at all). They allow the possibility that although, with hindsight, mistakes may have been made, perhaps some events simply weren't predictable when the plan was originally made.

By unveiling the entire four-step process at the beginning of the discussion a leader makes clear that her main outcome for this meeting will be a new plan and an improved performance, not a witch-hunt.

One Voice: Samuel

Samuel is 28 and has been working since he was 18. He has had two careers so far, law and subsequently, in entertainment. He is used to being one of very few black men in the office.

'I always had the initial feeling that it was going to take a very long time to make diversity really happen in the office. There's a very big difference between law and entertainment. Law, changes have been taking place as people set up their own firms. Entertainment seems very based on white culture. Different sectors have different cultures but none of them seem to really focus on inclusiveness. At senior levels you can't see more diversity in business. Nothing specifically seems to be changing. I think it is thought about at an intake level, but not anywhere else.

'When I first joined in my current role, things that I would do in my spare time were different from here. The inclusive way of enjoying themselves for most people here is just drinking. In my culture going out includes going out to the theatre or to a club. In ents [entertainment], it is only drinking. That is the only way of bonding. If you don't drink, if you don't go out and bond, then I don't know how you fit in. I was once told in order to be successful, by my director, that you have to drink. I thought, that can't be the case. I'm not a heavy drinker, I will have one and leave, but that's the culture in the industry. It feels very old-fashioned.

'It's specifically standing in a pub. It's as if there isn't any other way, as if most people need to get to the pub, so if you suggest anything else then it falls by the wayside. Even a culture that prides itself on being inclusive, it isn't very inclusive if you don't drink. Furthermore, when you do go and drink with them, everyone is a lot nicer to you, they believe in you, they give you that vote of confidence because you drink with them. There's lots of people here who don't fit in *because they don't go drinking, they don't get taken on lunches, they just don't bond. I don't know if that will ever change, it is a very big thing. I'm sure people have tried, but it doesn't change.*

'*In the industry I don't see many people who look like me in senior positions, but I believe that I can be the one who changes things. If I see opportunity then I will go for it. I don't see myself as CEO because I don't tend to look that far – I look for short-term goals. Next role is manager and I see that as attainable. I don't know if diversity would come into play in my favour. There would have to be a culture change across the board in the sector. I would need to see more diversity at senior levels.*

'*My parents wouldn't have accepted this as a profession for me when I was 16. They came over to Britain to get a better life and they would have wanted me to be a doctor or a lawyer to live a successful life. To this day, my father worries, can I progress?*

'*I think there is a focus to progress young black men. I think there is caution about bringing people like me through, however. A white man might well think, what does this mean for me? On the one hand, change needs to happen, but on the other, people shouldn't be promoted just because of their race. I wouldn't want to get promoted just because of my colour. But if there isn't an active change, then how do you ever get diversity shifted? I think everyone is accountable for the situation. If everyone has a focus on equal balance, this will help.*

'*I actively find myself speaking in a different way when I come to work. One of my colleagues who is a white man, he talks to everyone the same way, but I will speak to different people in different ways. It's a weird balance. I'm not doing it intentionally, but I think I come across better if I speak to them differently. I have been doing it for so long, but it means that I am not relaxing.*

'When I first joined here there was a black woman in my team. Everyone else was really nice to me, but for some reason, she wouldn't talk to me at all. I thought, why won't she talk to me? This makes no sense. And it went on for about a month or so. She's left now and I am going to be brutally honest, this is what she told me six months down the line. We got talking and I found out a lot more about her and she about me. Eventually I told her that I used to dislike her because she never used to talk to me and she said: "I won't lie to you, at the start, I thought you were a bit of an Oreo." I was so baffled, I thought, why would you even think that? But now when I look back and think about how I behaved, and the way that I treated certain people, and always make an effort to come in, smile and talk to everyone, she perceived me like that because of this. It felt like a harsh judgement, but she considered my trying to fit in with all my colleagues meant I wasn't being true to myself. I don't know how that changes, I don't think that it ever will.

'Why don't we make more of an effort to make people be included? A lot of people aren't ready to face up to the fact that they aren't including people. In so many cases, it's passive aggressiveness. It comes across even more hurtful than actually being aggressive. As people, we all have to take responsibility for pulling people aside. I do it all the time. If someone makes a passive racist joke, I will make a joke back: I will say, "I'm about to call HR." But I think I should do more. If I hear it, then I have to do something. And if everyone did this, that would be good. It's just not on as it is now, everyone has to speak up.'

CHAPTER FOUR

Belonging in action

Great intentions around diversity and inclusion are all very promising in the abstract, but so often they fail because the task seems too big, too intractable and finding the role you can play just too much. Many men are scared of saying the wrong thing and making the wrong assumptions. It's simpler to let things be and hope that a change is going to come. This is nothing new. As far back as the suffragettes, leader Emmeline Pankhurst said: 'We have to free half of the human race, the women, so that they can help to free the other half.' By working together, addressing barriers, men and women can build a culture of Belonging that thrives and create genuine and lasting change.

Everyone has to play their part

Each of us has to play their part. Everyone has a role, we must all make a difference. Creating this culture of Belonging begins with looking for the people around you who can help and recruiting them. You must think about how best to deploy their individual talents and have a clear, measurable path. Lasting change takes thought, planning and a willingness to be flexible. It's people that create culture, not departments or process. You must create a momentum and sense of personal investment that resonates far more than any initiative or tactic could ever do. So where to begin? In this chapter we will look at the very start of the engagement with the workplace. Even at the beginning of the process of hiring people, certain language or approaches can act as barriers to feeling as if you belong in that organization.

It's not enough to recruit a diverse team. How you manage them so that they all feel a sense of Belonging is crucial

In addressing the issue of feeling isolated, not part of the 'gang', or in some cases, being made to think that you really, really shouldn't be there, we will offer guidance on managing diversity and creating a sense of Belonging that is very empowering and encompasses everyone. We all want to feel valued and to know that we are seen as individuals, with all our differences embraced. Exceptional cultures aren't created by a mission statement; they exist because individuals feel included, feel that they belong and able to contribute to the direction that's been set out for the team.

Each of us can make a difference, too

We will show how if you sponsor, ally or become someone's wing-person, you can create a greater sense of Belonging. And if your career needs momentum, we will show you how to find your sponsor, or ally or wing-person. We will offer a guide to how best to use sponsors and mentors – and will decode the difference between the two things. These important roles can be crucial in providing paths to success, better working practices and have benefits for all the participants.

Finding the right wing-person at work is a whole other layer of a crucial element of the process. As fond as we are of film analogies (well, *one* of us is), everyone needs a 'Goose' to their 'Maverick'. These co-pilots in *Top Gun* look out for each other at work. Having your own wing-man or wing-woman can offer support, advocacy and so much more.

Women, ethnic minorities, the LGBTQ+ communities and those with disabilities seeking to get some understanding of how the world works on the other side of the current balance of power, can find out how to recruit white men in power as allies and how best to build on that support. In offering mutual support, purpose and a plan for starting to create change, this chapter marks the start of being equipped to create a sustainable and credible path for inclusion. Many businesses now offer flexible working and the possibility of working from home. There are times when it is necessary to work outside the office, both for individual circumstances and in times of national exceptional circumstances. Of course it can be harder to create a sense of Belonging for virtual teams, but it is part of how businesses need to adapt for the twenty-first century and a crucial consideration for managers.

Recruiting for diversity

Recruiting new team members and colleagues is a process, and like many processes in most businesses, it just happens. As long as you fill the role, then the exercise has been successful, hasn't it? Well, perhaps not. Is the recruitment process designed to ensure that you get the best person for the job or simply to attract the person who feels that they fit the job description? As we will go on to show, these are not necessarily the same thing.

There is a much-quoted internal Hewlett-Packard internal report called 'Lean in, The Confidence Code'. It states that when applying for a role, a man is confident of his chances if he has 60 per cent of the required criteria whereas women don't feel confident until they have 100 per cent of the requirements.

Many women don't apply for roles because they are strictly following the rules about the requirements needed for a role. These women don't see the part where advocacy, relationships and a more creative approach to framing your expertise and experience could work to mitigate the idea that the requirements are the absolute and immutable minimum that candidates need to have. The fact is that the process of hiring someone is much more nuanced than it seems. Sometimes job roles are written by committee, so they become a collation of numerous views about the ideal candidate. Or they turn into an aspirational view of the qualities of the person holding the role (this often happens if this is delegated to the person who held that role before) alongside the actual job. They will imply that the job holder is a cross between a business superstar, a management innovator and possibly a spiritual leader.

Change the script

Instead of following accepted wisdom, this is how to ensure that you gain traction with the widest pool of talent. Commonly used words like 'expert' can be excluding. Who decides what level of experience makes you an expert? If you are an introvert, how comfortable would you be in asserting yourself to be 'an expert'? Why not try 'We are looking for at least five years of experience in X systems/workstream'? Keep your job descriptions minimal – the more you put in, the more you create a barrier for those people who don't exactly identify with the criteria.

'Motivated' and 'passionate' are far more inclusive descriptions and phrases than 'you constantly outperform the goals expected of you' or 'driven', 'relentless'. Also, avoiding the phrase 'the ideal candidate' is good as ideals are just that – ideals. Let's bring some humanity into the process. It may seem blindingly obvious, but don't use masculine nouns and pronouns. Using the words, 'you' and 'we' just resonates more.

Try to use the job role as an advertisement for what you're doing to drive diversity, inclusion and a sense of Belonging. This doesn't mean using one of those tired and transparent tricks like putting in a stock shot of a 'diverse' team, normally sitting around a long table and looking at a screen/whiteboard/whatever. It can also help to list the benefits you offer – flexible working, maternity and shared parental leave policy, any carer/childcare policies. It's tricky to ask for these things in an interview or chat without feeling that you may be excluding yourself from consideration or that you look as if you're only there for those specific benefits.

View the job descriptions/candidates' brief as a two-way street – you are asking people to commit themselves to you and you need to outline what the value exchange is – what you can give them back. Mutuality of interests makes people advocates of their workplaces. In creating a sense where it's the individual contribution that is recognized, where you have human values and that you are welcoming; great culture begins from the very start of the recruitment of colleagues.

Strategies for Belonging

RECRUITING FOR DIVERSITY

Ensure that your job descriptions are screened to make them inclusive and list all the benefits of flexible working and parental leave to ensure that the candidate doesn't have to ask about them and risk looking as if they are not dedicated enough.

Managing diversity

The Avengers is one of the biggest movie series of all time, taking billions at the box office. It isn't perhaps the most obvious reference that you would expect from Karen Blackett, OBE, head of creative transformation giant WPP UK, CEO of Group M and the first UK government champion of race. Yet she comes back to it, time and again, when explaining how to run a team of people.

'I believe that the best teams are made up of very different people, all excellent in their different ways. Just as the Marvel Avengers are. You need teams that complete each other, rather than compete. You wouldn't want a whole team made up of Incredible Hulks, but a Hulk, with a Captain America, with an Iron Man, Black Widow and the Scarlet Witch – that could be exactly what you need.'

Blackett's role is to be the Nick Fury of teams, the one who brings lots of talent with different skill sets and personalities together and to make sure that they get the best out of each other. It often isn't easy: the talent can get tangled in politics caused by ego-driven status anxiety. The key is to focus the team on winning. Her own experience, working at MediaCom (the UK's largest media agency), where she was the first and only black woman to ever run a media agency in the UK, until she took her role as CEO of Group M and running holding company WPP in the UK, helped her to develop her philosophy. Her bosses at MediaCom believed in winning, and in having the right person in place to contribute to that win, irrespective of race or gender. Based on this logic, and on the empirical success that it delivered, it's hard to see why so many businesses fail to manage diversity for winning success. And yet so many do.

Here's one reason why. Organizations, like organisms, tend to want to reproduce themselves exactly. (Most evolution is accidental in nature.) Most of the time, people recruit people like them, replace like with like and try to maintain a sense of togetherness through physical and behavioural alikeness. It is easy to understand why this happens. After all, it's very comfortable to work with people who are like you. And if your boss says that they want to promote you, but you must have a successor to take on your old role, well, it only makes sense that if you find someone exactly like you, then they'll be a safe pair of hands to deliver for the business. Except that there are two fundamental problems with this approach.

Disruption never stops

This doesn't allow for the disruption now inherent in every sector. Disruption literally never stops and will never stop. It isn't just that technology keeps developing, it is that customer satisfaction will never be the same again, thanks to organizations like Amazon, which are built to serve the dissatisfied customer. Jeff Bezos, Amazon's founder, talks about always serving the 'beautifully dissatisfied'. And as with most things, once Pandora's box is open, there is no going back to the old status quo. So disruption will continue, the beautifully dissatisfied will see to that. And if you only have people in your company who are a good 'safe pair of hands' then you are likely to find your business disrupted soonest by a more agile competitor, so that is reason one for not hiring for comfort.

Hiring people who are different is essential. But hiring them isn't enough: they have to feel they belong.

Glass Slipper

Many organizations have been built up with layers of people pretending to fit in, because that is the only way to stay in a job. This is really stifling and no way to get the best out of the team. It is known in academic circles as the 'Glass Slipper Syndrome'.

It's maybe not generally known that the original folk tales on which one of the greatest hits of panto is loosely based were really quite dark. The Brothers Grimm telling of *Cinderella* differs from the pantomime and Disney version in several respects. For instance, Cinderella's ball gown is not the gift of a fairy godmother but of a tree growing on her mother's grave that she has watered with her tears. The stepsisters end up getting their eyes pecked out by pigeons. And the glass slipper episode has a darker turn, too.

You'll remember from childhood that the only way the clearly rather unobservant Prince Charming can identify Cinderella after the ball is by searching the kingdom for a woman whose tiny foot fits the glass slipper left on the stairs of the palace. The so-called 'ugly sisters' can apparently fool the prince into thinking that they are the woman he intends to make his bride, apart from the fact that neither can squeeze her foot into the slipper. In the original version of the story they do indeed get the slipper on. The evil stepmother ensures that they do so by cutting off a toe or two. The prince only clocks that this is fake because of the blood, the blood that spills everywhere.

Unpleasant stuff.

As unpleasant as every day can be for people who work in an environment where they need to cut off aspects of their personalities in order to fit in. The Glass Slipper problem afflicts everyone who doesn't fit the culture and expectations of their chosen career. There are many unspoken expectations wrapped up in the job you take, fuelled by years of cultural imagery. For example, an investigative journalist is expected to be hungry, edgy, a bit tired-looking and fearless. A chef is meant to be sweary and aggressive.

If you're a comfortable, well-rested journalist, does that make you less good at chasing down a story?

If you're efficient and relaxed, are you a worse chef?

If you don't participate in media's drinking culture, are you less likely to progress?

A professor at the University of Colorado, Karen Lee Ashcraft, wrote a paper identifying this issue. Ashcraft writes that some occupations have come to be 'naturally possessed' of features that fit certain people much more than others. If you have ambitions to progress within an organization that is characterized with attributes that don't come naturally to you, then you may feel under huge pressure to adopt them, even if it means hiding your real identity, day in and day out. This can put an enormous strain on people, and the effort it takes is not only exhausting but of course therefore detracts from the energy that would otherwise be available for doing good work.

Sometimes the attributes are sexual orientation or skin colour. Sometimes it's subtler: do you ski? If you do, is it at the 'right' resort? If not, in some companies, you might as well not have bothered.

Squeezing your foot into a glass slipper that doesn't fit is always painful. Organizations that go along with this are missing out on the benefits of diversity and wasting their teams' energies on a fruitless exercise of conformity. It's a big mistake to assume that when everyone gives the appearance of getting on well that they are actually working at peak performance. Particularly of course if people have to hide their natural traits in order to fit in.

To manage well for diversity it is most important to allow authenticity, to encourage differences, and to go out of your way to hire people who might not like each other (just as Iron Man and Captain America really don't get on that well) but who are the right mix, in order to get an excellent job done.

Strategies for Belonging

MANAGING FOR DIVERSITY

Beware the 'Glass Slipper Syndrome', where your employees have to pretend to be other than their true selves. This detracts from their ability to do a good job and stops them from being happy, too.

There's a number of different types of people you need around your organization to create a culture of Belonging:

A sponsor	Someone who talks you up when you're not there;
A wing-man or wing-woman	Someone who helps you in ways you cannot help yourself;
A cheerleader	Cheers you on, no matter what;
An ally from the 'other side'	Someone from another 'cohort', who will provide unexpected support;
The buddy	Cheers you up, laughs with you, mops you up, has a good moan with you

Most people just have buddies in the workplace. That's all well and good, and very comfortable too, but not enough to create a great culture of Belonging. Look for a balance of different types in your team and manage them for their differences, not for them to be the same as each other.

The crucial importance of sponsors

Developing a network of buddies can provide you with an extensive mechanism of support, advice and release – there is nothing quite like the shared experience of knowing the circumstances of an event or situation and being able to laugh, commiserate or share the gritty detail. Here, we examine the value of support from above your current organizational level. What role could a sponsor play in your development and how do you find them?

A sponsor can talk about you and your abilities in senior circles. They can give you visibility and exposure beyond your current circle of influence and talk about you as a future leader.

For an individual who feels that the current structure just above them isn't giving them the framework to progress, simply finding the right sponsor may allow you to break out of a circle of dead man's shoes or overt favouritism.

Here's one case study… Middle manager Julia found herself working on a big internal project that was led from board level and which involved a selection of people from a number of different departments. It wasn't a glamorous high-profile project by any means; it was one of those projects that was never going to result in being carried shoulder-high by your colleagues as you triumphantly emerge with the implementation plan. However, what it did offer was the opportunity to work alongside more senior team members, who weren't part of Julia's day-to-day department operations. It was refreshing to hear different viewpoints and ways of working, given the different department requirements and spending time together was giving a wider view of the company.

As the project progressed, Julia found she really enjoyed her interaction with Simon, a senior member of another department. He seemed to understand the way that she worked and was always willing to listen to her ideas and suggestions. He also brought fresh thinking from his experience and was always happy to share his views and perspective. Feeling stuck in a career cul-de-sac, Julia decided that she would ask for his help. As a visible minority group in the company (she's openly bisexual), she sometimes feels as though she's not the 'right chap' for the board. She wasn't sure how to enlist Simon's support or even if he was happy to think about it, but as the project was coming to an end, she had nothing to lose.

Simon thought about it and responded with an offer to be her sponsor. He would check in with her on a regular basis but wasn't going to offer granular advice – what he would do is showcase her and her work where it was appropriate and he would commit to consistently actioning that. He was very clear that this might not result in immediate results and that he was only doing this because he thought she had a contribution to make.

Independent voice

To have an independent voice that speaks for you is very powerful, but it only works if you have created a level of respect and understanding with your sponsor. No one will heedlessly talk you up (that would damage their credibility) if you weren't able to demonstrate why they support you. Simon here showed generosity. There wasn't, on the face of it, much in it for him. However, as their interactions played out, he found that he could use Julia's support. She became integral to his own progress as a supporter from a very different background and indeed culture. He could get insider knowledge from her of a different team in the business to strengthen his strategies for progress.

If you plan to sponsor someone, be prepared for a long-term commitment and for your praise to be part of a long-term strategy. If you work in a culture that only recognizes talent and potential in people when they demand attention, then you have a talent and retention problem. When you sponsor, you may find that you learn something along the way. On both sides there needs to be a clarity around what each of you expects. We're not talking about setting KPIs for the arrangement, more of boundaries/limits to the input and outcome: No, you can't expect to be promoted within six weeks of the process starting. Yes, I am comfortable about doing this, but I won't negotiate your pay rise.

Strategies for Belonging

THE CRUCIAL IMPORTANCE OF SPONSORS

Find a sponsor who can talk about you and your abilities in the top echelons of the company. If you are not lucky enough to have this happen naturally, or the business doesn't have a sponsorship scheme, then seek that person out. If you are in the position to sponsor someone, then do so, but try and find someone different a different kind of person from you to help. And this may be good for you in more ways than one. Not just because you'll be helping talent to rise to the top. As the old expression goes, it is important to be nice to people as you reach the top, in case you run into them again on the way down. So it will be good for your career too, as well as your sponsee's prospects.

Finding your Goose

'I've always had a wing-man,' says Eric, a highly successful entrepreneur when we meet him. 'It was someone that I started out with and it came very naturally to us to have each other's back. Although it's a long time since we've worked together, I still use him to bounce ideas off, and solve problems with, in a way that I don't with anyone else.'

Eric is describing a unique kind of workplace relationship that isn't about your mates, sponsors or mentors. And if you can find your wing-man or woman in the office then it will help to ensure that your stance on issues is backed up by at least one other person. One person going against the normal culture is an anomaly. Two is another thing entirely and can help to create change. For many men and women in the workplace being a bystander is the current default position when they encounter toxic behaviours which contribute so much to people feeling like they don't belong. It can be a very lonely position to be always the person who speaks out and in fact if you do this alone, you risk becoming the one that the majority expect to speak out. This is turn can lead to you being the one that is routinely ignored. By developing the wing-person relationship, you ensure that you're not alone. However, it is essential that the wing-person is not the same kind of person that you are.

Your normal crew in the workplace will be those you have most in common with, perhaps educational experience, similar backgrounds, shared experiences. The wing-person comes from a different place, is the introvert to your extroversion (and vice versa), yet they will put your needs and aims even before their own.

Sounds too good to be true?

Another myth to smash

Well, here's another myth of the old-fashioned patriarchal workplace to smash: not everyone that you work with is entirely in it for themselves. Through generosity of spirit comes a more expansive outlook and this positivity is contagious.

A wing-man or woman can make a massive difference to your career. When you hit a career blockage, have a bad meeting or sink beneath pressure, your wing-person can help you to regroup and move on. Crucially, if you are the one taking a stand against toxic behaviour in the workplace, they will back you up. Not just in the immediate situation – they of course might not be present – but in their emotional support and in rooms that you are not in.

Jackie told us about the support that she received from her wing-person, Philippa: 'I was repeatedly in a situation where I felt undermined publicly by my boss. Last week, he called for a board meeting at 9 a.m. I'm the only woman on that board and I said that I couldn't guarantee that I could make the time because of the school run, I'd be there by 9.10 a.m. He said not to worry, that they'd start without me. When I walked in the first thing he said was that he'd told the boys in a certain team that they did not have to make the savings that I had said were essential for the business plan. He said, we agreed this before you turned up. And one of the other men on the board actually sniggered (there's just no other word for it).

'I tried to contradict him, but I felt on the back foot about the whole situation. But I do not want to lose my job. I'm divorced, I am really the only breadwinner. I've got three kids and I don't have time to look around. But you can understand that I felt really down and somehow guilty as well as angry and frustrated.

'When I talked to Philippa about it, the clouds cleared. First of all, she listened, properly listened to me. She didn't give me unrealistic advice as some people might do in that situation, but she did more than just listen. She found someone close to the top executive my boss works for and she had a quiet word. Not a complaint. Nothing that would escalate to HR, which I really couldn't bear at that moment, and anyway, I didn't believe it was worth escalating. But she mentioned that she'd heard that something was up with the culture of our office. Wheels were set in motion and while nothing has officially changed, the atmosphere in my section is way better and the politeness of my boss has improved significantly. I think she just indicated that she was very surprised to hear of such old-fashioned behaviour.'

Philippa had pointed out to the senior team that there was a discrepancy between the values of the company and the experience of her friend. She'd done this as a value equation. Here they were, hiring an expensive asset in Jackie and then failing to set her up for success by allowing her to be undermined.

Belonging behaviour delivers progress for everyone. Notice that Philippa didn't particularly spend time sympathizing with Jackie – this went as read. She invested effort in righting the wrong effectively instead.

Certainly, a wing-person will be there for you and cheer you up. Also, and importantly, they'll tell you some home truths about yourself. If they don't do this, they're not actually doing their wing-job properly. A work buddy is one thing – the person you moan to about your boss being short with you, or who makes you a cup of tea when you're flagging. Your buddy will comfort you when you're down, commiserate when you don't get a promotion, chat with you when you're bored, cover for you when you're late. This is not a wing-person. The wing-person plays a different role in your career. They will make connections for you and talk about you when you're not there; they will create opportunities for you. They will be thrilled at your success, even if sometimes it is better than their own. A truly great wing-person thinks about you when you're not around. They push you out of your comfort zone and they tell you what you got wrong. They make suggestions about how you should change that they know you won't want to hear. They keep on at you about those changes, even if you tell them not to, because they care as much about your career potential as you do, sometimes they care more. Listening to them and then acting on it is essential. It's a big part of having a growth mindset and that's the mindset you need to succeed.

Buddies can make you feel better but don't expect them to help concretely with your career. In proven fact, wing-people can definitely deliver what cheerleaders can't. In an interesting experiment, published in *Harvard Business Review* in 2018, Professor Serena Chen of the University of California, together with Juliana Breines from the University of Rhode Island, worked with participants in three groups, all of whom had been asked to name their biggest weakness. One set were asked to write themselves a letter talking about their weakness from a 'compassionate and understanding' perspective. Another set were asked to write in terms of boosting their self-esteem – to focus on validating themselves rather than on that weakness. The third group were the control and weren't asked to do anything.

Participants in the weaknesses seen with compassion group showed much more of a growth mindset and were much more likely to agree that with hard work they could change than either of the other two sets. A follow-up experiment showed that behavioural change was much more likely from people who experienced compassionate but clear understanding about what they'd got wrong than from those who had been given unconditional approval.

Here's how wing-person differs then from a buddy or a cheerleader. They'll point out your mistakes (with kindness and compassion, but firmly) and won't let you get away with being stuck. Self-esteem in this *Harvard Business Review* analysis is overrated: you need a wing-person (or a Goose, to come back to *Top Gun*) to make sure that you are really working on your weaknesses, not just glossing over them. If you haven't already, finding one so that you can together agree to stand up for the code of Belonging is worth devoting time and effort to.

Strategies for Belonging

FINDING YOUR GOOSE

Get yourself a wing-man or woman. They'll look after your interests and you will look after theirs. Nothing makes you feel like you belong like a wing-person at your side.

Want to win? Find an ally from outside your circle

One of the most depressing myths that has built up in recent times is that each gender must stick with their own. Women should network with women, men should stick with men. There are two reasons why this is bad for Belonging.

First, there is no particular reason why you as a man will identify best with all the other men in your workplace or as a woman with the women. This type of stereotyping leads to all kinds of dumb behaviour. Having a penis doesn't make every man the same! To apply biological factors to workplace operations is woefully anachronistic. The research for our earlier book, *The Glass Wall* did clearly demonstrate that there are misconceptions that separate gender. However, this doesn't mean that men must stick with men or women with women – you need a diverse tribe in the workplace.

For any man leading or managing in the workplace it is arguably essential today to have a woman as an ally to enable him to get the most out of a balanced workforce. Let's hear from Ian, the worldwide leader of an extensive service business, what his experience has been. Ian says that he despairs of the fact that he can still be in meetings where the majority of the room are who he himself categorizes as 'pale, male and stale'. He's very worried that many of the women he works with think that they have to behave like alpha males in order to succeed, since he thinks that the workplace would work better with fewer alpha attitudes. Indeed, he finds himself more naturally drawn to working with women and dreads being stuck in an alpha-male 'pissing contest'.

'My parents married in the mid-sixties and to begin with, they were fairly traditional – Dad worked, Mum looked after the kids – but by the late 80s, my mum was the only breadwinner in the house. All my ambition and drive come from my mum, not my dad. And I am proud to call myself a feminist. I much prefer to get things done at work by winning over women to my point of view than having to have tedious status arguments with other men.'

Ian calls himself a 'safe flirt' in the office. He's anxious to point out that this means nothing sexual, he just means that he'd sooner get things done by charm than by aggression and that women respond better to this than the men he works with. He believes fundamentally in being authentic and knows himself well enough to know that he'd rather hang out with women than with other men.

Kelly's experience too has been that she's benefitted more from relationships at work with men rather than women. Indeed, she found herself at odds with the women's network that she joined: 'Every woman in the network was just so ambitious for status and also seemed to be very concerned about where I fitted in the pecking order. This made me very uncomfortable. My natural inclination if there is a pecking order is to wander in the opposite direction. In all honesty, the emotional cost of joining this network was too high for me. It meant not being as direct or as spontaneous as I am naturally.'

When we probed what she meant, Kelly said she couldn't manage the small talk nor the etiquette of many encounters with the women in the network at her workplace. She felt that the rules didn't come naturally to her, nor was she inclined to learn them. 'But I did need allies in the workplace,' she went on, 'so I ended up looking for them in amongst men that I felt that I had more in common with.'

There's absolutely nothing wrong with either of these scenarios. The success of a Belonging formula at work is for it to be natural, authentic and above all based on decent human behaviour. There's nothing wrong with not bonding with the men if you're a man nor feeling distant from the women if you are a woman. Furthermore, there's a huge advantage in having an ally in the opposite gender.

Ask advice from an ally from outside your circle

Ian confides in us that he's frequently asked his women allies for advice on handling difficult situations with the women who work for him: 'I see many of the women stuck in a cycle of over-performance that just isn't sustainable. Some of them are ridiculously high achievers, with a background of school achievements of consistent A*s and firsts, and in an enormous hurry for promotion. They seem very happy to work 18-hour days, to talk about working harder than any man and to go out networking every night. I worry about this a lot, and have needed to consult with other women in my network of allies to understand the language to use to tell them to slow down.

'My first attempts were taken in a very hostile way. When I told one woman in my leadership team to pace herself, she basically had a meltdown. I talked to my allies and I've had to learn to lead by example – the other day, I had a very late night, so I slept in, had breakfast with the kids and worked from home. But I made it very clear to everyone in my leadership team that this was what I was doing, and that they could call me, but also that it was okay to follow my example.'

On the other hand, Kelly has learned a very simple lesson from one of her men allies – an apposite use of a sporting analogy: 'I was trying to sell a rather complicated change to a board of men who frankly were all rather negative about being told what to do by a woman. Also, when I was explaining the situation, they weren't really hearing me. I was suggesting that there was a need to avoid disruption from challengers in our sector. Mainly, they were hearing something very different. They were hearing me criticizing the way they currently did their job, which I absolutely was not. The way they were doing their job was completely fine, it just wasn't sustainable with the new competitors coming into our sector.'

Kelly took the problem to her ally and he suggested using the 2012 Champions League Semi-Final where Chelsea beat Barcelona as an analogy. Simply put, Barcelona, one of the best football teams in the world, played according to a set playbook. However, during the course of the match it became clear that every play had been studied by Chelsea and they had a defence against it. Barcelona was outplayed by a team who know what to expect from them and however good they were, they were countered. Barcelona fans around the world were shouting, 'Just stick it in the mixer!' – i.e. seek a goal by abandoning the playbook and making a spontaneous attempt.

When Kelly returned to her board and prefaced her proposals with this story, the men reacted immediately with positivity: she'd framed change and spontaneity in a way that attracted their attention. This kind of understanding and empathy would not have come so easily from a network exclusively made up of other women.

A warning note is struck by US research firm Promundo, who found that many more men think they're being allies than it seems to most women. The research found that 77 per cent of men said they were doing everything that they could to promote gender equality in the workplace, but that only 41 per cent of women agreed that men are doing this. Also, 89 per cent of men say they'd be good listeners to accounts of workplace harassment versus the much-lower proportion of women who think this at 58 per cent. As gender activist Shelley Zalis comments, it is important to listen to the person who has recruited you as an ally and pay attention to exactly how they want to be supported, when to step in and when to step back. The exercises that close this chapter show how to be a great ally, sponsor and wing-person.

Strategies for Belonging

AN ALLY FROM OUTSIDE YOUR IMMEDIATE CIRCLE

It's more and more essential to find an ally from another type of person to yourself to navigate modern work culture. Check your close circle: if they all look and sound the same as you, then you're missing out. If you become an ally, make sure you're doing it well, with good enough empathy and sensitivity.

Exercises and techniques for Chapter 4

So, a culture of Belonging means recruiting a diverse team, but also making sure that they work well together in a spirit where all are accepting of differences. Make sure that you have the right mix of sponsors, allies, wing-people and buddies around. Become a sponsor, ally and wing-person and help to spread the culture of Belonging. Here are some exercises to help power the Belonging culture.

It is possible for groups of people with a similar cultural background to make assumptions about how each other thinks, about how they will behave and how they will react in different situations. It's easier to 'read between the lines'.

It's also possible to take a few shortcuts because you are likely to have shared shorthand built on shared cultural references. The classic example would be the ability of a group of men to throw a football analogy into a conversation and for everyone to instantly understand all the nuances of the reference. (And no, not every man is into football, and yes, increasing numbers of women are; but nonetheless women report feeling excluded – and feeling that perhaps they're deliberately being excluded – by references that assume an esoteric knowledge of the significance of a particular male sporting event.)

Once we begin to work in more diverse groups, we can no longer work on the assumption that everyone is going to have the same shared attitudes, beliefs or ways of thinking. In fact, we can hope to expect the very opposite – we cannot as easily predict how everyone will react to a new idea of or proposal and we cannot fall back on easy shorthands. It may take a little bit longer to explain what we mean.

Because we no longer automatically have a shared culture, we must seek to actively build one. There may be some resistance to this idea. For one reason, because it sounds like extra work – and as we said earlier, nobody needs any extra work. But the benefits of building a shared culture with your colleagues *far* outweigh the slight inconvenience of actually sitting down and talking about this stuff.

Here's a way of building a shared team culture. We'll go through the process on the basis that we're working with a small team (up to a dozen people). At the end, we'll look at how we can adapt it to work across larger groups.

Exercise: Building a shared culture

Phase One: Individual work

First, within your team, ask every team-member to answer the following questionnaire, adhering to the instructions in the 'How to Answer the Questionnaire' paragraph on page 145.

Who am I at work?

At work, I add value by…
(up to three answers)

At work, my limitations include…
(up to three answers)

Who am I on a bad day at work?

On a bad day at work, I…
(up to three answers)

When I'm having a bad day, I need…
(up to three answers)

How do I respond to pressure?

When I'm under pressure, I…
(up to three answers)

When I'm under pressure, my colleagues can help me by…
(up to three answers)

How do I communicate?

I think email is a good way to communicate for…
(up to three answers)

But I think we need to have a face-to-face meeting when…
(up to three answers)

I try to answer all my emails (and other messages) within…
(up to three answers)

I expect my emails to be answered within…
(up to three answers)

A meeting should be…
(up to three answers)

A meeting should never be…
(up to three answers)

The best way to set an agenda for a meeting is…
(up to three answers)

How do I like to receive feedback?

I am happy to receive feedback from my peers, or I only want to receive feedback from my manager…

How do I like to resolve conflict?

The best way to resolve conflict is…
(up to three answers)

We should never resolve conflict by…
(up to three answers)

How do I expect to be treated?

Three words that describe how I expect to be treated at work are…
(up to three answers)

How to answer the questionnaire

Initially work through the questionnaire, answering all the questions. If you get stuck, it's okay to leave a few gaps. Then set it aside and return to review your answers after a period of at least 24 hours. Fill in any gaps and feel free to make any other changes that you now want to. Then set it aside again. After another period of at least 24 hours, look at your answers again. This time read them through as though the answers had been written by a colleague of yours (one that you like!). Ask yourself:

- What would I enjoy about working with this person?
- What might the drawbacks be of working with this person?
- If I wanted to improve my working relationship with this person, what should I do?
- If this person wanted to get on better with their colleagues, what should they do?

Take time to reflect on your answers to these four questions. Might they inspire you to make any changes in the way you behave at work?

Phase Two: Group work

Set aside three hours for a group meeting. Off-site would be great, but a meeting room will do. No laptops and all phones switched off (give them a break in the middle to check in with the digital world).

Ask a colleague from elsewhere in the organization who has trained as a facilitator to run the meeting. (If no one in your organization has ever trained to be a facilitator, remedy that immediately.) Ask everyone to bring their answers to the questionnaire with them.

Icebreaker

Give everyone three minutes to fill in the gaps in the following sentence:

If I had the time, I would like to learn much more about… because…

Go round the group, with everyone giving their answer. Allow for brief discussion if any starts ('I didn't know you were into…' etc.)

Now the serious stuff begins… Using the relevant answers to the original questionnaire, the group is now going to create a shared protocol for how it behaves – which will underpin the emergence of a shared culture.

Getting to know you

Go round the group, asking everyone to share their answers to these questions from the original questionnaire:

At work, I add value by…
(up to three answers)

At work, my limitations include…
(up to three answers)

On a bad day at work, I…
(up to three answers)

When I'm having a bad day, I need…
(up to three answers)

How we will communicate

The facilitator writes each of the following questions – from the original questionnaire – on an individual Post-it note and places them all on a wall, spaced out:

I think email is a good way to communicate for...
(up to three answers)

But I think we need to have a face-to-face meeting when...
(up to three answers)

I try to answer all my emails (and other messages) within...
(up to three answers)

I expect my emails to be answered within...
(up to three answers)

A meeting should be...
(up to three answers)

A meeting should never be...
(up to three answers)

The best way to set an agenda for a meeting is...
(up to three answers)

The team members then look through their answers to the questions. Each chooses one or more of their answers, writes it on a Post-it note and places it under the relevant question. When everyone has added as many Post-its as they want, the group wanders along the wall, looking at everyone else's replies.

The facilitator then calls out the commonalities that they can see, asks for others to also call out any themes they can spot, and leads a discussion. The outcomes of this discussion will be a series of statements that set out guidelines for how the group will communicate. These should cover: what can be discussed via email or other digital messaging and what subjects must be addressed face to face; how quickly team members are expected to answer email to each other, to clients and to other stakeholders; how agendas for meetings will be set and when they will be circulated.

The facilitator should allow the discussion to wander into related areas that seem important to the group. For example, which social media we send work-related information on and which we don't. At what time can team members 'switch off their phones' (i.e. they're no longer expected to reply to work communications). The outcome of any of these side-discussions should also be a written guideline.

In all discussions, the facilitator's role is to ensure that everyone feels heard and listened to. This does not mean that everyone will agree with all the guidelines. If someone is particularly unhappy with any of them, the team leader should note this and commit to discussing the point individually at a later date.

How we will treat each other

Split the group into sub-groups of three or four people. Each sub-group should discuss their views on the following questions and should feel free to allow their conversations to wander into related areas:

I am happy to receive feedback from my peers, or I only want to receive feedback from my manager…
(up to three answers)

The best way to resolve conflict is…
(up to three answers)

We should never resolve conflict by…
(up to three answers)

Three words that describe how I expect to be treated at work are…
(up to three answers)

After 15 minutes, end the sub-group discussions. One person from each sub-group should now write their sub-group's conclusions on a flipchart and talk them through with the wider group. If there are widely different views within one sub-group, allow another member to add their thoughts briefly, but the facilitator should manage this process carefully by surfacing the fact that there are different views but not allowing the whole process to be about this.

When all the sub-groups have added their conclusions, the facilitator should call out commonalities, ask others to do the same and the whole group should use these as a basis to write a series of further guidelines that will govern the team's behaviour when interacting with each other.

At the end of this session, the facilitator (or an agreed team member) will collate all the outputs and distribute them to the team as an agreed set of Team Behaviour Guidelines. They should also be made visible on a noticeboard or poster in the team's area. You may also choose to share them with other teams that you regularly work with and other stakeholders.

These Team Behaviour Guidelines are not corporate values. Nor are they meant to replace or contradict any corporate values you already have. They are simply specific instructions for how team members will treat each other. They might say things like…

'In meetings, we allow people to finish what they are saying and do not interrupt each other.'

'When any individual in the team delivers work to senior management they will credit all team members who have contributed to the project.'

'Team members are allowed (and encouraged) to take a five-minute screen-break every hour – and will not be criticized for doing so.'

'The daily team catch-up will last no more than 10 minutes.'

Spreading a shared culture throughout the organization

Most organizations will have top-down cultural initiatives. These are extremely important in indicating a general direction of travel, but any sensible leadership team knows that they can only have a limited role in defining the actual culture of their organization. Indeed, one definition of corporate culture is 'what happens when the leadership isn't looking'.

So long as your Team Behaviour Guidelines don't actively contradict corporate behaviours, any enlightened HR department will welcome them. The fact is teams are extremely unlikely to come up with any guidelines that contradict any company's corporate values or behaviours; they will almost always be an expression of them. So the simplest way to make this work for larger groups is to allow and encourage each team to go through this process for themselves and create their own Guidelines.

This isn't a recipe for anarchy. Most teams will come up with roughly the same guidelines. How can we be so sure? Because all these guidelines are effectively saying is: 'We are human beings and we commit to treating each other respectfully'. Shouldn't that be obvious? Do we really need to go through a whole process and have a bunch of written guidelines? Yes, because as we work with people from different cultural backgrounds or different generations or different genders, or those who have joined from other companies, they will have slightly different ideas of what is respectful and what isn't.

For example, research suggests that if the most senior person in the room is sneaking looks at their phone, not only have they switched off from the meeting but everyone else in the room will too (because, well, if they're not concentrating, what's the point?). The senior person doesn't mean to be disrespectful. But they are. And everyone else is demotivated as a result.

In that situation, it's hard for a more junior person to call out the behaviour, but if the team has a written guideline…

'We do not look at our phones during team meetings. If meetings last longer than half an hour, we will have a five-minute break to check for urgent emails/calls…'

…then the behaviour can be gently challenged. The meeting is more effective, the team does better work.

One Voice: Stephanie

Stephanie is in her early 30s and works in a creative team at a large employer. She is dyslexic and talks here about what happened when she opened up to her current employer about her condition:

'I currently work in the creative team, but before that, I was working in a very numbers-based job at the same employer. It was very audited and had very high levels of procedure, which I found very difficult.

'I was diagnosed with dyslexia at school, where at GCSE level, I did get help. I had one English teacher who could see how passionate I was about English and how much I enjoyed it but that I was definitely struggling in regards to the pace of the work. I could do it all, it just didn't necessarily make sense to the examiners, or the grammar wasn't correct, and the punctuality wasn't great. We had a discussion and I got some extra tuition classes and extra time in exams. Then I went to college, where I chose practical subjects and did really well, and finished with distinctions, and this gave me the confidence to go to university.

'I chose subjects where I thought that most of the work would be practical again, but it absolutely didn't work out that way. It was very theoretical, very essay-driven, with strict timelines. There were a lot of aspects that made me panic and troubled in the first two years. But quitting wasn't an option. (I come from a Nigerian background and that is just how I was brought up.) In my final year, I was able to ask for more assistance and a number of things were put in place to help me.

'Then I entered work and a very different situation. In education there are good teachers that you can talk to about the help that you need when you are struggling. And there's good awareness. This isn't the situation in most workplaces, where you are paid to do the job and then you go home.

'I started work in a jewellery store and there I could avoid the things that were difficult. But as I got older, I decided that I wanted to change careers.

'The next place I worked, I didn't tell them about my dyslexia. It was heavily numbers and process based, and there were many areas that I really struggled with. I've been dealing with my dyslexia for forever and so you find the little ways that help you avoid making errors. Or whenever I did make an error, I would try and fix it and apologize. I didn't talk to my employer about the situation because I didn't feel in the position to raise it. I still had the stigma about being different and being treated as though there was something wrong with me. I didn't feel as though I could ask for help.

'And then I changed jobs again to my current employer. If anything, the new job initially made me struggle even more. There were lots of numbers and letters that I kept getting mixed up. And lots of customer communication that had to be absolutely correct. But where I work now, they have a neurodiversity community. The woman that runs it is absolutely amazing. I joined the community because I knew that I needed somewhere that I could go and speak about the struggles I had in my role. And I now have a really solid support system to help my career. I had discussions about my strengths, not just my weaknesses, and about what I am passionate about. They asked me what I enjoyed, where I really fly and what kind of stuff I would like to stop doing. They helped me find a role where I could be more creative and play to my strengths, as well as helping me with software that could help my difficulties. I found that I could have an open and *honest conversation with a group of people that understood what I was going through and had shared experiences, whether this was dyslexia, autism, ADHD. That there were loads of us going through certain challenges at work and that there are solutions to them. Sometimes it is very difficult to have a conversation with your line manager and admit that you are struggling. They helped me to have that conversation and ask whether there is something that we can do together to create a better working environment.*

'Before this, the role wasn't conducive to my mental health. I was struggling quite a lot. I was really upset. It just didn't work. With help, I was able to start doing things that would help me for the future. I was able to connect with people in the team I am in now and be confident to have a conversation about my condition. I now know that being dyslexic is not a problem, not an issue, it is part of who I am. If you are in a position where you can do something that you love every day, you find that the neurodiversity challenge isn't going to stop you, in fact it makes you better.

'I used to feel for a fact that I didn't belong in the workplace. It didn't feel like a safe space. I worried that maybe the job just wasn't for me. I used to struggle to live with my truth. It was difficult to even think about talking about it. It added to the hysteria that is already in your head about not being able to measure up. Now I can see that there are great strengths in neurodiversity and I know that the business I am in supports me. I can be an advocate for neurodiversity now because I am in a safe space. Our brains are wired differently, we bring a different way of thinking about problems and I can champion this. I know that there's lots of us around. And we are, you know, absolutely smashing it and doing amazing things. If you still think that this

is a problem, can you change your mind? Because you need to be more open, more aware and educate yourself to see the amazing, wonderful talents that a neurodiverse person has because we've got loads and there are lots of us around that can show you. Come into the light!'

CHAPTER FIVE

Making Belonging the winning culture at work

You know the scenario... You're sitting there with an opinion that differs from the consensus. Perhaps you have some inside knowledge of what's really going on. Or a strong instinct that doing what the louder voices in the meeting believe is right would be... well, just wrong. But you can be frightened to speak out – to say what you believe is the truth – because you think it will put you under pressure to conform and perhaps end up with you being quashed.

Have you ever swallowed your words, only to then watch as the problem you kept quiet about just builds and builds? Author and TED speaker Margaret Heffernan recalls her experience running a major US company and being told firmly not to tell the whole truth by her advisors. She believes that the desire for senior executives to smooth over problems and not face up to the truth of bad situations is one of the key problems with business.

A champion of whistle-blowers and dissenters, she points out that when you do speak up in those situations, you are nearly always saying something that everyone is thinking anyway. Once the problem is out in the open, you can do something about it. The role of senior management is to create a situation of trust, where dissenters are heard and the option to zig when everyone else is zagging doesn't carry the risk of ridicule or dismissal. Without a culture in which people can take the risk of speaking up, you can't fix anything.

Heffernan quotes research that says up to 85 per cent of businesspeople fear they can't tell the truth, either through fear of retribution (predominant in the US) or because there isn't any point (the UK reaction). We need to celebrate our dissenters and cherish those who point out what is being left unspoken. Without telling the truth, we end up with unbelievable spin and that's as true in our day-to-day working lives as it is in our communications strategies for brands.

What would happen, the next time you are in a meeting in which you feel there is a truth that isn't being said, if you were to be the one to speak up? Disturbing the equilibrium and rocking the boat may have consequences. So too does silence. A Belonging culture is one where everyone feels safe enough to speak up. Yet we all care what people think of us. It's impossible to disagree if you know that is going to make you the most unpopular person with your boss.

Canadian sociologist Erving Goffman described in the 1950s how in general human beings are always on the alert to how others react to us, continuously adapting our outward demeanour to ensure the best possible image. And this was long before social media gave the socially worried the somewhat addictive hits of the 'like' or 'share'. The neuroscientist, Susan Greenfield, extrapolates from this development that everyone now has three possible selves: the true self, expressed in safe, anonymous environments without the constraints of social pressures; the real self, the conformed individual who is restricted by social norms in face-to-face interactions; and the hoped-for, possible self – displayed on social networking sites. Which you is the one you take to work, or are we all shifting constantly between one version and another depending on which meeting we are in and who is present? Everyone has had the experience of colleagues saying one thing when the boss is present and saying and doing another behind their back.

However, as artificial intelligence revolutionizes our workplaces in the future, the importance of showing up at work as a fully rounded human being becomes more and more crucial. Increasingly, we will rely on algorithms for decision-making, and the jobs that can be done better by robots will no longer need humans. Which means showing up as your authentic self at work and being able to focus your energies on the very human capabilities of debate, challenge and even rebelliousness are essential to a successful career. If all you are doing is doing what you are told, we suspect a robot or an algorithm will be able to do that more cheaply and more efficiently, 24 hours a day and seven days a week without taking time off for parental leave or holidays.

Anxiety stops us being our best selves, of showing, if you like, our best human traits. This then is why the Belonging culture must be the winning culture at work. As we have seen in earlier chapters, this is not only the job of senior managers. However, as the old Chinese proverb has it, the fish rots from its head. This colourful saying simply underlines that the top bosses must have the right attitude. If they can't take criticism, if they can't bear any kind of challenge, then the chances of anyone speaking up and being themselves are slim.

As we will see, if they can create a forum for debate, with the understanding that it is the policy that is being critiqued, not the person who has proposed it, then there is every chance of better decisions and better profits. As co-founder of investment firm Hargreaves Lansdown Peter Hargreaves says: 'Bosses should welcome dissent – engender it, even. I love criticism. If you look at some of the people who have gone downhill bigtime, it's the ones who would never listen.'

In high-performing teams, people are not afraid to take risks. There's safety in arguing and an understanding that disagreement is useful, so long as it is followed by a commitment to execute the policy once it is debated and decided upon. The most effective teams fight for what is right and then once that is decided, they fight to deliver the strategy, acting independently to execute the company vision and mission. Creating space for disagreement, challenge and dissent is crucial to a culture of Belonging.

If you don't get passed the ball, you can't drop the ball

Despite the huge steps forward in the women's game, and the progress made by the likes of Siya Kolisi (the first black man to captain South Africa and who led them to victory in the 2019 World Cup), it's unlikely that most people would look at the world of Rugby Union to seek insight regarding diversity and inclusion. Top-level sport is where the highest achievers are and you either make the team or you don't. Many a teenage nightmare has come from being the last person to be picked for the game of netball, softball or football. So, what can we learn from the insight offered by former rugby player Will Carling, who captained his national team at the age of 22?

Will joined a team that had never achieved its potential and was failing. Hearing him talk about those days is inspirational and insightful. When he joined, just getting an England cap was enough – you had achieved your goal and the key thing was to amass as many international caps as possible. Winning was of secondary importance. This had resulted in a playing style that was risk-averse and lacking dynamism, but some of the senior players seemed content with the situation. Holding on to their place was the main aim. Their only aim, perhaps.

It was brilliantly summarized when Will was told by another player to avoid, at all costs, getting himself into a situation where he was passed the ball (an interesting tactic, as being passed the ball is one of the key rugby skills and in fact how you win games). You see, if you were in a position where you might be passed the ball, you were also in a position where you might then drop the ball, or make some other handling error, like knock the ball on (giving possession to the other side). If you didn't make those mistakes, the logic ran, then you couldn't be accused of messing things up. This way, you kept your place.

You never put your team in contention, but who cares about the team?

Will Carling is open about the fact that when he got his captaincy at 22 it was a last roll of the dice for the team management. They had nowhere else to go and so this young man found himself in charge of much more experienced players and expected to lead them to new heights. All amidst the glare of public attention and a management that needed him to succeed in leading his 21-strong squad into a new way of thinking and playing.

It's hard to create excellence and team vision when your culture is one founded on fear of any level of failure and an attitude to risk that makes any change impossible to contemplate. In creating that type of thinking and attitude, you are, at best, just achieving stasis and you will smother any possible creativity or progress. You can all exist in a self-congratulatory glow of mutual admiration, but the next onward push is probably beyond you. After all, what might happen if you tinker with the system? You might all be found wanting and that must never happen…

F.A.I.L.: First Attempt In Learning

Embracing failure is a very difficult concept and indeed a very harsh reality. No one ever won prizes for failing, only for winning, being the best and beating the competition. And yet making mistakes can be one of the healthiest events to happen to you.

In order to create an environment where we are free to pass the ball, we need to start by acknowledging that, as a team, we aren't achieving all that we could do, given our talents and experience. We should start by asking the question of our teams about what it is that we need to change in order to improve our output. In this way, we aren't assigning blame, or looking for an excuse; we are aiming to get the individuals who experience the day-to-day rhythms of the processes and workplace to sit back and analyze those systems and to suggest their own solutions. They own the answer and so they are invested in making it work. It is a collective effort and so there can be no individual blame. Everyone, in a manner of speaking, is safe in their place in the team. We free them up to play the game, in a different way that they are part of devising. However, we need to think about how we do handle any mistakes or failure, should that happen.

The essential element is that we approach it with both fairness and honesty. Honesty in that we acknowledge the problem and the situation and circumstances of it happening, and fairness in the way that we deal with the consequences. When there is a problem or mistake, we need to acknowledge it openly – after all, if you cover up small mistakes, what else might you be hiding? You run the risk of building your culture on suspicion and the encouragement of duality, perhaps a perception that there is one rule for some people and another for the rest of them. That honesty underpins the application of fairness.

Fairness is one of the most fundamental elements of a great culture. If you know in your heart that where you work operates with no bias or favouritism, you will be more willing to share your successes and failures. We can all recall examples of workplaces where there is a great amount of chest beating about meritocracy, the rewards that hard work and talent can bring and a celebration of an open culture. And yet the people at the top all look the same, the pipeline of senior management looks like the team at the top and it's all just words. You know you won't get promoted unless you play golf/suck up to senior management at every opportunity/have a skill set that replicates the career path of the CEO/COO.

Committing to change is a very frightening concept and is sometimes forced on workplaces when they have run out of road. The background of uncertainty adds to the pressure in the teams and colleagues come into work each day unsure whether it will be their last. Apprehension, or even out-and-out fear, is no foundation to changing or admitting your failures. If there is already a habit of attributing blame, heightened concerns about whether your job will or even can exist in a new set-up ensures a complicit silence. Or everyone can blame the last person who left, who can't be damaged now. It can be astonishing to discover the level of influence some departed employees have had, creating disruption and problems in divisions where they were only in marginal contact.

The cliff edge

Impending cliff edges do at least focus the teams on the task at hand. One of the most difficult times to deliver change can be when there is a sense that everything is just fine, there are no alarm bells ringing and everyone is cruising along, knowing what every day will bring. Moving people on from a comfortable place can be very challenging. This situation can often be one where a new initiative just withers away, rather than being rejected outright. If there is no clear objective or benefit in a fresh approach, the reflexive approach from many people is to question the reasons behind the change and to question the motivation or thinking behind it. Suspicion, double-think and a gradual smothering can all follow.

One of the best paths for approaching this type of change is to gently feed ideas into the system, rather than announcing some grand new plan. A small meeting of colleagues rather than a big announcement can make people feel part of the change – they can work together for a new initiative, rather than mutely acknowledging and then ignoring it. A personal note from a senior person can be highly effective in encouraging the team to keep faith with changes, to thank them for their work and in some circumstances, to address any problems or mistakes that might have happened and which people may be worried about. Holding a note in your hand that is solid proof that another person is aware of your situation, understands where you are at and what is needed can be reassuring, relatable and just the little element that creates momentum and belief.

Change will inevitably involve the admission that you might fail or make mistakes. Learning from those mistakes and moving on can be a useful lesson and great teams recover and refresh. The teams that do this the most effectively are the ones where there is a genuine level of emotional support for each other.

Support

Let's be clear about what we mean by emotional support. Most people don't usually identify with the effusive statements of how much you love your colleagues. You are lucky if you do, but as most workplaces are a random selection of people sharing a geography and a structure, it's highly unusual to find it piled high with your lifelong soulmates. There will be people you really like and others who you don't like quite so much. Interestingly, we do spend more of our time during the week with people we didn't actively choose to spend that time with, so you need to be mindful of that (they didn't choose you either, so be kind).

Emotional support can be as simple as the active practice of kindness. Someone didn't recognize how you had put in extra effort on a tricky issue? It may be that they were so caught up, they forgot. If they don't acknowledge you regularly, raise it with kindness.

Supporting colleagues is as simple as realizing that there are rhythms and issues in their lives that they might not want to openly discuss, but which you can see are affecting them. Offer a cup of tea, a listening ear or pick up a sandwich for them when they are working flat out and can't break for lunch. Say that you are happy to help in any way you can. Keep saying that.

Consider the impact of your actions, too. Putting in a meeting at 5 p.m. might work for your diary but how does it affect others who might have caring duties/an evening class/a long commute? The busyness of people's lives can affect their ability to take care of themselves and to achieve their potential. One-off deadlines might not have a long-term effect but regularly emailing after 10 p.m. (because you're on a bit of a mission to address an issue and it works for you) creates a tension for people who don't want to respond before they have even eaten their breakfast.

Emotional support allows people to fully be themselves and to be open. Open to talk and to innovate and to change. Who wouldn't want that?

Strategies for Belonging

IF YOU DON'T GET PASSED THE BALL, YOU CAN'T DROP THE BALL

Start by asking the question of everyone in the team about what it is that might need to change in order to improve the overall output so that everyone owns the issues and then comes up with solutions together. Let the unspoken fears be aired and create a reassuring climate where people can be bold enough to create change together.

The England football team until recently seemed according to most pundits to suffer from the same concerns. Players looked reluctant to be passed the ball, reluctant to take a penalty. The risk of making a fool of yourself and being rubbished by the tabloids was far greater than the chance of heroism from scoring. Only when Gareth Southgate took over as manager did the tide seem to turn and England's performance in tournaments become less laughable. Southgate of course had himself famously missed a vital penalty in the Euro '96 semi-final. So, he'd been through the worst of it himself and we'll see in Chapter 6 the power of empathy. There's another way though, exemplified by Barcelona.

There's always someone to pass the ball back to

Is the footballer Xavi the best midfielder of all time? The Barcelona team that he played for during most of his career has been called the best team of all time. And Xavi was core to its success. Commentator Duncan White described his performance in the *Telegraph* during the 2010 World Cup, playing for his country – Spain – like this: 'Xavi is the beating heart of this Spanish team, the man dictating the tiki-taka pulse of pass after pass. He may be just 5ft 7in with a curiously hunched gait but no player more influences the way his whole team plays. He doesn't score, doesn't really tackle: he just passes and passes with a precision and wit unmatched by any of his peers.'

Note the reference to his height. When Xavi started his career, he would have struggled to get into the team at all at most clubs. They would have rejected him simply for being too short. Then in most teams he would never have been played in the midfield position, reserved usually for the big and strong. Xavi brought something unique to his team: an extraordinary ability to be there for the other players.

Describing his role in the game in one of the humblest utterances from a world-class footballer, Xavi said it was simply: 'Receive, pass, offer':

- Receive the ball.
- Pass the ball to a teammate.
- Get yourself into a position where that teammate can pass the ball back to you.

Let's put aside the brilliance of being able to describe everything that you do in three simple words. Let's focus instead on what that means for every other member of his team. Xavi's role here is not focused on scoring goals. It's not focused on tackling the competition, nor specifically on defence. Nor is it about him looking good. It's entirely to be at the service of his team members. Truly if you played for Barcelona at its peak, there was always someone to pass the ball back to, so you didn't run the risk of being the idiot that let go of possession to the striker from the other team who might score the winning goal.

Xavi was entirely focused in fact on the whole team's success and on making everyone else's job easier for them to carry out.

In an environment at work where people are largely given individual KPIs to succeed in to get the next pay rise or promotion, the chances of having a Xavi naturally appear are low. What if instead you create a culture of Belonging, where the whole success of the business is more important than individual stardom or each person crushing their own KPIs? If you can galvanize the culture in this way, the chances of success over the competition are much greater.

Contrast Xavi's work ethic with that of many professional golfers. When golf goes wrong, often they blame the club, the wind, the caddy or even the noise from the crowd.

Just consider the comments golfer Jordan Spieth was overheard making to his caddie, Michael Greller, during the opening round of the US Open in 2019. After two bad shots at the eighth hole, Spieth commented audibly: 'Two perfect shots, Michael, you got me in the water on one and over the green on the other.'

You got me in the water…? Who is wielding the club and taking the shots here? Golf is a solo game. Running a twenty-first-century business is not.

Former Barcelona president Joan Laporta said about the club: 'Football is all about the collective. Solidarity is even more important at Barcelona than anywhere else.'

Your business too could benefit from deliberate solidarity.

Psychological safety

In business, you need to create an atmosphere of psychological safety. This needs to be the priority of all of the leaders and managers of the business at every level. And if this were written into people's personal KPIs as soon as they became managers, you'd get a very different culture in the office.

There are some easy ways of signalling your loyalty and passion for a football team. Of creating that sense of Belonging. With a football team, everyone wears the same kit, of course – Belonging is literally signalled. When Jose Mourinho took the job as manager of London club Tottenham Hotspur in 2019, at a moment when many fans were unsure of his loyalties, he announced that he would even be wearing the team's pyjamas.

Without the option of physical signalling, a key question for every forward-looking business culture is how to make sure that everyone feels the sense of Belonging that leads to success. Mission statements and values written on the walls disappear into insignificance in the face of unconscious signalling. It's crucial everyone in the team really feels just that – part of the team – however differently they might show up.

James is a director of a worldwide team in a manufacturing business. He talks about going on a team bonding awayday a few years ago. There was a task that involved a great deal of running around – a bit like an *Apprentice* scavenger hunt. He was given a team to run that included lots of bouncy outgoing people and one older woman, very introverted and not very able physically. James says that he could immediately tell that she felt threatened by the whole afternoon, even though its purpose was to bond people together: 'I couldn't bear this, that the team bonding exercise was actually making her feel excluded. She was upset that she might not be helping us win, but she really wasn't physically up to most of it, not compared to the other people around (it was a very young team generally). The exercises included literally climbing through hoops and jumping on trampolines among other things. I took her aside, before she could properly get upset, and asked her to do whatever she felt comfortable doing. And nothing else. I suggested that she be the go-to person for the rest of the team when they needed advice or to check in with someone. And I could feel her relax immediately – there was an antidote to her anxiety.'

The team didn't win the task by any means, but they didn't score badly either. They achieved the top five out of 20 teams. And as far as James was concerned, the team were winners because they succeeded in ensuring everyone belonged. Remember, the actual objective was bonding, not winning a plastic trophy.

In a way, James set up his colleague for a mini version of the Xavi role: receive, pass, offer. It's not always your job to score the goals. Sometimes it's more useful if you can make your colleagues feel safe to take risks and be there for them, be a backstop, be the support they need. And he gave her a positive role when she had been feeling excluded. This didn't just mean something to her, it meant something to the whole team. No one wants to have to ignore a team member because they aren't bouncy enough.

James exhibited real empathy to every member of his team. And he managed things so that each could perform in their best possible role. Problems arrive at work when people think that they are being truly empathetic when actually they aren't. Imagining how *you* would feel if you were in someone else's shoes is not the same as imagining how they *are* feeling and acknowledging that this may be a completely different, even an opposite, emotion. This is real and useful empathy. The problem with superficial empathy is that it doesn't actually let you put yourself in their shoes. And you are not that other person.

So, if James had just thought about how he would have felt, as a more naturally outgoing team member, he would have imagined that his fellow team member couldn't wait to join in. Maybe he would have seen her diffidence as shyness and given her the most outgoing task to get her out of her shell. Which would have been guaranteed to make her shrink into it. Instead, he empathized with her, her relative physical slowness and her embarrassment about letting the team down. As a man in his early thirties, he instinctively put himself in the shoes of an unfit and inner-directed woman in her mid-fifties. This is rarer than it should be amongst leaders. A focus on psychological safety, a sense of Belonging and deploying valuable and diverse talent in the role that it can deliver most powerfully against is the key to running a successful team.

Sympathy and empathy

Just for clarification, let's talk about how sympathy is different from empathy. Do you have a cat? Pet cats like to bring their owners presents. The best way in which they can show their love for their owner is to bring them a present that they themselves would love to receive. This is usually a dead bird or a dead mouse. It is usually of course received with horror by the recipient. This sort of present is sympathy, not empathy. Sympathy without empathy might pass for leadership in the workplace, but in the end, it's like giving your colleagues or team members a dead mouse. And that is no recipe for psychological safety. The modern leader needs to ensure that empathy is valued as well as sympathy, and that creating a sense of Belonging is the first responsibility of every manager.

Strategies for Belonging

THERE'S ALWAYS SOMEONE TO PASS THE BALL BACK TO

Many cultures only reward the goal-scorers, the rock stars, the Elvis. Yet as the Barcelona team culture shows, if you can recognize and reward players like Xavi, who create a safe environment for everyone else, the whole team will benefit.

Creating a positive culture at work

The good news about this is that it is actually quite simple. It also relies on just a few people, even in a large organization, to make a difference. So long, that is, as they are supported unequivocally from the top of the organization and their efforts are magnified by positive reinforcement from internal comms teams and reflected by the HR posse.

Michelle remembers her first boss at a new job. She arrived as the very first woman associate director; there were no other women except in junior roles. Her boss Charlie sat her down in one of the first meetings they had: 'Well, Michelle, you're our first woman into a middle management role and it's important that we make you feel welcome.' This was nice, but he immediately continued with an instruction that made her feel anything but welcomed. His next comments set her up for what felt to her like cage fighting. Charlie continued: 'Your opposite number, Tim, is really, really good at what he does. He's one of the top performers in the organization. Your job is to beat him, to compete with him. To convince me and the other directors that you are better.'

Michelle had an immediate gut reaction and a very different point of view to this. She replied to Charlie: 'You're setting me up to compete with Tim. Why? Surely the competition is outside the organization? Surely I should help Tim, and together we can beat our competitors and grow the business?'

It's said that women are naturally more collaborative than men. Whether or not this is true, this was the first time that this system of internal collaboration had been suggested at this business. Sure, the men had got on with each other as colleagues, the banter was fluent, but the overriding culture was that you got on by doing each other down.

Michelle's speech resonated with Charlie. He repeated it to his senior colleagues and encouraged Michelle to work with Tim almost as a bit of an experiment. When the internal collaboration worked, as the business grew, it became the dominant culture for success.

Michelle's firm started as a small challenger company in an established sector. She came in with a different and more strategic outlook than the firm had experienced up until then. It proved a recipe for success and grew the business. But crucially, as the business grew, it continued to employ the practice of collaboration rather than internal competition. As time went on, the types of people at the business shifted. People who came there with the normal attitude that you got on by putting others around you down stopped succeeding at the company. Those who came there to help each other were promoted instead and there were a lot of promotions because there was a good deal of fast growth.

Michelle, now a senior director at the same, much-larger and market-leading, firm explains: 'When I interview candidates now, I try and explain to them how it works around here. I say everywhere, if you do some really good work, you get a gold star. A gold star which counts towards your next pay rise and promotion. Well here, if you do really good work, you get a gold star too. But if you help someone else do some really good work, you don't just get one gold star, you get 10. The candidate will sometimes look at me blankly. They'll ask: "But how do you know that I've helped someone else? How do I know that I will get that credit for helping?" When that happens, I know that this probably isn't the right person for our organization. That even if they are a huge talent, they won't thrive here because they are too anxious about being personally recognized. It's too much about them.'

The saying goes 'Success has many parents but failure is an orphan'. The only way that you can truly build collaboration into the culture, so that it is regarded as inappropriate to say, 'I did this' rather than, 'The team did this together' is if failure is owned by the leader of the business and successes are shared with everyone, the widest possible circle of contributors. When Michelle's company celebrate a success, they will thank not just those who participated in the bid, but also everyone who took up the slack that was created when the pitch team had to focus away from their day jobs. When Michelle's company face a failed bid, the common practice is for the most senior people involved to get together and analyze what went wrong, learn from it, but publicly to shoulder responsibility for the failure entirely. In this way there is psychological safety for everyone involved.

Very few businesses get everything right all the time in the long term. No one can place every bet in the right place. The cultures that thrive will be those where success belongs to everyone, not just the rock star performers, and failure only belongs to the top team, who must learn from the mistakes and course correct along the way without pointing the finger at more junior levels.

Happiness matters

Unsurprisingly, this makes for a happier culture in the workplace – and happiness at work matters.

Madhuleena Roy Chowdhury is a certified psychiatric counsellor and has collected together proof of the impact of happiness on the workforce including evidence from the University of Warwick, who in one of their studies revealed that happy workers are up to 12 per cent more productive than unhappy professionals. They are more likely to be the proud owner of good health, have smooth-flowing professional and personal relationships, and prove to be more beneficial for the organization as a whole. They will of course be more likely to cross static work-life boundaries to deliver more when the business needs them, too, and because they're less stressed, they're less likely to be off sick.

Chowdhury quotes the Danish term 'Arbejdsglæde', which means the happiness that we derive from 'doing' something. Essentially, job satisfaction, pleasure from productivity. She says: 'It is an emotion, a sense of well-being that comes when we feel good about the work we do, when we feel involved in the 'professional commitment'.

With 'Arbejdsglæde'...

- We enjoy doing the tasks assigned to us
- We feel right about the people we are working with
- We are happy with the financial benefits we get from the job

- We have the scope of improving our existing skills
- We feel respected and acknowledged at work

People usually say it is other people who make them happy. The social psychologist Jonathan Haidt suggests that this is because, deep down, we are mostly still pack animals. We want approval from the leaders of our communities. This is one reason why great management can make people happy: people want the recognition of the alpha. Our survival is no longer as dependent on it as it once was, but in the workplace, it can feel crucial to have your boss recognize and approve of you.

If you work at a company where your boss never appears except on their way to an important meeting (or golf course) without you and they do not notice what you do, then it can be very hard to be happy about your working day. We are like chimps in that respect – we want affirmation from the leader. There are bosses who use the technique of bestowing praise on and acknowledgement of team members as their main method of motivation. When they are not around, though, then what does that culture consist of? People sitting around waiting for the chief to notice them is not the most productive situation. There is also the problem that disagreement with the boss, which can be crucial to creativity and innovation, tends to be disapproved of in this kind of environment. If you are the one who does not properly fit in, who always gets passed over, then you are more likely to fade into the background.

Haidt, however, adds that we are also 'part-bee'. (We expand on this important point in the next chapter.)

Finding this happiness at work is not just up to the individual. Once again, it's where everyone can contribute, should they choose to do so to the happiness of each other. Every time you stand up for inclusion and Belonging in the workplace on behalf of other people, it makes the workplace a little bit happier for all.

Haidt explains that human beings are multi-layered: 'We were shaped by individual selection to be selfish creatures who struggle for resources, pleasure and prestige, and we were shaped by group selection to be hive creatures who long to lose ourselves in something larger. We are social creatures who need love and attachments, and we are industrious creatures with needs for effectance, able to enter a state of vital engagement with our work... just as plants need sun, water and good soil to thrive, people need love, work and a connection to something larger.'

Back to Michelle. By making a simple suggestion that the organization value collaboration over internal competition, she sowed the seed for the culture to change radically from an alpha male chimp-inspired internal battle, where only a very select few survive and thrive to a culture that mixed strong hive elements into its makeup. Where people sought to find out each other's strengths and weaknesses, not to destroy each other, as had been the case in the past, but to enhance one another. And all credit to her boss Charlie for listening to her challenge and endorsing the change.

This is a step we can all take at work. Create a culture of collaboration, not competition. Support each other's weaknesses instead of exploiting them. Celebrate the differences and ensure that the prevailing culture is one of daily micro-affirmations. It must come from the top, or it won't stick, but it can start with everyone who has the insight to model this better way.

Kate Rowlinson is the CEO at co-author Sue's media agency, MediaCom. Taking over the role just as the agency won a prize for being agency of the decade for the second time in succession, she is clear that she has great heritage to build upon. She believes that MediaCom's culture is based on the idea that you succeed on merit and on being a 'we' person rather than a 'me' person; in other words if you value collaboration and team effort over being the star of the show and trying to garner credit for yourself. Yet she knows that day-to-day, in a business as large as the one she has begun to run, which is over 1,250 people across the UK, there are still improvements to be made to the culture to ensure that the spirit of 'People first, better results' is lived daily.

She is introducing a new concept: the inclusion ally. People who are trained to make those difficult interventions and to speak up when there are cases of micro-aggressions and to encourage micro-affirmations too.

Rowlinson says: 'Whoever you are, you can build an amazing career here. We reward performance, good citizenship and great work. The idea of the inclusion ally is somebody who has a role and training to deal with the kind of situation where a comment is made or a gesture happens that makes people feel uncomfortable. The inclusion ally is the person who will step forward and call it out. We'll ask for volunteers, because this could be really tough. I think that many people aren't aware that they have caused offence, so alongside this we will build a campaign that builds awareness too.'

A culture of collaboration and an atmosphere where everyone feels safe and as though they belong. This is the new normal in business that everyone can help to create.

Strategies for Belonging

HOW TO CREATE A POSITIVE CULTURE AT WORK

Make a simple switch from a culture where people succeed by putting others down to one where success is based on how much you help others up.

Safety in arguing

Wouldn't it be joyful if, during every workplace experience, we were all in unanimous agreement and there were none of those tedious conflicts?

Our every suggestion was met with a resounding 'yes' from our colleagues and we didn't have to deal with that really annoying man in compliance?

Sadly, of course, your authors must bring you crashing back to reality and the truth about working with other people. You are, at some point, going to have to deal with a divergence of views and perhaps ways of operating. Your treasured beliefs will be challenged and sometimes your motives and even right to object will be questioned. How you deal with this is the difference between corporate harmony or the existence of a long-running resentment/outright hostility and sabotage.

Avoiding conflict might feel like the easiest path to follow but this is not the answer and will lead to longer-term issues. You may feel that you have the moral high ground in refusing to participate in a playground fight, but in reality, you run the risk of not becoming an effective leader. Putting your head in the sand and hoping it all just blows over might feel like the more mature option, but conflict rarely resolves itself and what may start out as a spat could turn into a full-blown problem if you cannot deal with it thoroughly and so move on.

The reasons for conflict are as varied as the manifestations of arguments themselves. Conflict can start from holding opposing views on a situation, from the notion that people are in competition with each other in the team or just someone turning up for work and having a bad day. You can sum up the root causes for conflict and argument in the simplest terms as being about either emotions or communication.

Emotions

Emotions are a driving force of our humanity and their ability to derail your workplace position is limitless. Feeling angry because your position isn't being listened to, the fact that a colleague's remarks appear to be a personal slight against you. Fear of losing face, the fact that you are tired and you just want to cry can all drive you into turning a niggle into a full-blown row.

Emotions are tricky and it's just best to acknowledge that. I can never fully know how you are feeling unless you tell me. You might not be comfortable in sharing the full story with me and so we stumble along, each interpreting actions and behaviours through own particular prism. This is once again where empathy must come into play for us to be comfortable with arguing. I might not agree with you, but I can understand where you're coming from and, more importantly, I know that it isn't about me, it's the way that you see it. As we have said earlier in this book, it's easy to mistake sympathy for empathy, but the two are different. Remember, I can feel sympathy for you but that might not include the emotional recognition that makes empathy so powerful in creating a fully functioning workplace.

Deploying cognitive empathy in an argument is a way of putting yourself in someone else's position without the accompanying impassioned engagement. This can be a rational and logical way of getting a different perspective and for taking some of the 'heat' out of the discussion. The process of exploring where their perspective has come from – whether it be previous experiences, a long-held view or just the familiar way of operating – takes the pressure out of the encounter. Asking someone what has led them to think in a particular way, if articulated in a manner designed to encourage rather than disparage, can help all parties to examine the why and wherefore of their position. In turn, you must be willing to explain and explore why you got to your particular view without bringing heated emotions into play.

Language plays a key part too, in that we can frame the dispute in a way that takes away any personal element to reduce the 'sting'. Saying, 'You always insist on having your own way' is confrontational. Turning that into, 'You have made me feel I can't make a contribution to the discussion' puts the onus on them to allow you to express your point of view. If things continue to escalate, you can take time out and review by exploring whether you need to resolve the conflict right now (hindsight is very helpful when we look back at an argument and can lead to a change in position from both sides towards a more mutual position).

Another good question that can be asked is what is the other person's biggest concern? It could be that it is loss of face or a worry about what the outcome might be for them. This can enable de-escalation of the situation as you are asking them to step back and distill the conflict into a simple articulation.

Balance

What we are trying to aim for is a balance between pure logic and emotional empathy. No one feels comfortable ground down by relentless logic (and it can make you feel very vulnerable if your emotional input is just ignored). However, the opposite extreme of emoting at a very personal level can be destabilizing too. While we advocate bringing your whole self into work to create an authentic version of the wonderful person we know you are – that's why you are reading a book about creating a more inclusive workplace – some situations are not the most appropriate for revealing your inner struggles and issues. If it's relevant then share it, but if it isn't, save your sharing for another day.

We should all go into work believing the best of our colleagues. Gently and honestly revealing your less appealing side as a way of 'winning' an argument may well reduce the chances of your workmates doing that for you. Conflict is a sign of a healthy culture, as long as the resolution and the recognition of that conflict is clear and thorough. The last thing any workplace needs is to have a long-running dispute about who was right in the endless meetings about a new personnel review process in 2018.

All parties need to acknowledge that the conflict took place. Pretending it never happened will never fool anyone and if anything, it prolongs the lifespan of the argument. It becomes a source of gossip, unresolved resentment (amongst all participants, even the 'winner') and can create a sense of management pitting people against each other.

To move things on, it can be wise to wait and then set aside time to explore where the conflict came from. Not in the sense of going over all the nuances of the disagreement again, but to reframe what was said and how to move forward from that point. By all means talk about what the views were, but consider getting another participant in to provide the summary. This clearly needs to be someone who is dispassionate and isn't seen by either side as a 'plant'. Then we would suggest getting people to listen – tricky, we know, as everyone loves to score points in meetings – there shouldn't be interruptions allowed while people articulate their views and perspectives.

Encourage the exploration of other options. One manager we spoke to said that sometimes, when resolving an issue between two views, he took an extreme position to try to encourage those in disagreement to unite against him. They then feel they have a mutual position and that creates a jumping-off point for working towards a solution that everyone can participate in. It might not be possible to create a true win-win, but giving time and space to exploring the argument (with the agreement and participation of those who argued) can flush out issues and develop a sense that everyone's views are welcome and that they are heard. It may be that the resolution is obvious, but we need to encourage meaningful participation and the creation of a true team, rather than individuals who just share a geographic location.

As much as we can, we should work towards the feeling that we are safe in disagreeing with our colleagues while recognizing that certain people find conflict very hard to handle. Your personality, upbringing and culture may predicate your colleague from being comfortable in raising disagreement. This can be explored one-to-one to try to find a way where everyone feels that they can express a view.

Of course, if you are a fan of radical candour, you'll be happy to embrace the nuances that this brings into your work life. Those who find this style a little confrontational will need an introduction into the way that you like to work and that although it might feel rather a robust way of negotiating interpersonal relations, you really do value what they have to say.

Strategies for Belonging

SAFETY IN ARGUING

Arguments are inevitable in the workplace. Resolving them positively is essential for inclusiveness and Belonging. Acknowledge that individuals from different backgrounds and cultures have a very different reaction to arguing. Openness and empathy are essential to work through any complex situation. We all have to be able to grow emotionally, and above all else help each other through the difficulties of disagreements.

Disagree and commit

Emotions can be very gendered when you analyze their role in the workplace. 'Cold-hearted' may be viewed as a great quality in a leader who is a man, with some perceiving this as being driven by an analytical mind, hard-wired to just facts and progress. In contrast, 'She's so emotional' is a common put-down of women, implying their only motivation are those silly feelings that she keeps on talking about.

When you are highly invested in your work and passionate about outcomes, strong emotions can easily come into play and they can be hard to handle. Someone offering a mild critique of your approach to a project becomes your nemesis: at every interaction, you look for ways to pay them back and to put them down. There is a famous line from American writer Gore Vidal: 'It is not enough to succeed, others must fail.' In fact, the writer W. Somerset Maugham, took this even further and said, 'I realize that for most of us, it is not enough to have personal success, one's best friend must also have failed.'

For best friend, read work colleague.

As we have stated earlier, we spend a lot of time in the workplace and it's easy to allow the day-to-day issues to assume an importance that they don't really have. The tension between behaving in a professional way and just wanting to let rip can be a daily concern. The issue that must be tackled, for every organization except those with a strict hierarchy, perhaps is how to allow people to express their true opinions and air their views and yet to move on speedily with a common purpose. In other words, to allow people to disagree with, but then ensure that they commit to the decided path forward.

There are various theories about where this disagree-and-commit concept comes from. Scott McNealy, co-founder of Sun Microsystems, used the phrase in the late 1980s: 'Agree and commit, disagree and commit, or get the hell out of the way'. In recent times it has been adopted by Jeff Bezos at Amazon as one of its leadership principles.

In the abstract, it sounds like a great idea. You can exchange your well-honed views and experiences with your colleagues and they in turn respond with their views and perspective: you clash, things get a bit heated, but then you reach the very best outcome, shake hands and go off to deliver corporate excellence.

'Hang on,' we can hear you saying, 'I didn't buy this book from the fiction or fantasy section, there's lots that can happen in my world that might make this tricky.' Of course, this is the case. One of the fundamental issues that affects many initiatives and ideas is the reluctance of those colleagues who didn't subscribe to the idea to deliver it. It may be annoying, but it is understandable.

If your resolution of disagreements assumes that any majority is a good enough measure of a commitment from the whole team, you could be storing up trouble. Yet it may be that exploring every nuance raised can feel like counting grains of sand and that it is obvious what the correct course of action is. But that isn't the best foundation for commitment and the subsequent delivery of the action. If time is short, if your lunch appointment is waiting, if this is your fourth meeting of the day (and it's only 11 a.m.), if the phrase 'Well, I think we're all agreed' comes to your lips even if everyone is not in agreement at all, then the desire to sweep everything up and just decide to do something, whatever it might be, can be strong.

Those meetings run the very real risk of not doing what they set out to do. After all, if you're the one who thinks the course of action your colleagues have strong-armed you into is wrong, why would you put more than a minimum amount of effort into delivering it? You weren't convinced that everyone had explored every possible plan and it's all a massive waste of time as it won't work. If you are a thoughtful and considered introvert, in a meeting where your more extrovert and gung-ho colleagues are determined to do the exact opposite of your view of the optimal decision, it can be hard to raise your point. How many times have we heard of situations where a company embarked on a project that ended up going very wrong only to discover that people had doubts but no one wanted to listen to the opposing view? If a disgruntled participant isn't joining in the collective effort, businesses run the risk of missing key deadlines and losing momentum.

How to handle dissent

The optimum way of handling dissent is to encourage questioning in the meeting where you decide on your course of action (unless of course you have the immediate support of 100 per cent of the participants, but more on that later). By questioning, we mean a strong line of enquiry that explores every why and wherefore of the options open to you. Get people to do the due diligence on your various ideas. Explore the possible downsides. Even if those downsides might seem to be highly unlikely, you are also preparing your teams for those unexpected eventualities. Knowing that you had discussed the possibility of certain scenarios happening can help to avoid the frozen brain syndrome that can hit teams – where the scene around you is so unexpected that you simply can't think of what to do and how to handle the situation. If somewhere in your collective memory you know that this might happen, and you acknowledge it, this can give teams the confidence to reappraise, regroup and move on. Some leaders are open about the fact that things going wrong has helped them and their teams; knowing your colleagues have the flexibility and depth of talent to absorb the stress, think of a new path and then execute it is really healthy and reduces the onus on the manager. By using your doubting colleagues to stress test any strategy or plan, workplaces can embrace a great way of stretching the idea as well as helping to avoid the dragging feet of a sceptical participant.

In contrast to this strategy of embracing challenges is the workplace culture where it is an unwritten rule to never question the ideas of your bosses. This can also smother the concept of disagree and commit. After all, no one disagrees, do they, in this environment – at least not openly.

This unquestioning path is a dangerous and deluded one. We don't know about your working environment but none of us has ever met any manager who knew everything there was to know about the businesses that we worked in. A good manager is not there to role micromanage every situation to the point of paralysis. And so much time is wasted in the insidious scenario where teams waste time attempting endlessly to second-guess what the boss might think or do and how to work around that, rather than deal with the situation in a manner that is the most appropriate and best for all the parties involved.

Your authors have experience of having worked in places where the most senior person in the room has dominated proceedings to such a degree that instead of debating possible courses of action and their upsides and downsides, we spent 90 minutes listening to various augmentations and delivery options for a flawed plan. No one wanted to be the person who raised any doubts. We then spent months on trying to make this idea work, only to waste our efforts and expense on a doomed project. The team got the blame, of course, for not delivering. But in the moment, for everyone concerned it just felt a lot easier to take the collective blame rather than raise your hand in the initial meeting and bring the focus of the disapproval on to just you. There were no gains, we shared the pain.

Anyone, senior or within a peer group, who is part of a culture that truly embraces disagree and commit, needs to realize that you aren't always on the right side. Hanging on to your pet notions when they have been rigorously examined isn't courageous; it can be stubborn, and mule-headed. Leave your pet notions at the door and enjoy the cut and thrust of the debate or you run the risk of being excluded and ignored. You are preventing yourself from Belonging by not allowing yourself to be challenged, thinking a different way and seeing the point of view of your colleagues. In doing so, you can earn yourself the right to push back and explore your colleague's ideas rigorously. If done with the intent of improving the idea, rather than doing down your workmate, everyone can benefit.

Crack on!

We all just need to make sure that when a course of action is decided on, whether it's our idea or not, we step up and crack on. A healthy culture can handle tension and friction that a multiplicity of viewpoints can bring. If there is a clear value system and a management that can absorb, address and hone the friction, you should be able to allow everyone to have their own views heard and valued. While the idea of a 100 per cent happy and harmonious work culture is appealing, it may be that you are only seeing one side of the picture and ignoring some inconvenient truths. Or you are surrounded by nodding heads who aren't capable of, or feel unable to, offer an alternative view.

Committing to a course of action is just that: your commitment. It doesn't mean just going along with a notion because it is convenient; it is the embracing of a joint venture and of giving it your best.

Strategies for Belonging

DISAGREE AND COMMIT

It's vital to any Belonging culture that disagreements are aired, that any plan undergoes the stress test of a devil's advocate. Don't allow any discussion that involves second-guessing what the boss might think. Ask them, or move on. Create a clear line in the sand when objections have all been fully aired after which everyone must commit to the plan. But always have a Plan B and flexibility to react to what happens as the planned idea hits the real world.

Your boss is not infallible

What's taboo in your organization?

Taboos are an interesting concept. A taboo is something that isn't allowed by society. Some taboos are also against the law and many, such as talking about certain topics in some societies, are simply heavily frowned upon and often then simply unheard of in the office. For instance, talking about how much you earn is taboo in many organizations. It suits management to keep comparative salaries quiet in many businesses. And now this taboo has been challenged.

In November 2019, the Fawcett Society, a charity that campaigns for the rights of women, said that women should have the right to know what their male colleagues are being paid if they suspect pay discrimination. They add, perhaps more challengingly, that men can help by simply telling female colleagues what they earn. The fact remains talking about money in general is still taboo in British society. In fact, talking about money is a bigger taboo than sex, religion or politics, according to YouGov research commissioned by Lloyds Bank. Half (50 per cent) of UK adults believe that talking about personal money matters is taboo in everyday conversation; higher than sex (42 per cent), religion (26 per cent) or politics (14 per cent). This is one of those rather British taboos. Others are more universal and of course change over time.

In 1974, US First Lady Betty Ford spoke publicly about her breast cancer diagnosis and treatment. It now seems remarkable that, at the time of her action, public discussion of breast cancer in the United States was seen as off-limits. Four decades later, in some countries and particularly in the developing world, cultural barriers to women's health still exist. What's clear is that some taboos therefore clearly outlive their usefulness (if indeed, they were actually useful in the first place).

Arguing in public at work in most organizations is very taboo. Saying, 'With all due respect, I can't agree or I must say no' to your boss is almost unheard of in many companies, unless it's very private and carried out behind closed doors, one-to-one. This kind of thinking needs challenging and dismantling. Why shouldn't you disagree with your boss? Are they meant to be infallible? Unless you're working for the Pope, this is unlikely (and even then, but let's not go there...).

No one is *always* right

The idea that the person at the top of the hierarchy is always right is of course wrong. Yet somehow even though few bosses would claim to know everything, disagreeing with them isn't usually encouraged in front of other people. Of course, continued rows and aggression in the workplace (or elsewhere) is unacceptable and unproductive, but a situation of not daring to disagree is unhelpful and unhealthy.

Who benefits from insisting that the bosses shouldn't ever be challenged in public? A clear indication of great bosses is that they are open to challenge and more than able to take on new, even disruptive ideas, no matter who or where they come from. So perhaps it is only weaker bosses who benefit from this and that's not a healthy situation.

Not arguing with the boss stifles dialectic. Dialectic is when an argument builds from one theory, or thesis, when confronted with a different point of view or antithesis, to a synthesis or better idea based on rigorous debate and logic. If one of the participants is intimidated by the other, as you might imagine, it doesn't work as well. The answer to this is sometimes therefore to ensure that no one is ever challenged so that no one is afraid to speak up. This too backfires as there can be no open arguments. It is far better to create a culture where rigorous debate is not just tolerated but encouraged.

There's another effect too. If no one sees anyone speaking up to someone with power (i.e. to the person who writes their review, who has the potential to block their pay rise or promotion), then you'll get much more conformity of thinking and behaviour in the business. Without diversity of thought, there's no freedom for people truly to be themselves in all their diverse glory.

Paddy runs a department of about 150 people. He remarks that in the past he used to struggle to run departmental meetings and tell them what he thought all at the same time. He's a head of business strategy at a large third-sector institution: 'When I first took the role, it was the first time I had managed so many people. It didn't take me long to work out how I wanted the work to change. However, it took me months to finish the new ways of working presentation because I was paralyzed by insecurity.'

Paddy goes on to explain that his biggest fear was making a statement that was challenged by his team: 'In all honesty, my biggest nightmare was giving my carefully thought-through new process to the people that worked for me and having one of them put their hand up and say that they didn't agree with it.' For this reason, Paddy took at least six months to get round to unveiling a process that he had thought through in about six weeks. When he did unveil it, his direct reports and their teams took to it immediately. But his boss, the CEO of the company, had got very frustrated by the delay.

When they discussed it, Paddy explained how he felt, but his boss challenged him on his attitude: 'She said that she was worried that I was anxious about disagreement. She pointed out that if someone had said something then it would either have been not a good point and therefore easy to deal with, or it would have been a great point, one that despite all my analysis I hadn't considered, in which case that would be a fantastic build on my thinking. I know she's right, but I just couldn't set myself up for being challenged in that way – any questions almost felt like an attack.'

Paddy's reaction is all too common. He's taking questions and even critiques personally. Yet his reputation for quality thinking and deep analysis was established. By being fearful of questions, he was creating a situation amongst his team and his peers that actually is unhelpful in today's VUCA (see below) times.

VUCA

As mentioned earlier, VUCA – a term coined by the US military – stands for Volatile, Uncertain, Complex and Ambiguous. It applies to modern business and the world in general. It perhaps explains why binary thinking – either/or decision-making – seems so reassuring to people. Reassuring, but not helpful. Answers in leadership are often nuanced and great leaders are open to this. Allowing disagreement from those who work for you, and in particular, publicly embracing challenge from those who work for you and who look and sound different to you, is crucial for great leadership and creating a sense of Belonging to drive healthy argument and positive debate. No one in business usually finds VUCA times easy, at least outside of spy and *Star Wars* fiction. However, there are exercises in this book that can help everyone deliver a culture where disagreements are acceptable and that could have helped Paddy get his new policies out in a more agile and timely fashion.

Agile ways of working, in fact, are fuelled by the idea that no plan is perfect, nor does it survive getting into the ring with your opponent, or, as former world heavyweight champion Mike Tyson famously said: 'Everyone has a plan, till they get punched in the mouth.'

In their book, *Building the Agile Business through Digital Transformation*, Neil Perkin and Peter Abraham write: 'Just about every organization is finding that navigating the ever-changing environment in which they find themselves is like riding a surfboard on a choppy sea of uncertainty.

'Yet, for many, their approach to strategy has not changed. We need a new kind of strategy for a new world. A strategy that is far more adaptive than the fixed, inflexible forms of strategy that are still prevalent in many businesses.'

Ultimately, this comes down to people and how they are managed.

For businesses to be adaptive, they need to foster a culture of challenging the status quo in every part of their organization. This requires two fundamental behaviours to be in place:

1) Welcome challenge from everyone.
2) Replace fear, uncertainty and doubt with acceptance and validation.

If you want to navigate change, if you need bright ideas, you need a culture where people feel and trust that this is welcome.

Without internal challenge, organizations are going to move too slowly to survive. Yet if challenge is built up to be something that is a big deal, then most of the time people will be too fearful to raise an issue. You need to replace that sense of fear with an atmosphere of trust.

The burning platform

Human beings largely have two states of mind. At its simplest, we've evolved either to be frightened or curious. While necessity is the mother of invention, when we're panicking, we're not that curious about change: we're too busy battening down the hatches against the storm.

That paradox is well-described by Maria Konnikova, author and writer at *Scientific American*, who explains: 'Organizations, institutions and individual decision-makers often reject creative ideas even as they state openly that creativity is, to them, an important and sometimes even central goal.'

If you want change, if you need bright ideas, you need a culture where people feel and trust that this is welcome. Which isn't just a question of slogans or rhetoric.

As John Kotter and Dan Cohen, two experts on business transformation who have drawn up an 'eight-step process for leading change', argue: 'The core of the matter is always about changing the behaviour of people. Behaviour change happens in highly successful situations mostly by speaking to people's feelings.'

Often the idea is to create a 'burning platform' – an argument that forces everyone to change, and to change fast.

Authors Chip and Dan Heath warn that negative emotions have a 'narrowing effect on our thoughts… Most big problems we encounter are ambiguous and evolving… To solve these, we need to encourage open minds, creativity and hope.'

Psychologists write that only when all levels of your being are aligned and interlocking are you adaptable and open to new ideas. Your physical actions and emotional thoughts need to cohere and you need to feel part of your community. If you're running a work community and excluding some people, then you're failing to get the best out of everyone.

In the climate of disruption we're facing, you need to get the best out of everyone, especially those who are different from the norm. An army might do as it's told and obey orders, but the challenges of today's workplace require real commitment and the involvement of the whole team. An old-school, traditional environment of minor humiliations and locker-room banter means people are on edge, awaiting alpha approval or dismissal.

Keeping a low profile to avoid being the next recipient of exclusion or alienation from the pack is no way to encourage change and innovation. Diversity is good for business, as is challenging the status quo. With today's economic outlook, a business has to be agile and adaptable. Conformity and hierarchy slow this down and no business can afford to be late to transformation and new ideas.

A culture where people are confident enough to argue their point of view is essential for strong growth and a really happy team who can grow together to be the best. If arguing with the boss is taboo in your organization, then it's a taboo that should be overturned.

Strategies for Belonging

THE BOSS IS NOT INFALLIBLE

The management of the organization will create a winning culture if they allow the idea that they welcome ideas, challenges, criticism. No one wins if the boss is meant to be perfect.

Exercises and techniques for Chapter 5

We value and encourage diversity of thought, but we know in a company that doesn't have a Belonging culture, diversity of thought can be held back by:

- Bosses who don't want to encourage people to disagree with them.
- Individuals who – in a fear culture – are worried about disagreeing with anyone more senior.

In both cases, much of the problem arises from the fact that we tend to assume that disagreement will lead to conflict and that conflict will lead to an argument, or even a blazing row. Disagreement does not have to lead to a row – if you know how to disagree and can follow an emotionally intelligent path through any disagreement that occurs.

Disagree and Commit

First, the lead person in the meeting needs to explain that they want the meeting to disagree and commit (as we have seen above). This is an idea that's been keenly adopted by Jeff Bezos at Amazon. But in fact, its roots go all the way back to Cyrus the Great. Founder of the first Persian Empire in the sixth century BC, Cyrus the Great expressed disagree and commit like this: 'Diversity in counsel. Unity in command.'

The idea is simple, but extremely powerful. As the leader, you explain that there will be two distinct stages to the decision-making process. At the first stage, everyone is free to express their opinion, even if it disagrees completely with yours. In fact, you would welcome other opinions as they might help you to reach a better conclusion. However, in the second stage, when the decision is made, you expect everyone to get behind it – even those who may have argued against it in the previous stage – for the good of the company.

The process works because the core fear that stops people speaking up to express an opinion that is different from that of the boss is the fear that they will be seen as a problem or an obstacle, even an enemy. The boss will eventually just want to get rid of them. This basic (and entirely understandable) fear prevents true diversity of thought.

The disagree and commit effectively says: 'I'm happy for you to disagree with me. I welcome it – as I welcome all diversity of thought and opinion, and perhaps I will be swayed by your opinion. In return for this freedom of expression, we all commit to getting behind the decision when it's finally made.'

Because, as we've already noted, a Belonging culture is not some wonderful fairy-tale place; the simple reality is that the leader will usually make the final decision and it might not be what everyone in the meeting wants to happen. But because they have all agreed to commit to this decision, the leader will not see disagreement in the initial stage as the sign of a 'troublemaker' – anyone can disagree with the leader and still belong.

How to disagree

Surface your thoughts and feelings

If you know you are in disagreement with someone, then before you begin the discussion, take a moment to identify what you are thinking and feeling. You need to acknowledge thoughts like, 'I'm right', or even, 'Why can't this idiot get the point?' but then let them go. If you have feelings of anger and frustration, find them in your body, accept them,* and then you can enter the discussion without the feelings driving the discussion.

1) Understand that there are three kinds of disagreement
Disagreements usually centre round three areas:
(a) We are using different facts and evidence to reach our conclusions
(b) We are interpreting the facts and evidence that we have differently
(c) We actually fundamentally disagree

Work out which disagreement you are having. If it is (a) or (b), then the disagreement can usually be sorted out without a row. Share the facts and evidence you both have, discuss your different interpretations. This allows someone to say, 'I did think x, but in the light of these new facts, I agree with you that Y'. Taking this approach allows someone to change their mind without having 'lost the argument'. If it is (c), then following the next steps is more necessary.

* We'll show you how to do that in the exercises following Chapter 6, pp. 233–38.

2) Use non-inflammatory language

Use 'My opinion is…', 'I think that …', or 'I believe…'

Avoid using 'You…' as in 'You are wrong about this', 'You should…', 'You never…', 'You need to…'

Here again, you may need your emotional intelligence. If you start to feel angry or frustrated, you will want to use more aggressive language. Instead, breathe, feel the emotion in your body, mentally acknowledge it, then continue with the non-inflammatory approach.

3) Follow the Rogerian argument model

The psychologist Carl Rogers proposed a model for arguing your case, which allows both parties in a discussion lots of wiggle room to shift their views, compromise and come to agreement without anyone having to lose face:

- Highlight the problem that needs solving, stressing – if possible – that a solution will benefit both you and the other person involved.
- Outline the other person's position first and do so in enough detail that they will realize that you fully understand it. If you don't fully understand it, ask. Do this politely. Avoid saying, 'Why the hell would anyone think…'.
- Now, outline your position.
- Emphasize that the other person's view has merit. If possible, concede that there may well be many situations where the other person's view would be the right one.
- Point out how, in this specific instance, *they* will benefit from your solution.

4) Look beyond positions to interests

Throughout the process, try to find out what underlying interests lie behind the position that your opponent has taken up. It might be that their position doesn't really matter at all and that you can meet their real needs in other ways. For example:

Positions

Your partner wants to go out for dinner.

You want to stay in.

A row ensues.

Explore interests

You alternate cooking and clearing up. It's your partner's turn, they don't want to do it.

You want to stay in and watch the big game. You could time-shift it, but you're bound to hear the score.

You offer to take an extra turn cooking and clearing up, if you can eat before the match.

Both interests are met.

Exercise: Reducing conflict between silos

Almost every business these days is promising to put an end to silos between teams of people through restructures, or new processes. It's a nice idea, but it will never actually happen. You need generalists and systems thinkers, but you also need specialists – and as long as there are specialists, there will be silos. The trick is to make the silos work better together to reduce conflicts. Two of the best ways to do this are to create liaison officers and to rethink your metrics.

Appoint 'Liaison Officers'

In his book, *Team of Teams*, General Stanley McChrystal identified one of the major downsides to having an effective team. When a team is really good, it reaches 'the point at which everyone else sucks' – that is, the team gains much of its identity by the belief that it is better than all the other teams. This can happen quickly in the workplace – each department 'knowing' that it is doing a fantastic job but that it is constantly being let down by all the 'jerks' in the other departments.

Then when you have to pull a multi-disciplinary team together, or you need different departments to collaborate quickly and effectively, this antagonism surfaces and slows things down.

The military answer is 'liaison officers' – people whose job it is to forge better relationships with the other units. They don't have to know everyone in the whole organization, just one person in each unit. Assigning one person in each department with the job of getting to know at least one individual in each other department can significantly reduce conflict within a company. All that matters is someone in every department knows someone in every other department so that when co-operation is required, there is a 'friendly face' to approach, not 'those jerks'.

Re-think metrics

Much of the conflict between departments arises for the very simple reason that each has been given separate metrics and they are working to meet those metrics. If department A is trying to meet target A and department B is working to meet target B, a collaborative project between them that doesn't help either reach their targets will be low down on everyone's to-do list.

Where departments struggle to work well together, senior managers should consider rethinking their metrics to come up with a new shared target that they can work towards in harmony.

How to say 'no'

Ideally, we would always be able to say 'yes' to all our colleagues' requests, but that's never really going to happen. Sometimes we will have to say 'no'. One important way to reduce the overall levels of conflict in an organization is for everyone to know *how* to say 'no'.

If a colleague or your boss (or, for that matter, a client/customer/ stakeholder) makes a request that is simply impossible to fulfil (perhaps the timescale is completely unrealistic), merely saying 'no' isn't enough.

They need to know that they have been heard and understood. To minimize the negative fall-out (and subsequent conflict) from having to say 'no', follow this process as closely as you can:

- Acknowledge that you understand the request: clarify exactly what they are asking for and explain clearly why you are unable to respond to their demand in the way they would like.
- Show understanding and compassion for their issue/problem: make sure they know that you have fully understood how important this is for them and that you would like to be able to help them.
- Explore different ways to meet the request and make sure they know you are doing this.
- Ask 'why' questions to find out the underlying needs that lie behind their request. It's possible that you will be able to meet their underlying needs without fulfilling this request – or help them to do so.
- Explore alternative ways of meeting their need in a problem-solving way, looking for any way in which you can contribute or support them.

Disagree and Commit: Making it work for you

The technique of 'disagree and commit' is a powerful one when used well, but as we have outlined above, it can be very hard for an individual to truly get behind an idea they believe is wrong. If you leave a meeting thinking that maybe the wrong decision has been taken, the following thoughts may help you to commit to the idea. Any leader who wants to use 'disagree and commit' could usefully share these ideas at the end of a meeting when a decision has been taken (except number 6 – that's purely for individual reflection; from the boss's mouth it's a threat and should be avoided).

1) *You don't know everything*
   Even if you're the smartest person in the room, it is actually possible that you are wrong. You have been wrong before (no, really – you definitely have.)

2) *Nobody knows everything*

Business decisions are usually taken before all the facts are in, or in an unpredictable environment. No one can be sure how any strategy will play out.

3) *Things may have changed*

If you're thinking 'we've done this before – and it failed miserably', perhaps market conditions or consumer behaviour or the competitive set has changed so much that a different outcome will be possible this time.

4) *An average strategy delivered brilliantly tends to beat a brilliant strategy delivered averagely*

Even if this isn't the very best idea possible, if the team get behind it, it might work very well.

5) *You scratch their back…*

If you get behind this idea, you are more likely to find that others get behind your ideas in the future. In fact, you might have another idea right now that you need support for.

6) *So what if you are right?*

If, after all this, you are absolutely definitely 100 per cent convinced that you are right and everyone else on the team is wrong, and there is no way you can convince them of this, and they are making a huge mistake (and this isn't the first time this has happened), you may want to think about finding yourself a job where your wise words will be better appreciated!

One Voice: Noel

Noel runs his own business and is a senior figure in his industry, featuring as a counsellor on many significant advisory boards. He is absolutely a supporter in the most vocal terms of diversity, yet knows the current senior representation on his own board is not yet what it should be for historical reasons. He also worries about the pitfalls of using the wrong terminology, about positive discrimination backfiring, and making a mistake as a straight successful white man in a position of power.

'Diversity is a complex area because as we know, a shift needs to take place. And we know it's a long time coming. Yet we can't have positive discrimination. And we can't have quotas. Yet the reality is that historically, it's been a problem. I would say that the direction of travel in terms of the understanding of diversity and inclusion is a very good thing for lots of reasons. But there can be a danger that you end up almost flipping the other way and you are worried about saying the wrong thing.

'I could imagine if I was spending a lot of time in the States working in an American organization, I suspect I'd be worried about when to use certain language, because the reality is the terminology changes every couple of years. A friend is a corporate banker, who works in an American firm. He would say that it's obviously a critical issue, even more so than it is in the UK.

'What it all comes down to fundamentally is a belief in tolerance. So, we're privileged enough to grow up in a Western democratic society. We've grown up with diversity of thought. If you're intelligent, why would you ever discriminate? Is anybody better or worse on the basis of their race, sex, gender, whatever? You know, I'm not saying there's not an unconscious bias here and I appreciate that there sometimes is, but I would firmly say that I have never

discriminated. I've never said to myself, that person will not get employed or promoted, for anything other than merit.

'The diversity movement is right because we've got to redress the balance. There's no question about it. I think it's partly a legacy because many people who run the organizations have come from that kind of world where it has been white men running things. Obviously, there's a big shift that's taken place over the last 20 years. It's gradually changing, but it's slow, it's slow. It's very slow. No, there's no debate, that is the right thing to do. But I do also agree that you've got to be a little bit careful that you don't fundamentally then exclude people who are as strong or stronger, and from more traditional backgrounds.

'If I take my board, at the moment, it's not 50 per cent female, which it should be. But unless I fire some men or they all decide to leave, it does mean it's going to take a while. Of course, I am acutely aware of that and I think that good people, who are tolerant people, who are non-discriminatory people, genuinely believe that.

'I think that we have to work a lot harder to achieve diversity and inclusion, it's a constant re-education you go through. Whereas you know, 20 years ago in business, if all the board were white males, you wouldn't really think about it. Not that you would necessarily think it was right, but you just wouldn't think about it. What you do now is you think about it and that's all of course very good. But obviously, you know, changing the board takes longer than you'd hope it would.

'You cannot use quotas of course, but having said that, personally, I would be happy if my business from a gender perspective was, you know, disproportionately female for lots of reasons. There's a consultative relationship to our business and I think that kind of sensitivity and EQ [emotional quotient] is an advantage that women have over men, and that ability to be self-critical. Some industries, it is still a bit of a boys' club, you know, and the truth is, there is still that kind of sense of employing people from your school and your background. But I don't know what to do about the fact that, if you are a young white man, now in business, you might well think, what are my chances of getting on our board? Unfortunately, in a way, they've almost got to do what women have done historically: work even harder to ensure that their voice is heard. The table has rightly turned. The reality is, if somebody is vital and brilliant, and is genuinely delivering for lots of reasons, then nothing is going to stop them.

'There's a difference between knowing the right thing to do and being physically able to execute it for lots of reasons. And sometimes it takes time. So, I don't necessarily know if shaming is the right thing to do, which is a strategy, let's be honest, that people use sometimes. I think the key is, have you got the right attitude, the right empathy, the right understanding, the right tolerance? Do you believe that it's all about talent and meritocracy or not? Do you believe that?

'And things have changed. And that is good. It's a better world in many ways. A young man today is allowed to have that sense of empathy that probably my father would have said meant that he was very in touch with his feminine side! That's a good thing. They've just been brought up to be more natural. So, you know, I'm very hopeful, in a way, about the next generation generally.

'The elephant in the room, I actually think, is not really gender and ethnicity. I think it is social background. I would argue that that is probably where even more work needs to be done.'

CHAPTER SIX

The inner journey

'Remember me as the one who is awake.'

Buddha

There's a story that one day a priest came across the Buddha sitting under a tree and was astonished at how serene he was. The priest asked: 'Are you a god, sir?' The Buddha replied that he had simply revealed a new way of living in the world, free of egotism and want. He ended with the reply above.

Now, we're not suggesting that in order to have a thriving workplace it is essential for everyone to be free of all ego and need. Clearly, that would be nice, but practically, it is frankly unobtainable. Nor are we invoking 'woke' jargon. However, the more that you, as a reader of this book, focus on being aware of your fellow workers, on fully empathizing with their points of view with real understanding, while still remaining clear about your own standpoint, then the more of a sense of Belonging there will be – the more everyone will in fact belong.

'Do as you would be done by' is considered by some to be at the root of all major religions since ancient times. This golden rule is both beautifully simple and hard to deny. It is frequently similarly hard to live by in the workplace. Back to Buddha for why this is so: 'It is easy to see the faults of others, but difficult to see one's own faults. One shows the faults of others like chaff winnowed in the wind, but one conceals one's own faults as a cunning gambler conceals the dice.'

Enough of religious theory. There's a basic evolutionary reason for this. Brains evaluate everything in terms of potential threat or benefit, and they do so instantly, for without this instinct we wouldn't survive. As behavioural economists write, these instincts come before reasoning. We're making those snap judgements constantly all through the day.

Everyone is wrong, apart from me

It is a natural instinct to need to begin with the assumption that we are right. We live in a world where others will hold us accountable for what we do. Our society is based on co-operation. When nobody is answerable to anyone else then society falls apart, as the seventeenth-century philosopher Thomas Hobbes pointed out. Living through the civil wars in England, he wrote of the social contract of government and pointed out that without this, the human condition was: 'solitary, poor, nasty, brutish, and short'. Human beings are very good at holding *others* accountable for their actions for the social good. We are also, instinctively, very good at having to survive and navigate a world where other people hold us accountable. Our instinct is to act like Shaggy with his best-selling pop song: 'It Wasn't Me'.

Frequently, we assume that people who seem similar to ourselves are more likely to be right too. Where does reason and logic come into play? Mainly, we initially use it to back up and justify our instincts. Essentially, our instinct is to behave like plausible politicians maintaining the position of being right and proper at all costs. In the era of 'Fake news' and social media identities this tendency may be proved to have been magnified further than at any other time in history.

Nobody is perfect

Of course, nobody lives up to their desired image or persona. Nobody is perfect. Most places of work were built on the notion of continuous excellence and perfection. If you don't measure up at all times, there are consequences professionally. After all, most have been designed with an alpha-male minority in mind. This is unrealistic, and it is excluding, and it is making people sick. In the twenty-first century the workplace needs to adapt. The benefits of a more whole human workplace are well-documented in terms of retention of talent and better decision-making. We need to move beyond an obsession with things being perfect. Does this strike you as irresponsible? It's time to get real. If everything is perfect, then nothing can change and without change, businesses get disrupted and fail. We've seen this in the first two decades of this century; the pace will become faster. The coronavirus pandemic of 2020 forced business leaders and governments to think not only of short-term profits and key performance indicators but in terms of humanity, of society and the wellbeing of their employees. Optimistically, some hope that this will mark a step-change in business. But history proves that when society recovers, businesses quickly resume their focus on the pursuit of profit.

Therefore, we need to wake up in order to think and behave beyond our innate, understandable and lazy instincts. Beyond instinctive patterns of behaviour and beyond traditional allegiance to old masculine and feminine stereotypes. We have to go on an inner journey. This might take extra concentration. The rewards will be plentiful, both in terms of your career, your business success and your personal life.

Happiness at work

People usually say it is other people who make them happy at work. But remember though, as we said in the last chapter, the social psychologist

Jonathan Haidt suggests this is because, deep down, we are still pack animals. We want approval from the leaders of our communities. This is one reason why great management can make people happy: people want the recognition of the alpha. Our survival is no longer as dependent on it as it once was, but in the workplace it can feel crucial to have your boss recognize and approve of you.

As we explained earlier, though, that alpha leader recognition, so crucial to pack animals, is not a substitute for a good culture. Apart from anything else it tends to collapse when the alpha is not present. Relying on this as a way of keeping people happy in their jobs is not the answer.

Haidt also says, we are 'part-bee'. This is crucial to our happiness too. Bees work for a common cause, not just for individual recognition. They don't compete with each other within the hive. The hive works together to make honey and ensure the survival of the next generation. A hive-like workplace is one where teams work together for a common goal. There is less focus on an alpha leader recognizing an individual and more on celebrating everyone in the team.

Haidt goes on: 'We've been told for years now that human beings are fundamentally selfish. We're assaulted by reality TV programmes showing people at their worst…. It's not true. We may spend most of our working hours advancing our own interests, but we all have the capacity to transcend self-interest and become part of a whole.'

The beauty of difference

What do we need to do? We must all daily attempt to wake up to the beauty of difference. We must attempt to have the humbleness to acknowledge that it is possible that we have been wrong; the energy to debate a point of view on the basis of equality of opinion, no matter what the hierarchy status of the people arguing; the capacity to acknowledge different points of view, from people from very different backgrounds and cultural experiences. These are the attributes of champions of Belonging in the workplace. This is leadership and in a healthy workplace there are leaders of a kind in every seat.

You don't get to have no hands

In an editorial for the leaders of the advertising industry, global editor-in-chief of *Campaign* magazine Claire Beale wrote in 2020: 'We need strong leaders, brave decision-makers as never before, not just to steer a survival course of the industry but for the world around us too… you have the potential to corral power and love, to strap them together and wield them in the name of a better future… to drive positive change.'

In her commencement address at Oberlin College in 2015, First Lady Michelle Obama told the graduates to make use of their privilege, saying: 'Graduates, with a degree from this amazing school, and all the status and connections that degree confers, you don't get to have no hands. No, you don't get to be precious or cautious or cynical. No, not when the earth is warming and the oceans are rising. You don't get to be cynical. Not when too many young people still languish in communities ripped apart by violence and despair. Not when women still make less than men for the same work. Not when millions of girls across the globe never set foot inside a school. No, not when many young people just like you – the men and women we honour this Memorial Day – have sacrificed their lives for your freedom to make your voice heard. You don't get to have no hands.'

If you have any privilege, and most of the people that we have interviewed for this book have acknowledged privilege of some kind, then we believe with Obama that you can use that platform to make the workplace a better place for others. Can and indeed should. And we know that if you have read this far that you can and you will.

In this chapter we will examine how emotional intelligence, active mindfulness and sincere empathy can shift the workplace culture into one where the benefits of diversity are truly realized. The exercises that follow will show how we can transform ourselves and deliver Belonging for everyone.

Fix your private life

The delightful thought that you should bring your whole self to work is one that is very prevalent in today's workplace. No more hiding of any issues or concerns, just pure unadulterated you. What a refreshing change from old-fashioned workplaces, where you worked from behind a mask of being just the same as everyone else and conformity was the name of the game.

So here we are, open and sharing with our colleagues, every aspect of ourselves and our lives out there. This can be really invigorating and fun for some people. For others, who may be more introverted, it can be an unsettling experience. Why would you want to do this? It's private and personal and frankly, has nothing to do with the job that I am doing. I am here to do my job to the best of my ability, not join some commune of oversharing strangers. Is this a workplace or a cult?

So how do we approach the workplace and construct it so that it allows you to be your true self, but without what can feel like pressure to take part in a daytime confession show? What steps do we take to allow honesty but without oversharing and a sense of discomfort? How do we ensure that those who aren't as comfortable with sharing aren't made to feel as if they are being cold or stand-offish? To ensure that we are supportive and not prurient?

Work and home are different spaces

Initially, it starts with us, as people who work within the organization. More specifically, it begins with the acknowledgement that work and home are different spaces; we operate between the two (and we usually spend more of our time working), which can skew our perspective. Working parents talk about the fact that they live with the constant split between feeling bad that they aren't there for their children all the time and at the same time they feel that they aren't perceived to be fully committed to and available for work. In working flexibly, or compressed hours, they wrestle with the sense that they aren't in the key meetings they need to be in or that they are not seen in the same light as colleagues who don't have family commitments. Workplaces that address any tensions that can exist between parents and non-parents do so by offering flexibility where it's needed on an individual basis. It can be for any caring responsibility for elderly parents or for a myriad of other reasons that require a blend of work and home.

Take control of your blend

Blend is the key word here. Your blend changes over time and with the differing demands that occur in your life. Sometimes the 50/50 mix you aspire to may actually be 70 per cent work and 30 per cent home – to maintain your personal equilibrium, you will then need to ensure that you get a 70 per cent home and 30 per cent work at another time, so that you aren't torn between a continual either/or. You can have both, but you need to fix it. You will have to take control and be mindful of the blend and how it's working for you. Also, we all need to be mindful of other colleagues' perspectives. One of us recently issued five meeting refusals to an invitation because the organizer just picked a time and issued the invitation. It was turned down with the reason that it clashed with a funeral we were attending. The next invitation was for 30 minutes after the original suggested time. And this pattern continued – it felt like a blank disregard for valid reasons not to go to the meeting or call in remotely. I had to get a colleague to intervene and point out the issue. The point is to be *mindful* of other people's time and pressures – the way that you would want your colleagues to be mindful of your time and pressures.

Be match fit

While we are contemplating our perspective on work, we need to be rigorous with ourselves too. As much as we can, we should endeavour to be 'match fit' for work. By this, we don't mean that you embark on a regime entirely centred on giving your all to your company (as that isn't healthy in the long term). What we are trying to unearth is, what is your racket? What are the reasons you give to stop you doing things? What narrative has gained traction for you as your reason to not fully belong?

One of the people we interviewed talked about how they have frequently heard the line: 'I am not able to do that, it's just the way that I am'. In one case it was from a person who said he couldn't be expected to network with colleagues because it was just not comfortable for him. While this might be true and we all know that introverts do find networking hard, by giving yourself an achievable target it can be done. Sue is an introvert and conquers this by talking to two new people at any networking event until she has properly established a bond with them and then she has hit her target and can go home. It's not too onerous and with practice, it gets easier. The excuse of 'I can't, it's just the way I am' was a narrative designed to defend themselves and the way they chose to operate. It was a very limiting behaviour in this case as building alliances across the company was important. He refused all offers of help to get him closer to other team members and ultimately, his tool of self-defence and protection just held him back.

Minimize self-limiting narratives

When we listen to our inner voices, we can give undue prominence to the self-limiting narratives. We continually hear the lines: 'I am bad at maths'; 'I don't have anything interesting to say in meetings'; 'I can't be expected to do that, it's not in my KPIs'; 'Someone else would be so much better at doing that'. As we listen to these voices, they become what we believe and we act accordingly.

To fix this, you need to get these voices to quieten down or even shut up for ever. A way of doing this is to substitute your inner critic with the advice that you would give a close friend if they were saying what your inner voice repeats to you, day in and day out. If you said that you didn't have anything interesting to say in meetings, they would encourage you to participate by asking questions that build on any points that others might be making. When you do this with a friend and tell them that they have come up with an interesting solution and ask them how they came to it, this achieves two things: your colleague now sees you as a supporter, and you have also seen their transformation and learnt about how their thought process has played out. This now means that you might use that process to discover your own interesting solutions to talk about in meetings when you are a bit more comfortable with speaking up. You can also ask your colleague to give you support when you choose to explore speaking up.

A unique lens: it's not a competition

The other challenge in fixing your private life is to realize that everyone views life through their own, unique, lens. Your colleagues' challenges are not the same as yours. Those issues may feel less important than yours, but you don't know how big and dominant they seem to them. This is where you need to exercise a lot of empathy and also be aware that you aren't in some game-show challenge contest. Try to avoid comparing one person's situation to another's in an attempt to make them gain what you feel is a sense of perspective. If you do that, you still have your own lens on life fully in play. Instead, put your view aside and try to look through the lens of the other person. How you support and interact with them after seeing the world through their eyes then dictates how you build on that knowledge. If you feel that you don't know how to do that, just ask. 'Would it help if...' is an open question that encourages a response. 'God, your life is a mess, let me tell you how many ways I can help out. When do I start?' is far less inviting. This isn't your life and it's not your lens – be kind.

Tending to feelings is part of your job

Changing the narrative is just part of the picture as it changes how you make people (and yourself) feel. They forget the words, but they remember the feelings you created. Looking after your feelings may feel like a strange pursuit – after all, they are your feelings and they just happen, don't they? Tending to them might appear to be a strange use of your time and completely unrelated to your workplace but it can play a huge role. Think back to when colleagues seemed to be distracted or removed from what was going on. This might not be entirely due to the rather tedious sequence of events that are currently typifying your company (the trinity of writing up performance reviews, budget-setting and a series of ill-judged brainstorms strike me as the worst confluence of events, but that's just me, we are sure you can imagine your own).

Asking someone how they are might elicit a glib response but asking how they are feeling may be a richer seam of discovering exactly what is going on. Try it on yourself too. How are you feeling? Are you nervous at the moment? Why is that? If you are anxious about a meeting, run through all the times that you have been in that meeting before and how well you have handled it. Or, if it's a new meeting, give yourself a chance to review how you can handle it, and if you are concerned about any agenda points, get a colleague to buddy up with you to offer support if you need it. Have a plan to use those feelings as a fuel to get you to where you want to be, rather than allowing them to limit you.

Some nerves are good as it means you will be attentive and invested in what is going on, rather than running the risk of appearing to be dialling in your participation. Review and recalibrate how you see your feelings and how you work with them, rather than letting them work you. You may not be able to control them, but you can choose how you react and respond.

By recognizing your humanity, in all its strengths and weaknesses, you are opening yourself up to make stronger connections beyond those things that other people see. Fixing your private life means addressing those facets that prevent you being fully able to be part of a culture and belief in a sense of Belonging, and to support and enjoy the humanity and quirks of the colleagues you work alongside. You also allow them to enjoy your whole self and the benefits that this can bring.

Strategies for Belonging

FIX YOUR PRIVATE LIFE

It's crucial that you take care of yourself in every sense at work. You need to be match fit, and as with all modern top performers, this means your emotional and mental well-being as well as your physical health. If you look after yourself, you will be better able to tend to the feelings of others. This will help you spread the Belonging message in your workplace and it will help your career path too.

Using Method to create Belonging for all the team

Oscar-winning actor Robert De Niro is famous for his method acting. For his role as Vito Corleone in *The Godfather*, he spent three months living in Sicily learning the language and the way of life. For his role in *Raging Bull*, he gained 60 pounds to play the older Jake LaMotta and trained as a boxer with him for over 1,000 rounds as well as fighting in three professional bouts (and winning two of them). For the movie, *The Untouchables*, he tracked down Al Capone's actual tailors to make him an identical suit and insisted on wearing identical underwear even though it was never shown on screen. Perhaps most famously, he got a cab licence and worked for 15 hours a day for a month for the movie, *Taxi Driver*.

You don't need to win an Oscar in the office, but method techniques will help you put yourself in other people's shoes and make it much easier for you to champion others.

Sometimes we need a jolt truly to begin to imagine the position that people who aren't like us in the office are in. We heard from one man who shared with us his very shocking experience that led to a re-imagining of the office.

Diversity shock

At the top of his profession in media and entertainment in the US, Paulo found himself on the receiving end of a barrage of criticism after he made what seemed to him at the time a not-unreasonable comment about the importance of balance in terms of talent versus diversity. Paulo's comment was widely misunderstood. It came across to some people that he was saying that it might be easier to recruit for the latter rather than the former. After all, potential talent can be hard to judge or predict, especially perhaps in the creative sector whereas you can visibly see some forms of difference. In a public forum he stated that he was concerned about diversity being given more emphasis than specific talent.

To say this caused outrage is to understate the reaction he provoked. Paulo has told us that he actually meant that he thought there were too many people who were just engaging in a tick box exercise and looking for the 'woman in the room' or the 'ethnic minority' in the room, rather than really finding the people, from a range of backgrounds, who would add value.

He explains that he'd come out of a long meeting, where he'd had his phone switched off, to a torrent of social media reactions, most of which were negative, some even threatening. Paulo says that at this moment he learnt that his perspective on the workplace at that point was really very naïve. He woke up to recognizing an established capitalist system that he now thinks is very sophisticated in its design and that ensures that the white middle class will thrive at the expense of everyone else.

'Until this happened, my basic view of the world was I've succeeded against the odds and so can you. If you want it enough, you can do it whoever you are. I now know this to be absolutely untrue. That if my profile (as a straight white middle-class man) changes by one increment, the journey becomes harder. If I change it by two or three or four, it becomes impossible. Very, very quickly. So the way I view the world has just completely transformed.'

Change of mindset

Paulo goes on to say that his old mindset, which he still sees all around him, is very difficult to change. There needs to be an acknowledgement that the more power and privilege you hold, the more responsibility and accountability you hold, too. By undergoing the shock of the widespread reaction to his comments, Paulo underwent a strange and involuntary form of the method. He found himself suddenly on the wrong side of an argument that he hadn't even intended kicking off. By speaking up, he suddenly felt what it was like to have the white masculine privilege called out. Until then it had been invisible to him.

But it's not invisible to others, especially the few women in the roles of creative chief. One interviewee, Vicki Maguire, told us that at some stages of her career, she felt embattled: 'Every day, the battle comes out of the blue. Usually a battle against white masculine privilege.

When can I breathe out?' Logically, creative agencies should excel at diversity – after all, they're trying to reach a diverse range of consumers who might buy the brand advertised. But the twenty-first century has hit creative agency business models hard and she points out that when times are tough, as they are in most sectors, when the landscape shrinks, everyone reverts to old patterns of behaviour, forged in the past, even though this is exactly the opposite of the actions that managers should be taking in order to grow. Many businesses have had to fight for survival because of the global pandemic in 2020 and a growth mindset, and a Belonging culture, are even more crucial at these times.

A culture of outrage?

Of course, there are those who feel that the outrage culture has gone too far. Bill and Jake work in the media sector. They each run big teams and confide in us that in their view, what they call the 'outrage culture' has gone too far. As straight white men leaders, they're feeling that they are seen as bigots and blockers to change simply by being in their hard-earned roles. And in some sympathy with Paulo's experience, they believe that everything is made worse by social media. Social media, which can be virulent in its judgements, but which has also given the oppressed and silenced sectors of society a voice.

The way forward

There's a way through this. The way forward, particularly at times like this, is to endeavour to imagine fully other people's situations, as president and CEO of Western Union, Hikmet Ersek, advises: 'Top leaders should put themselves in other people's shoes and listen. If you listen to people, whether they are rich or poor, white or black, male or female, old or young, they make you grow, they keep you innovative, they keep you active.'

Dan Brooke, consultant and former CMO and board champion for diversity and inclusion at Channel 4, goes further. He advises that people need to begin to see each other as 'champions of diversity and inclusion'. He explains: 'It is everyone's special job to think hard about how you encourage everyone around you at work that the best kind of Belonging behaviour will be rewarded.'

It's actually always useful to ask yourself the question: When it comes to the people at work that you recommend, are they people who look or appear like you? If the answer is broadly yes, then you're probably not doing enough to encourage diversity and the solution will be to spend more time and energy on the method.

Using the method

What does this mean? It means listening to people who aren't like you. If your team likes to bond at the pub and this is the only way you hang out together, then you're excluding people who don't bond in this way. Maybe they don't drink, maybe they're introverts, maybe they have to get home for the childminder or to help other dependents who rely on them. Question why there's just one form of bonding. Work harder to find more ways to deliver this by asking the members of the team who don't participate.

Do you pride yourself on the cohesiveness of your team? It might mean that everyone is the same and difference is excluded. It might mean that to do well in the team, some people constantly have to code-switch, i.e. to pretend to be other than their real selves. The only way you'll find out is if you really examine what is going on, honestly and humbly. It might be that lots of you love to go skiing in winter. Nothing better than talking about the excitement of the black slopes and luxury of the resort. Except for those who can't afford it, or aren't physically able enough or simply hate snow. The great champion of Belonging will keep antenna focused on spotting those who lean back, those who are faking enthusiasm, and make it their responsibility to be truly welcoming of difference.

Method every way

It plays out in every way in truth. A team where women are the leaders must be inclusive of men and mindful of their perspective. A predominantly youthful team must allow older members to feel relevant. Can the university graduates respect and nurture the school leavers? Are the school leavers, who are proud of their 'university of life' qualifications, dismissive of the 'over-educated'? Is a team of southerners inclusive of people from the north? And in every case vice versa. It's so easy to go with the majority flow and let the status quo continue as it is. If this continues, those who are different in each team will continue to be crushed just a little every day and fail to thrive. What if, instead, we all set out now to be champions of inclusiveness, sensitive to each other's cultural references and different backgrounds? This will also make a huge difference to the mental well-being of the team.

Mental well-being

Penny James is CEO of Direct Line Group. In fact, she is the first ever woman to be CEO of the company. She tells us that every business is heading into a fast-moving and disruptive world and the cultures that bred success in the past are not those that will succeed in the future. She's sure that successful businesses will be built on trust and openness amongst their employees: 'The more we can invite people to trust us by telling us about themselves and what does and doesn't work for them, the more chance we have to succeed.'

Direct Line Group has worked hard to promote mental health and well-being and has found that this works well because it cuts across many other apparent divides, and frankly, if you have a culture where you encourage openness on this topic, you will have created a much freer and more supportive culture in many respects. Staff churn will be minimized, loyalty spikes and that increasingly important metric to many organizations of employees recommending working there to their friends goes up.

Walking in the shoes of others, and creating an environment where mental health and well-being are cared for, are two actions for everyone championing Belonging in the workplace.

Strategies for Belonging

METHOD

Don't just go with the flow and fit in with the status quo. Use the method technique from the world of acting to understand all the differences in your workplace and help to champion them. Great companies encourage people to add to the corporate playlist, not just replicate it.

Breaking free from parent-child transactions

Bringing our whole selves to work, as we said earlier, is, of course, a good thing. It means we can be free of many of the code-switching constraints that we have talked about earlier in the book. It means being free to be yourself, not a carbon copy of the senior management, no matter how difficult an act that is. However, behind this worthy idea lies another truth that might not be as helpful to a diverse and Belonging culture. This is that we are incapable of leaving our unconscious beliefs about others at home and out of the workplace, particularly if we don't take some time to recognize what they are.

In the business guide *The Loudest Duck: Moving Beyond Diversity While Embracing Differences*, Laura Liswood explains that many of our deepest beliefs come from early years and from our families. She suggests that we all need to 'tell grandmother to go home'. We all take our unconscious selves to the workplace, bringing beliefs, perceptions, understandings, misunderstandings and importantly, archetypes, or indeed stereotypes, of other people, based often on very deep-rooted, even ancient, understandings picked up from our parents and grandparents. Those people who, as children, we normally believed were the authority. Now, normally we go through a period of assessing those understandings when we are teenagers and young adults. And some of the beliefs we reject, even insist on doing the opposite of what our parents may have taught us. Other beliefs we may well simply accept, never challenge, not even notice.

Frequently, new parents will find themselves suddenly behaving as their own parents did. Even when they promised themselves that they would never do so. The phrase: 'Because I said so…' has an uncanny way of repeating itself from generation to generation of exasperated mums and dads. Or we will suddenly notice that we have acquired traits that we recognize in family members. A sigh when we're tired that reminds us of our mother or father. A characteristic whoop when we're excited or joyful that echoes a parent. Together with this sudden consciousness of a similarity of body language or behaviour, there are a whole load of unconscious habits and beliefs that we have picked up and may not be aware of at all. For example, there are stories that we loved as kids that have cultural relevance in our lives. Maybe with a part of ourselves we may all hope that the prince might turn up at any moment to slay the dragon (and so not deal with a furious client ourselves, but leave it to a rock-star boss). Or that a wicked witch has joined the meeting (when a senior woman expresses a contradictory point of view). It's crucial to be aware that this is going on, or we can't change.

One in three don't belong

Is this one reason why one in three people in the workplace don't feel as though they belong? Our original research (*see* Appendix, pp. 246–52 for more details) shows that over a third of the workforce in the UK and over a quarter in the US don't feel they belong. If you are in a meeting with two or three colleagues and you *do* feel a sense of Belonging, then one of the others will not share that feeling. It has to be you that does something about this, and understanding as much as possible what your heritage has taught you about difference is crucial to this.

Getting to grips with the role playing at work

An understanding of T.A. (Transactional Analysis) can help. T.A. is a type of therapy that uses the role play of parent, child and adult to help people break out of repetitive cycles and escape the traps of their personal heritage. It uses the logic that in your interactions with others there are basically just these three roles that you can inhabit. Anoushka, now a senior manager at a large retail business, told us how thinking about T.A. helped her establish a much better relationship with her boss: 'I kept having really frustrating meetings with him. I'd go and see him, with positive news about reaching a sales target, and instead of congratulating me, he'd find a problem with something else. He would have a rant about whatever this was and I would become defensive and upset. I really felt that I was getting nowhere.'

Anoushka is, in fact, highly ambitious. Her eventual aim is to be CEO of a large business, so eventually she went to HR and virtually demanded coaching of some kind. The coach she saw introduced her to the T.A. idea. Now it became clear to her that she had always entered the meeting with her boss with two personas. Yes, she was going in as an adult, with great sales figures. But in addition, she took in the more childish persona of someone who not only *expected*, but actually *needed*, the praise of a father figure. Without getting too deep into psychological theory, she was able to recognize that her dad had in fact been sparing in his praise of her as a child. If she got a good result at school, her parents had been sometimes dismissive: 'Well, she's not like that at home'. She hadn't felt that her father in particular was proud of her.

When she entered a meeting with her boss, and he took her success for granted, then asked her about where she hadn't been perfect, this triggered a childish reaction in her. Working with a coach allowed her to acknowledge this, even to understand that her boss was a little intimidated by her success and her ambition. At one point he'd rebuffed her request for promotion by saying that she was over-ambitious. Anoushka certainly wasn't going to let that stop her, and understanding that she had a choice in the encounter, the choice to continue as the adult in the room, transformed her experiences. She rejected the alienation that the meetings with her boss provoked, focusing instead on the positives, and when he did critique her, she acknowledged the challenge but reinforced the wins too.

It's important to point out that sometimes the sense of disapproval that one person might pick up from another that triggers a parent-child role play to take place might not be verbal at all. You're probably familiar with the idea that actions speak louder than words and that over 90 per cent of communication is non-verbal. Some of this is body language, some is tone of voice. A large amount is based on micro-expressions. Tiny and involuntary, they're impossible to control and therefore impossible to cover up. They only last for a few seconds, but a few seconds is enough to trigger a response in the person that you are with, no matter what you might consciously be planning to say.

So, Anoushka's boss might even have meant well, but have had a dysfunctional relationship with a woman in his life that had nothing to do with her and this might have been impossible for him to account for. Especially as, from her account of the interactions, he wasn't particularly trying hard to create good and comfortable conditions for her in the first place. Although only in his very early forties, he was from a traditional background and really they had little understanding of each other's very different situations (she was the mum of two young children, back at work full-time now and determined to succeed, while he was a father of three, but with a full-time, stay-at-home wife, who took care of every domestic detail; he had started work at 18, she had delayed entering the workplace while doing a degree followed by an MA and felt anxious to catch up; he spent his weekends watching rugby, which she neither watched nor understood... the list goes on). He'd only ever had men like himself as bosses, so fitting in had never been something he'd had to work at in order to get ahead professionally. He fitted the blokey pub culture of the sector and she didn't. So they found themselves at odds, and eventually Anoushka had to recognize that he wasn't going to do anything about it: he hadn't got the motivation and so she had to.

Drama

We all need to recognize that this pattern can easily occur in the workplace and at times it becomes addictive. Robbie Steinhouse coaches clients who become trapped in the 'Drama triangle', where the parent, child and adult participants instead exhibit as persecutor, victim and rescuer. Steinhouse points out that this triangle plays out in most actual drama that we watch in movies and on TV: 'This is the plot of all the James Bond films, with the cycle repeated numerous times throughout.'

When in the victim state, we tend to mainly feel sorry for ourselves and that 'it's just not fair'. The persecutor insists that it is all someone else's fault and likes nothing more than shifting the blame. The rescuer delights in going to the rescue, but doesn't think about the dependency that they are surely creating by solving the problem in a 'deus ex machina' way (where the victim does nothing to solve their own problem, but a solution is created magically from above).

You have a choice, however: you can choose to maintain an adult perspective. (There's lots more information about these roles in material by Eric Berne, Acey Choy and Steve Karpman.)

If you're in the victim, or the child, role, accept that you're vulnerable and triggered, yet try and solve the problem in your adult persona. If you see that you're the parent in the situation or indeed have slipped into the role of persecutor, then try and use language to ask for what you want that isn't patronizing or demanding, that simply states what you think the situation requires as neutrally as possible. And in the adult role, reject the persona of the rescuer. Ensure that you help people help themselves and don't be the one that saves the day all the time.

The Power of TED (The Empowerment Dynamic) author and creator in chief David Emerald recommends that anyone who finds themselves in the role of 'victim' adopts the alternative role of creator, views the persecutor as a challenger and enlists a coach instead of a rescuer.

Emerald recommends the following transformed roles:

Creator – victims are encouraged to be outcome-oriented as opposed to problem-oriented and take responsibility for choosing their response to life challenges. They should focus on resolving 'dynamic tension' (the difference between current reality and the envisioned goal or outcome) by taking incremental steps towards the outcomes he or she is trying to achieve.

Challenger – a victim is encouraged to see a persecutor as a person (or situation) that forces the creator to clarify his or her needs and focus on their learning and growth.

Coach – a rescuer should be encouraged to ask questions that are intended to help the individual to make informed choices. The key difference between a rescuer and a coach is that the coach sees the creator as capable of making choices and of solving his or her own problems. A coach asks questions that enable the creator to see the possibilities for positive action and to focus on what he or she does want instead of what he or she *does not* want.

Defy expectations

We believe that above all you can try and defy the expectations that people form about you in the workplace and thereby find a place to belong. You might find that there are expectations based on your appearance. Many men who don't show up as diverse (not only Bill and Jake, *see* p. 214) have told us that this means that they're expected to be against all D+I (Diversity and Inclusion) initiatives and that this is unfair. Women still tell us that they're 'accused of being over-emotional' or, like Anoushka, are told that they're 'over-ambitious' for simply wanting to get on. And, in addition, an assumption might be about the role you have played in the dynamic of your team so far. Perhaps you've got stuck as the one who always challenges the norm. This is a very useful role, but can also be limiting if people assume that your response to every situation is to challenge it every time. It can mean that you are excluded from decisions so mix things up by being seen to back the norms sometimes, because some principles in any sector remain true over the long term. Alternatively, what if you are the one who always remains quiet and submissive. Again, you might find yourself completely overlooked and treated like the backing singer to the main act. Imagine the impact you will have with a carefully chosen stance against the majority view that shows that you belong in any meaningful debate.

The key point here is to make sure that you carve out a real space for yourself, and for the team around you to gel, to belong in the workplace. By stereotyping people for the role that you have attached to them, for whatever reason, or by being unconscious of how you are treating them, unhappiness and alienation are inevitable. You can, and must be, the agent of change for the better.

Strategies for Belonging

PARENT-CHILD

Break free from playing the role of either parent or child at work. Defy expectations and take the conscious adult role to lead Belonging for everyone.

Zen management: less is more

There are any number of social media threads on work. Those fascinating threads that give you a sneaky insight into the workplace and the behaviour that happens every day. One particular favourite of ours was the manager who insisted on being emailed whenever anyone planned to spend more than £5 on anything, so that he could give permission. For context, this is in a department with a high monetary turnover. While it's a great discipline to keep an eye on costs, this just creates a log jam of requests and a build-up of resentment at the lack of trust it implies. It also looks as if this particular person feels insecure in their role and needs to make sure that everyone knows it is them, and only them, in charge. Be in no doubt about that.

Micro-managing is a temptation for every manager. That way, nothing can really go wrong, can it? Okay, your team can only move at the speed that your various other commitments allow, but at least you are sure that things are running to plan. It's all good! Except that when it becomes time for you to look up at the next job you might want, you realize that in fact you are doing the jobs of the people who work alongside you. You haven't really learnt anything about managing people and process because you are too involved in the day-to-day delivery. Plus, your team are now so sat on and squashed that none of them has developed so that you have a replacement ready to step up. Zen management – less-is-more management – is hard to deliver. You have to do a lot of groundwork and be willing to sit on your hands when you might want to muck in.

Be clear about team values

It starts with you being very clear about what your values are as a team. Are there no-go areas that you would never, even if it was lucrative, consider taking on? Are there behaviours that aren't part of your culture? Are you prepared to call them out? How can you ensure that there isn't any 'special interpretation' of your values that allows certain people to put themselves in a position of greater influence?

In essence, Zen management is ironically nothing like minimal when you first start to implement it. The teams involved need to be rigorous and committed and to understand how the practice will work out. It is clearly not a situation that suits people who work best under a higher level of supervision as you are expected to be self-starting and willing to act independently. You also have to be prepared to stand up behind your actions and your decisions and this can be hard for people to take on. Walking into an organization that operates this way can be a real Marmite experience: some people relish the autonomy, others find it too risky and find the individual emphasis that it requires to be too demanding. This is not a criticism of those who don't want to work that way. After all, different companies have very different requirements.

The best of both worlds

For managers who join this type of operation the adaptation can also be problematic. Should you be a person who likes to take a close personal interest in your team members and have a hand in their day-to-day work, the distance that a more detached style creates can be frustrating and challenging if you don't want to adopt it. The questions that arise about being held accountable when you aren't fully responsible for your team members can quickly start to bother you. The way you approach this dilemma may allow you to have the best of both worlds. Give yourself the time to consider what is really important for you to know about and keep track of. You might find that it is not as much as you think it is. Are you setting targets that are really contributing to the success and development of your team or are you writing four that are key and six that aren't helping your colleagues, or your team, grow? The temptation to write a long list of targets that address every eventuality can be so strong. Ask yourself the questions – where is this person now? What do they need to be more successful or fulfilled in this role? What do they need to do or learn to get better or get promoted? How do we motivate them? Once you have distilled this down, you will probably find that the target KPIs write themselves and they will form a core few points that show that you, as the manager, have focused on that team member.

For each team member, the deployment of a minimalist management style is a chance to step up and show what they can contribute. In accepting the values of the organization, there must be a strong sense of what is appropriate and which behaviours are valued. 'All of us together is stronger than one of us alone' is the mantra at a company that we know and the emphasis is interesting. The possible interpretation is that yes, we are made up of lots of talented individuals but guess what, our combined force means we are formidable. So, muck in, everyone, we are all in this together!

Strategies for Belonging

ZEN MANAGEMENT

Stop micro-managing! Create clear values and behaviour guidelines with just a few key targets tailored to the individual.

Being comfortable with being uncomfortable

If we are going to create a workplace where everyone feels that they have a stake and an understanding that they can and will be valued, we will all need to experience some awkward and uncomfortable times. We will need to accept that we might be challenged and our usual 'safe' methods of thinking and working might require some readjustment. Or even radical change.

Many of us worry about the unknown. Speaking to a woman CEO, recently, we were told that she was still concerned if her chairman (a man) rang her when she wasn't expecting a call – she thought it must be because he was going to tell her that she had messed up. Or that she was being fired. Even when she realized that sometimes he just rang to see how she was – in a friendly and amiable way – the gap between him calling and her talking to him in response was still dominated by concern.

Fear and apprehension

The human desire to survive is innate and change can feel as if it is threatening you. Unlikely as it is that reorganization of the management responsibility bands will result in you taking part in a fight to the death (that would be one heck of a way to determine the outcome!), we are fine-tuned to any hint of menace. Our restless intellects look for clues and patterns to help us navigate the new and the unknown and we feel threatened. And yet we live in a world of relentless change: to both our workplaces and the societies we live in, and we can't live our lives in fear and apprehension of what might, just might, be around the corner. If we do that, our worlds will become very, very small.

Stepping away from our natural concerns is a requirement if we are going to embrace change and create new paths and practices in our workplaces. One of the first steps towards achieving this is to accept that, to paraphrase a famous quote, 'There are known unknowns and we know that there are things that we do not know'. We can plan and strategize to our heart's content, but frankly, stuff happens and you might not have accounted for it. It is easy to believe that we are in control and that brings a sense of comfort to all of us. With me in charge, what can go wrong? I am in possession of the knowledge and I know what the plan is, so let's just crack on! However, the best-laid plans can go wrong and sometimes do go wrong and you can't plan yourselves out of every eventuality (after all, you have got to deliver and do rather than plan for the rest of your life).

The advantage that planning gives you is confidence and confidence is a key factor in being comfortable with discomfort. If you believe that you have the attitude and skill set to be able to navigate the unknown, then you have an advantage. Notice that we call it 'the navigation of the unknown' rather than any notion of conquering the situation. In finding a path, you know that what faces you isn't beyond you, even if you may not have achieved everything you might have hoped for. You have laid the foundation of future success and can build on that. It may be an incremental build rather than any huge stride forward, but if you are intent on changing your company culture or inclusion policy, you will have a mix of both as you recalibrate.

Creating confidence in your colleagues is a key challenge for managers. How many times have you heard of 'the management' announcing a brave and bold new direction without laying firm foundations for the change? Managers who fail to properly assess what their colleagues and workmates are capable of or who aren't aware of the challenges they are facing may be struggling with both the innate resistance to change but also a sense that the building blocks to change aren't in place. Someone failed to check the computer network so it doesn't have the bandwidth to accommodate a new IT system, meaning it won't deliver the promised transformation.

Confidence and resilience

Inner confidence at work comes from feeling valued and knowing that your contribution is recognized. Those managers who regularly check in with their team members to ensure that they have the skills they require and that they have a clear role within the team are laying good ground for the future. For team members to know that their manager values them is a foundation for personal confidence in work. Creating that confidence can help smart management to push for change at a quicker pace than those who manage less resilient teams. Confidence also encourages you to share any concerns without fear of appearing to be failing or making excuses for your own performance or even being perceived as a negative voice within the team.

Confidence can also be a good base in developing resilience in team members. A measure of resilience enables teams to weather the ups and downs of change. Colleagues who have a lot of experience can be an excellent source of perspective in terms of navigating difficulties (just make sure that you haven't enabled them to unleash unbridled cynicism to pepper the anecdotes). Seeing colleagues who have experienced pressure or situations before can help team members feel that as the team has survived tough times before, it will probably survive again, even if it is a worrying time. Once you have expanded your comfort circle, you don't mind pushing it out again. After all, you survived the last time, didn't you?

Difficulties can be great growth experiences. Being uncomfortable can be a good way of recharging and reevaluating your thinking and opening yourself up to new experiences.

Shared experiences

Another key element of being comfortable with being uncomfortable is the ability to be able to talk about how you are feeling. Suppressing the questioning voices in your head doesn't keep them quiet for long. Sometimes just sharing your concerns can be a way to address them and they lose their power to trouble you. Hearing that one of your colleagues doesn't quite get the nuances of a work initiative and talking through how they might approach it can be the first step into having a fully open culture that anticipates problems before they get a grip. This listening needs to be handled in a way that fully airs the concerns rather than allowing people who feel 'in the know' or more onside with change to just shut down any perspective other than theirs. More introverted characters need to be allowed to share, even if you have a sense that they are fine with discomfort. Make sure rather than assuming.

What if you don't have the answer?

One of the most uncomfortable situations you face as a leader is that you might not have the answer. Of course, the internet offers up a huge variety of answers but this might make your search history look a bit strange (just imagine looking up 'we've employed someone who has sexual history with an existing employee – what do I do?' which, by the way, was a question we have been asked). Let us be honest with ourselves: we don't have all the answers off pat. This is where you need to take your time to explore the options rather than just going with the first thought that might come into your mind. Telling your team that you want to think about something gives them the sense that you are giving time to a problem rather than just trying to move on as quickly as you can. There is no weakness in admitting that you would rather give a situation the appropriate analysis before committing rather than just appearing to dismiss it without thinking it through or considering the situation from the other person's point of view. Sometimes your quick answers can appear to minimize a concern and it could lead to fewer instances of you being asked for your input. You also give weight to the situation that you are being asked about, which can then create rapport with a colleague. They go away thinking they were right in seeing the situation as one of concern and you are now viewed as sympathetic and measured. Which is a great reputation to have with your team.

Ride it out

Another aspect of being uncomfortable is that you will have to get used to just sucking it up. If you are in a period of change it can sometimes just be best to ride it out until what is and has happened resolves itself. Of course, not having a clear path can feel debilitating, but in the long term will a few weeks of uncertainty really be that damaging to you and your career? Can you just hang on, try your best in the circumstances and wait?

One of the most damaging things in difficult circumstances is to succumb to the notion that you must *do* something, *anything*. Actually, in the majority of cases you are better off just sucking it up rather than running the risk that your impulse to act creates even more instability or confusion. It may look decisive and brave, but it could just as easily be impulsive and foolish. Just hang on in there. Take a breath, let it wash over you for a while: now, isn't that better?

Once you have weathered the storm it's a good idea to look back after a period of time (not too long, you need the team memory and recall to be strong) and work out what you did that was good and what was bad. Not in the sense of it being a full-blown inquiry into the rights and wrongs of who did or said what, with the subsequent allocation of blame, but just so you can learn from what you did and embed it into your behaviours. The good bits, that is. Depending on the personalities and perspectives of the team members, you can learn who is good at what aspects of change and challenge. With that in your armoury, you can then deploy people appropriately next time you face a period of uncertainty. It may seem obvious, but putting someone who doesn't have a strong reputation for empathy in charge of delivering tricky personnel news doesn't remove the emotion from a situation, it just looks as if you may have employed a robot to impart bad news. So, put yourself in the position of the recipient of that chat and ask how you can best deliver it with the most humanity.

Human values

Humanity is the very essence and the key element in dealing with feeling uncomfortable. If you are feeling uncomfortable, you should gain comfort from the fact that your feelings and perspective are entirely human. It would be strange if you were never uncomfortable. Once you have accepted that it is normal and that it's not a weakness or a feeling to be brushed under the carpet, you can gain the perspective that allows you to deal with it.

It may be that amongst your colleagues you are better equipped or have more experience with the uncomfortable. If that is the case, use your empathy to find ways to help other colleagues and to develop their skills in being comfortable with being uncomfortable. Most of all, do use this time of discomfort to equip you to expand the breadth and width of your confidence and repeat the behaviours and beliefs that allowed you to develop your skills and capabilities. We all know that yet more change is probably nearer than we think…

Strategies for Belonging

BEING COMFORTABLE WITH BEING UNCOMFORTABLE

Recognize that you may not have all the answers and that it's better to suffer some uncertainty than to avoid change at all costs.

Exercises and techniques for Chapter 6

In this chapter we have discussed many ideas and strategies that involve high levels of emotional intelligence: Staying in the adult position, rather than getting stuck in child or parent; being comfortable with being uncomfortable; tending to others' emotions; challenging your self-limiting narratives; practising Zen management and several others. Specifically, they require you to first be aware of your thoughts and aware of your emotions, and then to be able to manage your thoughts and emotions very skilfully. In particular, they require you to be able to stay with uncomfortable emotions. So, in this section we will look at techniques to help you be aware of your thoughts, be aware of your emotions and manage your emotions – particularly the uncomfortable ones

Awareness of your thoughts

The simplest technique to help you be more aware of your thoughts and form a better relationship with them is meditation. Thanks to the recent craze for mindfulness, many of you will have meditated before, but for those who haven't, rest assured: there is nothing weird or difficult about it and it's a remarkably simple technique that anyone can practise.

Meditation: noticing your thoughts

Find a quiet place. Sit in a state of relaxed alertness – comfortable, but not so comfortable you're going to fall asleep. Close your eyes.

Take a few long, slow, deep breaths and gently turn your attention to focus on your breath. Focus on the in-breath and the out-breath. Gradually tune in to the rhythm of your breath. In a sense, this is the whole exercise but in another sense what really matters is what happens to you when you try to focus on your breath. You will notice over time – and usually quite quickly – that you are unable to focus on your breath. Your mind will be taken over by random thoughts. This is not because there is something wrong with you, it is because you are human.

Some of these thoughts will be plans for the future. Some of them will be reviewing and quite possibly regretting the past. Others will be thoughts of judgement about what you're doing or how well you're doing it, or whether it's worth doing. And still other thoughts will be completely random. As this starts to happen, notice that it is happening. And each time it happens, label it. Say to yourself 'thinking', then let the thought go and return to the breath. It's important that you say 'thinking' very kindly. You're not judging yourself as having failed to stay on your breath, you're simply remarking on what is happening.

After 10 minutes, move your focus from your breath to any sounds that you can hear – traffic outside, people talking in the next room, a clock ticking, air conditioning humming, birdsong – and after a few moments, open your eyes.

After you have finished your meditation, reflect on what has happened and on how easily and how often you were distracted from your actual aim of focusing on your breath. Reflect also on the fact that you weren't trying to think. In fact, you were trying to *not* think, but thoughts occurred anyway. What does this tell you about your relationship with your thoughts?

Crucially, it tells us that we are not in control of our thoughts (for much of the time anyway). Our thoughts happen whether we like them or not, whether we want them or not. And we have very little control over this. This is an important learning. To behave in a more emotional intelligent manner at work it helps to understand that our thoughts are not necessarily thoughts that we want to have. They are not necessarily true. They are not necessarily helpful, and they need not necessarily be acted upon.

The second learning is that you are not your thoughts: you are the observer of your thoughts. You do not consciously and deliberately think most of your thoughts, you observe them. Knowing this, when you're at work – when you are *not* meditating – you can also observe your thoughts, as they occur and then calmly and rationally decide:

- Is this true?
- Is this helpful?
- Should I act on it or should I just let it go?

Managing uncomfortable feelings

Have you ever been taught how to feel a feeling? Almost certainly not – very few of us have been. It's a strange omission in our education system and in our culture. To be emotionally intelligent, you need to be able to stay with uncomfortable feelings. Everything in our training, education and cultural upbringing suggests that we should run a mile from uncomfortable feelings, but this is exactly the wrong way to handle your feelings and has very little benefit for us or for anyone else around us.

We either suppress the feelings, perhaps by having a drink to 'take the edge off', or indulging in some other addictive behaviour – in which case the negative feelings are going to bubble up at some point in the future because what we resist persists; or we act out or displace the feelings, creating havoc around us as we behave irrationally and aggressively towards people who haven't got a clue why this is going on. So, let's go through another simple meditation, which will illustrate a healthier way to deal with your feelings: by simply staying with them, by simply feeling them. Use this when something has happened at work that has left you with an uncomfortable feeling:

anger, fear, sadness, frustration, etc. Just as an example, we'll say you were angry.

Meditation: dealing with uncomfortable feelings

As soon as you are able (you may well have to wait till you get home), find a quiet place and sit in the state of relaxed alertness. Close your eyes and focus on the breath.

Once you've tuned into your breath and stayed with it for a few minutes, conjure up the memory of the event/comment/phone call/email that made you angry. Vividly recall it. Visualize yourself there and visualize the other people there. Replay the moment in your head so that you can once again feel the feeling that you felt them.

Now, scan through your body to find where the feeling is.

Every feeling has two elements: some thoughts and a physical sensation in your body. Right now (as we did in the previous meditation), we're going to let the thoughts go, but this time we're taking this additional step of looking for the physical sensation in the body.

Everyone is different and everyone reacts differently, but we will have a physical reaction of some kind. It may be a tightness in the chest, a heaviness in the stomach, tension in the shoulders, dryness in the throat, a feeling of having loads of energy in the arms or legs, or something quite different. Scan through your body until you find it. Now, label it, but label it using this slightly unusual form of words: 'I am aware of a physical sensation in my body, which I identify as anger'.

By using this form of words, we are underlining the space between our Self (the observer of the feeling) and the feeling. We are harnessing the power of defusion (understanding the difference between yourself and your thoughts or feelings).

Your next task is simply to stay with that physical sensation for a few minutes. You will notice that once we have removed thoughts and found the physical sensation and labelled it, even some extremely unpleasant feelings are surprisingly easy to stay with. As you stay with it, notice if the feeling changes or moves around your body. Quite often, this will occur.

When you have stayed with the feeling for two or three minutes, place your hand on your heart.

As you continue to breathe slowly and deeply, send yourself a message of love.

If 'send yourself a message of love' sounds a little bit too hippie for you, then just send yourself a message of kindness or a message that things are okay. Stay with this for another couple of minutes, then turn your focus back to the breath. Take three long, slow breaths, then turn your attention to the sounds you can hear. Then, after a few moments, gently open your eyes.

If you use this meditation regularly, you will find over time that you can use its component parts to deal with uncomfortable emotions as they happen, without having to sit quietly and close your eyes. Even when triggered in the heat of a highly pressured meeting at work, you can remember to…

- breathe more slowly and deeply;
- let the thoughts go;
- feel where in your body the physical sensation has occurred;
- label the sensation.

When you can do this, your actions and words can be calm, measured and reasonable, and designed to promote and enhance a culture of Belonging.

One Voice: Anita

Anita is one of the most successful business women in the UK, with a range of roles from being in government, to running a large retailer and leading 3rd sector organizations. In mid-career, she is taking some time out to consider her next role.

'We've been having conversations about gender roles in our household. As I am at home more at the moment, much more of the domestic burden is falling to me. My partner said to me, "But you like to cook." And it's actually true I love cooking, but he is missing the point – liking to do something and having to do it are very different. I feel a pressure to have to do it. And when he's under pressure then he doesn't do his share of the chores, but I see this and I pick up his share. And when I am under pressure, he doesn't do my chores.

'And he doesn't ever look ahead.

'And I think, is it my fault that I pick up the slack?

'We have to change this balance for the next generation. However, I think that my parents had this exact same conversation when I was growing up. They raised me as feminist because they are feminists but I think they have really gendered roles. In part that was inevitable because of the times they lived in, but how much has changed? People are much more willing to talk about the feminist agenda though than they are about race. No one wants to talk about class. People have a high degree of comfort talking about sexuality. No one really wants to talk about disability, except when it comes to neurodiversity.

'At the place I just left, we were having a very big conversation about gender. There, they justify the gender pay gap because they have a big retail element to it, which is predominantly staffed by women earning relatively low salaries compared to people in head

office earning big salaries. One solution that therefore was aired was to hire more men in the frontline staff whereas my view was, let's bring in more senior women to redress the balance.

'I argued about this. I said: "Today, without even trying, I could find 10 women to interview for open roles at the top of the company." They really weren't interested in addressing the imbalance in this way. And they just don't accept that they need to behave differently because, although they understand it's an issue, they still don't really get how you tackle it. It was a very driven retail business with a massive sense of macho 24/7 delivery.

'The reality is, until we make clear, until we can demonstrate to all of them that there is something in it for them personally too, then some of the men in positions of power, of comfort, will hate us. Because we are making their lives difficult. If you have a full-time wife at home dealing with everything, if you're in an organization where you haven't been used to lots of women in leadership roles, then diversity can feel as though it is bad for you as an individual.

'So long as we frame success only in terms of advancement, there are always going to be people disappointed when they discover that now it wasn't always inevitable they were going to be the CEO. I think there is a risk that some will think the reason is "the women", not because they don't have the smarts to be the CEO.

'Men have to see diversity programmes as good for them as well as just for women. About having the flexibility to go and play sport or music, or act as an active father. And that this means there can be great work because people are in better shape in the office because of the balance in their lives.

'We need to ensure that we can give everyone real opportunities. There are massive class/wealth issues. People get very defensive. I am clearly now middle class, but I wasn't born or brought up this way. I have the experience of coming from the working class. I see that people need access to resilience strategies and the ability to get access to all kinds of jobs.

'We have to be careful not to fight amongst diverse communities too though. I have experienced a situation where panels are created to be diverse at the expense of expertise. It is the result of lazy thinking. People putting a panel together think we need a woman or a black person but don't bother to think about their level of expertise. I mean, I have been asked to do a panel on blockchain! Me! This doesn't help anyone.

'In feminist circles, sometimes I have seen that some women forget that men can be feminists too. There are some men politicians too, who have done more for women than some powerful women in politics have.

'I want diversity of thought around me. I want people who can offer something different as a contribution.'

Afterword

There is much more emphasis on diversity and inclusion in the workplace than there was even five years ago. Yet despite all the time and money (billions, in fact) that has been spent on trying to change the status quo, it has proved very stubborn to shift. Only by recognizing that everyone has a role to play, and that every single one of us can and should be a champion of Belonging in the workplace, will cultures shift and real transformation take place. To be a success, the twenty-first-century workplace must be all-inclusive.

Thanks for reading our book. We are optimistic that when we all take responsibility and action, then the workplace will become a stronger, more inclusive environment, and that this will be a better future for everyone.

Kathryn, Sue and Mark
London, 2021

Bibliography

Introduction

Papers, reports and online resources

BCG. 'How diverse leadership teams boost innovation'. 2018.

McKinsey. Diversity matters, 2015.

Telegraph. 'Jeremy Clarkson BBC won't give jobs to men any more'. Jan 2019.

BBCNews. 'People of colour seem superglued to the floor', December, 2019.

Deloitte. 'Uncovering Talent', 2013.

Forbes.com. 'Evidence that better diversity leads to better profits', January 2018

Hampton-Alexander Review FTSE

Inclusion Works Pulse Report. 'Hive Learning', 2019

Leanin.org

McGregor Smith Review. 'Race in the workplace', 2018.

McKinsey. womenintheworkplace.com

Mehta, S. 'Review: The Failed Promise of a Billion-Dollar Business', November 2019.

S&P Global Essential Intelligence. SPGlobal.com

Weforum.org. 'Workplace gender parity', December 2019.

Wilkins, C. Wellman, J.D. Kaiser, C.R. 'Status legitimizing beliefs predict positivity towards whites who claim anti-white bias'. *Journal of Experimental Social Philosophy*, 2013.

Chapter 1: What is going on, and is it working?

Books

Harari, Y.N. *21 Lessons for the 21st Century*. Vintage, 2019.

Siebert, A. *The Resiliency Advantage*. Berrett-Koehler Publishers, 2005.

Papers, reports and online resources

Berman, J. 'White men who can't get jobs say they're being discriminated against', April 2019.

Chapman, B. 'Businesses apprehensive about hiring disabled people to senior roles', Independent.co.uk, July 2019.

Crenshaw, K.W. 'Intersectionality', www.racialequitytool.org

Hearst. 'The 4 paradoxes of modern man', www.hearst.co.uk/the-beacon/4-paradoxes-modern-man

Jones, C. 'Mountain to climb for women chiefs', CBI conference, November 2019.

Lay-Flurrie, J. Articles at linkedin.com

Maketwatch.com

Mediadiversified.org

O'Dell, L. 'If politicians won't caption videos for deaf voters, why should I support them?', Metro.co.uk, November 2019.

Schwab, K. 'Legal battle over future of web design', fastcompany.co.uk, May 2019.

Singh, H. 'What I have learned about Privilege: Never mind white privilege – being from a minority is a privilege too', *Huffington Post*, August 2017.

Times.co.uk

Chapter 2: The secret of Belonging

Books

Brown, B. *Dare to Lead*. Random House, 2018.

Guthrie, J. *Alpha Girls*. Piatkus, 2019.

Mowlem, M. *Momentum*. Coronet, 2003.

Syed, M. *Rebel Ideas*. John Murray, 2019.

Papers, reports and online resources

'100 leadership lessons', *Management Today*, September 2019.

Dalton, M. 'With the toss of a wig! Mo Mowlam and the Belfast Agreement', *Irish Times*, April 2018.

Everfi.com. 'Small acts of kindness', February 2020.

Fessler, L. 'How We'll Win. Quartz at Work', October 2018.

Petriglieri, J. 'What most people get wrong about men and women', *Harvard Business Review*, May–June 2018.

Chapter 3: Belonging for everyone as contents

Books

Miller, A. *All My Sons*. Penguin, 2009.

Papers, reports and online resources

Greengross, G., Silvia, P., Nusbaum, E. 'Sex differences in humor production ability: A meta-analysis', *Journal of Research in Personality*, 2019.

Lucy and Ethel wrap chocolates: https://youtu.be/WmAwcMNxGqM

McKinsey & Co. 'Women in the workplace', 2019.

Marriage, M. 'Men Only: Insider the charity fundraiser where hostesses are put on show'. *Financial Times*, 2018.

Stone, K. 'Men beat women in "Humour Production Ability"'. www.funnywomen.com, 2019.

Chapter 4: Belonging in action

Books

Grimm, W.J. *The Original Folk and Fairy Tales of the Brothers Grimm*. Princeton University Press, 2016.

Unerman, S. & Jacob, K. *The Glass Wall: success strategies for women at work and businesses that mean business*. Profile Books, 2016.

Papers, reports and online resources

Ashcraft, K.L. 'The Glass Slipper Academy of Management Review', 2017.

Avengers Movies: Marvel.com

Chen, S., Breines, J. 'The Power of Compassion'. *HBR*, 2018.

Hewlett-Packard Confidence Gap: https://hbr.org/2014/08/why-women-dont-apply-for-jobs-unless-theyre-100-qualified

How I Met Your Mother: https://www.imdb.com/title/tt0460649/

Top Gun: https://en.wikipedia.org/wiki/Top_Gun

Zalis, S. 'The Role of Men on IWD and Every Day'. Forbes.com, 2020.

Chapter 5: Making Belonging the winning culture at work

Books

Greenfield, S. *Mind Change*. Random House, 2014.

Haidt, J. *The Happiness Hypothesis*. Random House, 2006.

Heath, C. & D. *Switch*. Random House Business, 2011.

Perkin, N. & Abraham, P. *Building the Agile Business Through Digital Transformation*. Kogan Page, 2017.

Papers, reports and online resources

Chowdhury, M.R. 'Happiness at work'. positivepsychology.com, 2019.

Goffman, E. *The Presentation of Self in Everyday Life*. New York: Overlook, 1959.

Heffernan, M. MHeffernan.com

Konnikova, M. 'Why are we so afraid of creativity?'. *Scientific American*, 2012.

Kotter. 'Model for change'. Kotterinc.com, 2014.

'Why do we find it so hard to say the M-word?' Lloydsbank.com, 2019.

Chapter 6: The inner journey

Books

Armstrong, K. *The Case for God: What Religion Really Means*. Vintage, 2009.

Berne, E. *Games People Play: The Psychology of Human Relationships*. Penguin Life, 2016.

Emerald, D. *The Power of TED*. Polaris, 2015.

Haidt, J. *The Righteous Mind*. Penguin, 2012.

Liswood, L. *The Loudest Duck: Moving Beyond Diversity While Embracing Differences to Achieve Success at Work*. Wiley, 2010.

Papers, reports and online resources

Beale, C. 'Campaign Alist'. Campaignlive.co.uk, 2020.

Choy, A. *The Winner's Triangle*. Journals.sagepub.com, 1990.

Karpman, S. 'Karpman Drama Triangle'. Wikipedia.com

Obama, M. 'Remarks By The First Lady at Oberlin College Commencement Address'. Obamawhitehouse.archives.gov, 2015.

Steinhouse, R. 'Drama Triangle and Relationships'. nlpschool.com, 2016.

Appendix

In February 2020, we commissioned Dynata to conduct new research into Belonging in the workplace in the UK and US exclusively for this book. This uncovered interesting and troubling insights into workplace culture. They repeated the research in August 2021. Not enough has changed; more needs to be done.

As explained in our Preface (*see* p. xxvii), one in three people in the UK and one in four people in the US don't have a sense of Belonging at their workplace. And as the charts below show, much that is taken for granted in terms of being accepted is not the reality for those who are different from the norm. Too many people have either experienced or witnessed discrimination and too few are confident enough to challenge this. We need more champions of Belonging working to ensure acceptance for everyone. Here are some of the key charts from the research. The number who feel they belong is unchanged.

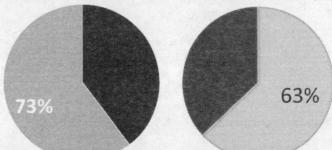

I FEEL I BELONG AT WORK (US)   I FEEL I BELONG AT WORK (UK)

73%   63%

Just over half the UK workforce, and now two-thirds in the US, believe that their leader is personally responsible for diversity.

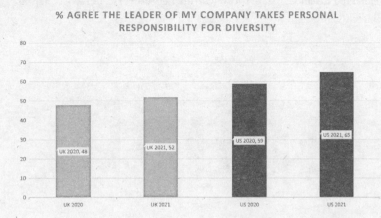

% AGREE THE LEADER OF MY COMPANY TAKES PERSONAL RESPONSIBILITY FOR DIVERSITY

Once in three people have felt excluded or marginalized at work because of their beliefs, personal circumstances or identity, and this has increased since 2020. It's significantly higher amongst some groups, including under-35s; those expecting their first child; those who are neurodiverse; and who are registered disabled.

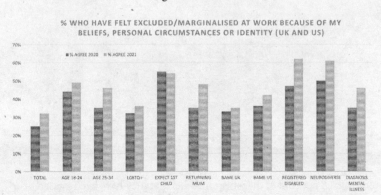

% WHO HAVE FELT EXCLUDED/MARGINALISED AT WORK BECAUSE OF MY BELIEFS, PERSONAL CIRCUMSTANCES OR IDENTITY (UK AND US)

Far too many people have *experienced* bias, harassment or inappropriate behaviour – nearly one in three overall and more than half of those registered disabled, half of those who are neurodiverse, or have a mental illness diagnosis.

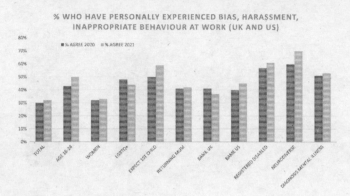

% WHO HAVE PERSONALLY EXPERIENCED BIAS, HARASSMENT, INAPPROPRIATE BEHAVIOUR AT WORK (UK AND US)

And far too many people have witnessed this behaviour: 36 per cent overall, 49 per cent LGBTQ+, 52 per cent under-25s, 72 per cent neurodiverse, 65 per cent registered disabled.

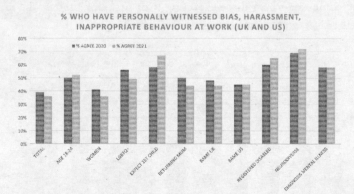

% WHO HAVE PERSONALLY WITNESSED BIAS, HARASSMENT, INAPPROPRIATE BEHAVIOUR AT WORK (UK AND US)

Overall, 18 per cent of the workforce feel that they have been passed over for a job or a promotion because of their identity. This rises to a quarter of

LGBTQ+; a quarter of mums returning to work; one in five people with caring responsibilities outside of children; 45 per cent neurodiverse; 44 per cent registered disabled; 36 per cent diagnosed with mental illness.

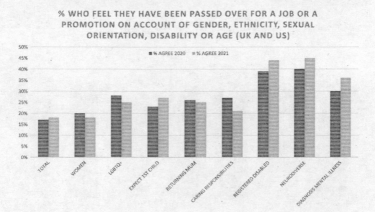

% WHO FEEL THEY HAVE BEEN PASSED OVER FOR A JOB OR A PROMOTION ON ACCOUNT OF GENDER, ETHNICITY, SEXUAL ORIENTATION, DISABILITY OR AGE (UK AND US)

We asked a new question in 2021: Do you consider your sector ageist? Thirty per cent of workers do think this, and many more younger people than older people; more men than women agree. Ageism is not just about older people but is any discrimination on the grounds of age.

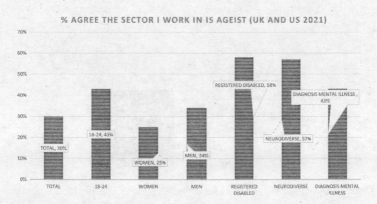

% AGREE THE SECTOR I WORK IN IS AGEIST (UK AND US 2021)

Overall, 64 per cent are very open about themselves at work (a slight increase). Women are less likely to be, especially if expecting their first child. So too are ethnic minority groups and LGBTQ+.

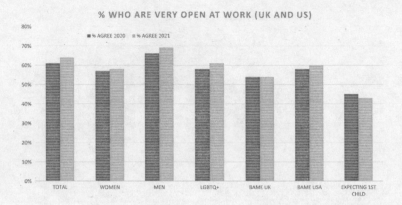

% WHO ARE VERY OPEN AT WORK (UK AND US)

More people are comfortable in challenging bias, harassment or inappropriate behaviour at work , but 40 per cent are *not*. More people doubt promotions and jobs only go to those most qualified to do them.

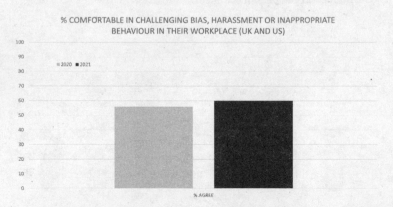

% COMFORTABLE IN CHALLENGING BIAS, HARASSMENT OR INAPPROPRIATE BEHAVIOUR IN THEIR WORKPLACE (UK AND US)

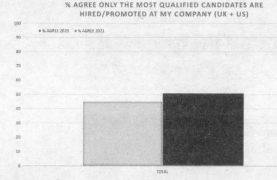

% AGREE ONLY THE MOST QUALIFIED CANDIDATES ARE
HIRED/PROMOTED AT MY COMPANY (UK + US)

Our research shows that there is a gap between how comfortable men feel about business trips with a woman and how comfortable a woman is on a business trip with a man.

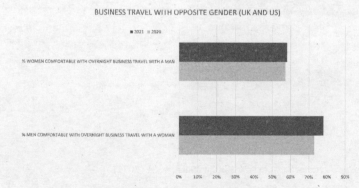

BUSINESS TRAVEL WITH OPPOSITE GENDER (UK AND US)

There are some gender differences in attitudes to diversity at work, although these are not as extreme as some might expect. There is a slight increase in those who think that there is too much focus on the issue at work, and more men think this than women.

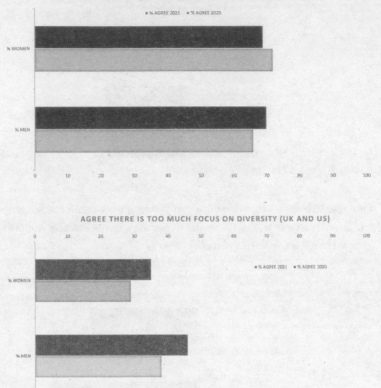

Source: Dynata. Sample size: 4063 (2020), 4011 (2021)

For more information on this research, please get in touch with the authors.

Our very special thanks for the research go to Dynata and, also, Pauline Robson, managing partner at MediaCom, for their invaluable insights and help.

Acknowledgements

We would like to thank our collective of advisors, whose support has been invaluable. We would also like to recognize the contribution made by the individuals we interviewed, who shared their experiences and insight with us and who shaped this book.

When we have talked publically about diversity and inclusion, our audiences have been inspiring and educational in their participation. For all of you who gave your time to us, thank you.

Thank you to everyone at Bloomsbury, our publishers, including Ian Hallsworth, Matt James, Rachel Nicholson, Allie Collins, Lizzy Ewer, Jude Drake, Louise Cameron, Jane Donovan and the wider team who have made this book so amazing. Many thanks to our agent Clare Grist Taylor; we are delighted to be some of the earliest clients of The Accidental Agency.

We believe and hope that this book is another step forward on the path to create a better workplace where everyone belongs.

Index